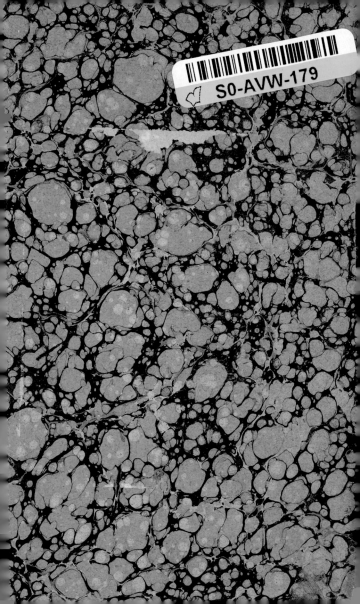

Edna Duff Briggs

THE

BRITISH ESSAYISTS;

WITH

PREFACES,

HISTORICAL AND BIOGRAPHICAL,

BY

ALEXANDER CHALMERS, A. M.

ↄↄↄↄↄↄↄ

VOL. XLII.

LONDON:

PRINTED FOR J. JOHNSON, J. NICHOLS, R. BALDWIN, F. AND C. RIVINGTON,
W. OTRIDGE AND SON, W. J. AND J. RICHARDSON, A. STRAHAN, J. SEWELL,
R. FAULDER, G. AND W. NICOL, T. PAYNE, G. AND J. ROBINSON,
W. LOWNDES, G. WILKIE, J. MATHEWS, P. McQUEEN, OGILVY AND SON,
J. SCATCHERD, J. WALKER, VERNOR AND HOOD, R. LEA, DARTON AND
HARVEY, J. NUNN, LACKINGTON AND CO. D. WALKER, CLARKE AND SON,
G. KEARSLEY, C. LAW, J. WHITE, LONGMAN AND REES, CADELL, JUN. AND
DAVIES, J. BARKER, T. KAY, WYNNE AND CO. POTE AND CO. CARPENTER
AND CO. W. MILLER, MURRAY AND HIGHLEY, S. BAGSTER, T. HURST,
T. BOOSEY, R. PHENEY, W. BAYNES, J. HARDING, R. H. EVANS, J. MAWMAN,
AND W. CREECH, EDINBURGH.

1803.

T. GILLET, Printer,
Salisbury-Square, Fleet-Street.

OBSERVER.

———Multorum providus urbes
Et mores hominum inspexit———   HORAT.

BY RICHARD CUMBERLAND, ES2.

N⁰ 44—83.

CONTENTS.

VOL. XLII.

THE

OBSERVER.

NUMBER XLIV.

WHEN I had parted from the old gentleman, I found
Mrs. Abrahams desirous to return home, being
somewhat indisposed by the heat of the theatre, so
that I lost no time in getting her and Constantia
into the coach: in our way homewards I reported
the conversation I had held with Mr. Goodison;
the different effects it had upon my hearers were
such as might be expected from their several characters; the gentle spirit of Constantia found relief in
tears; her grateful heart discharged itself in praises
and thanksgivings to Providence: Mrs. Abrahams
forgot her head-ach, felicitated herself in having
prevailed upon Mrs. Goodison to consent to her
daughter's going to the play, declared she had a pre-
sentiment that something fortunate would come to
pass, thought the title of the comedy was a lucky
omen, congratulated Constantia over and over, and
begged to be indulged in the pleasure of telling these
most joyful tidings to her good man at home : Ned
put in his claim for a share in the prophecy no less
than Mrs. Abrahams; he had a kind of a something
in his thoughts, when Goodison sat at his elbow,

that did not quite amount to a discovery, and yet it was very like it; he had a sort of an impulse to give him a gird or two upon the character of Sterling, and he was very sure that what he threw out upon the occasion made him squeak, and that the discovery would never have come about, if it had not been for him; he even advanced some learned remarks upon the good effects of stage-plays in giving touches to the conscience, though I do not pretend to say he had Jeremy Collier in his thoughts at the time; in short, what between the Hebrew and the Christian there was little or nothing left for my share in the work, so that I contented myself with cautioning Constantia how she broke it to her mother, and recommended to Mrs. Abrahams to confine her discourse to her husband, and leave Constantia to undertake for Mrs. Goodison.

When we arrived at our journey's end we found the honest Jew alone, and surprised him before he expected us: Mrs. Goodison was gone to bed a little indisposed, Constantia hastened up to her without entering the parlour; Mrs. Abrahams let loose the clapper of joy, and rang in the good news with so full a peal and so many changes, that there was no more to be done on my part but to correct a few trips in the performance of the nature of pleonasms, which were calculated to improve the tale in every particular but the truth of it. When she had fairly acquitted herself of the history, she began to recollect her head-ach, and then left us very thoroughly disposed to have a fellow-feeling in the same complaint.

After a few natural reflections upon the event, soberly debated and patiently delivered, I believe we were all of one mind in wishing for a new subject, and a silence took place sufficiently preparatory for its introduction; when Abrahams, putting on a grave and serious look, in a more solemn tone of voice, than I had ever heard him assume, delivered himself as follows:

There is something, gentlemen, presses on my mind, which seems a duty on my conscience to impart to you: I cannot reconcile myself to play the counterfeit in your company, and therefore if you will have patience to listen to a few particulars of a life, so unimportant as mine, I will not intrude long upon your attention, and at worst it may serve to fill up a few spare minutes before we are called to our meal.

I need not repeat what was said on our parts; we drew our chairs round the fire; Abrahams gave a sigh, hemmed twice or thrice, as if the words in rising to his throat had choaked him, and thus began:

I was born in Spain, the only son of a younger brother of an antient and noble house, which like many others of the same origin and persuasion had long been in the indispensable practice of conforming to the established religion, whilst secretly and under the most guarded concealment every member of it without exception hath adhered to those opinions, which have been the faith of our tribe from the earliest ages.

This I trust will account to you for my declining to expose my real name, and justify the discretion of my assuming the fictitious one, by which I am now known to you.

Till I had reached my twentieth year I knew myself for nothing but a Christian, if that may be called Christianity, which monkish superstition and idolatry have so adulterated and distorted from the moral purity of its scriptural guides, as to keep no traces even of rationality in its form and practice.

This period of life is the usual season for the parents of an adult to reveal to him the awful secret of their concealed religion : the circumstances, under which this tremendous discovery is confided to the youth, are so contrived as to imprint upon his heart the strongest seal of secrecy, and at the same time present to his choice the alternative of parricide or conformity : with me there was no hesitation ; none could be ; for the yoke of Rome had galled my conscience till it festered, and I seized emancipation with the avidity of a ransomed slave, who escapes out of the hands of infidels.

Upon our great and solemn day of the Passover I was initiated into Judaism ; my father conducted me to the interior chamber of a suite of apartments, locking every door through which we passed with great precaution, and not uttering a syllable by the way ; in this secure retreat he purposed to celebrate that antient rite, which our nation holds so sacred : he was at that time in an alarming decline ; the agitating task he had been engaged in overpowered his spirits ; whilst he was yet speaking to me, and my eyes were fixed upon his face, the hand of death smote him ; I saw his eye-lids quiver ; I heard him draw his last expiring sigh, and falling dead upon my neck as I was kneeling at his feet, he brought me backwards to the floor, where I laid panting under his lifeless corpse, scarce more alive than he was.

The noise of his fall and the horrid shrieks I began to utter, for I had no presence of mind in that fatal moment, were unfortunately overheard, far as we were removed from the family : the room we were in had a communication with our private chapel ; the monk, who was our family confessor, had a master-key, which commanded the avenues to that place ; he was then before the altar, when my cries reached his ears ; he ascended hastily by the private stair-case, and finding the door locked, his terror at my yells adding strength to a colossal form, with one vehement kick he burst open the door, and, besides the tragic spectacle on the ground, too plainly discovered the damning proofs of our apostacy.

Vile wretch, cried he as he seized hold of my father's body, unholy villain, circumcised infidel! I thank my God for having smote thee with a sudden judgment: lie there like a dog as thou art, and expect the burial of a dog! This said, with one furious jerk of his arm he hurled the venerable corpse of the most benevolent of God's creatures with the utmost violence to the corner of the room: whilst I tell it my blood curdles; I heard his head dash against the marble floor; I did not dare to turn my eyes to the spot; the sword, which my father had presented to my hand and pointed at his own breast, when he imparted to me his faith, lay naked on the floor; I grasped it in my hand; nature tugged at my heart; I felt an impulse irresistible; I buried it in the bowels of the monk: I thrust it home with so good a will, that the guard entangled in the cord that was tied about his carcase; I left my weapon in the body, and the ponderous bigot fell thundering on the pavement.

A ready thought, which seemed like inspiration, seized me; I disposed my father's corpse in decent order; drew the ring from his finger, on which the symbol of our tribe was engraved in Hebrew characters; I took away those fatal tokens, which had betrayed us; there were implements for writing on a table; I wrote the following words on a scroll of paper—'This monk fell by my hand; he merited the death I gave him: let not my father's memory be attainted! He is innocent, and died suddenly by the will of Heaven and not by the hand of man.'— This I signed with my name, and affixed to the breast of the monk; then imprinting a last kiss upon the hand of my dead father, I went softly down the secret stairs, and passing through the chapel escaped out of the house unnoticed by any of the family.

Our house stood at one extremity of the antient city of Segovia; I made my way as fast as my feet would transport me to the forests of San Ildephonso, and there sheltered myself till night came on; by short and stealthy journeys, through various perils and almost incredible hardships, I arrived at Barcelona; I made myself known to an English merchant, settled there, who had long been a correspondent of my father's, and was employed by our family in the exportation of their wool, which is the chief produce of estates in the great plain of Segovia, so famous for its sheep. By this gentleman I was supplied with money and necessaries; he also gave me letters of credit upon his correspondent in London, and took a passage for me in a very commodious and capital ship bound to that port, but intermediately to Smyrna, whither she was chartered with a valuable cargo. Ever since the unhappy event in Segovia it had been my first and constant wish to take refuge in England; nothing therefore could be more acceptable than these letters of credit and introduction, and being eager to place myself under the protection of a nation, whose generosity all Europe bears testimony to, I lost not a moment in embarking on board the British Lion, (for so the ship was named) and in this asylum I for the first time found that repose of mind and body, which for more than two months I had been a stranger to.

Here I fortunately made acquaintance with a very worthy and ingenious gentleman, who was going to settle at Smyrna as physician to the factory, and to the care and humanity of this excellent person, under Providence, I am indebted for my recovery from a very dangerous fever, which seized me on the third day after my coming on board: this gentleman resided many years at Smyrna, and practised there with great success; he afterwards went through a very curious course of travel, and is now happily returned to his native country.

When we arrived at Smyrna I was on my recovery, and yet under the care of my friendly physician; I lodged in the same house with him, and found great benefit from the air and exercise on shore: he advised me to remain there for a season, and at the same time an offer was made to me by the ship's captain of acting for the merchants in place of their agent, who had died on the passage. The letters of credit given me at Barcelona, and the security entered into on my account with the house in London, warranted this proposal on his part, and there were many motives which prevailed with me for accepting it.

In this station I had the good fortune to give such satisfaction to my principals, that during a residence of more than twenty years I negotiated their business with uninterrupted success, and in the course of that time secured a competency for myself, and married a very worthy wife, with whom I have lived happily ever since.

Still my wishes pointed to this land of freedom and toleration, and here at last I hope I am set down for life: such was my prepossession for this country, that I may say without boasting, during twenty years residence in Smyrna, no Englishman ever left my door without the relief he solicited, or appeared to stand in need of.

I must not omit to tell you that to my infinite comfort it turned out, that my precautions after the death of the monk were effectual for preventing any mischief to the head of my family, who still preserves his rank, title and estate unsuspected; and although I was outlawed by name, time hath now wrought such a change in my person, and the affair hath so died away in men's memories, that I trust I am in security from any future machinations in that quarter : Still I hold it just to my family and prudent towards myself to continue my precautions : Upon the little fortune I raised in Smyrna, with some aids I have occasionally received from the head of our house, who is my nephew, and several profitable commissions for the sale of Spanish wool, I live contentedly, though humbly as you see, and I have besides wherewithal, (blessed be God!) to be of some use and assistance to my fellow creatures.

Thus I have related to you my brief history, not concealing that bloody act which would subject me to death by the sentence of a human tribunal, but for which I hope my intercession and atonement have been accepted by the Supreme Judge of all hearts, with whom there is mercy and forgiveness. Reflect I pray you upon my situation at that dreadful moment ; enter into the feelings of a son ; picture to yourselves the scene of horror before my eyes ; conceive a brutal zealot spurning the dead corpse of my father, and that father his most generous benefactor, honoured for his virtues and adored for his charities, the best of parents and the friend of mankind ; reflect, I say, upon these my agonies and provocations, make allowance for a distracted heart in such a crisis, and judge me with that charity, which takes the law of God, and not the law of man for its direction.

Here Abrahams concluded, and here also I shall adjourn to the succeeding number what remains to be related of the persons, whose adventures have already engrossed so large a portion of this miscellaneous work.

NUMBER XLV.

THE reader will recollect that the worthy Hebrew, who assumes the name of Abrahams, had just concluded the narrative of his adventures, and that the next morning was appointed for a conciliatory interview between Mrs. Goodison and her father. Ned, whose natural indolence had now began to give place to the most active of all passions, had been so much agitated by the events of the day, that we had no sooner parted from honest Abrahams, than he began to comment upon the lucky incident of our rencontre with the old gentleman at the comedy; he seemed strongly inclined to deal with destiny for some certain impulses, which he remembered to have felt, when he was so earnest to go to the play; and declared with much gravity, that he went thither fully prepossessed some good fortune would turn up: ‘Well, to be sure,’ said he, I ought to rejoice in the happy turn affairs have now taken, and I do rejoice; but it would have given me infinite delight to have fulfilled the plan I had in design for Mrs. Goodison’s accommodation; she will now want no assistance from me; my little cottage will never have the honour of receiving her; all those schemes are at an end; Constantia too will be a great fortune, she will have higher views in life, and think no more of me, or, if she did, it is not to be supposed her grandfather, who so bitterly resented his daughter’s match, will suffer her to fall into the same offence.’ I must confess I thought so entirely with my friend Ned in the concluding parts of these remarks, that I could only advise him to wait the event of time, and recommend himself in the mean while as well as he could to Mr. Somerville, the grandfather of Constantia. Art and education, it is true, had not contributed much to Ned's accomplishments, but nature had done great things in his favour; to a person admirably, though not finically formed, she had given a most interesting set of features, with such a striking character of benevolence and open honesty, that he might be said to carry his heart in his countenance: though there was a kind of lassitude in his deportment, the effect of habits long indulged, yet his sensibility was ever ready to start forth upon the first call, and on those occasions no one would have regretted that he had not been trained in the school of the Graces; there was something then displayed which they cannot teach, and only nature in her happiest moments can bestow.

The next morning produced a letter from honest Abrahams, full of joy for the happy reconciliation now established, and inviting us to celebrate the day with Mr. Somerville and the ladies at his house. This was an anxious crisis for my friend Ned; and I perceived his mind in such a state of agitation, that I thought fit to stay with him for the rest of the forenoon: he began to form a variety of conjectures as to the reception he was likely to meet from the old gentleman, with no less a variety of plans for his own behaviour, and even of speeches with which he was to usher in his first addresses; sometimes he sunk into melancholy and despair, at other times he would snatch a gleam of hope, and talk himself into transports; he was now, for the first time in his life, studiously contriving how to set off his person to the best advantage; his hair was fashionably dressed, and a handsome suit was tried on, during which he surveyed himself in the glass with some attention, and, as I thought, not entirely without a secret satisfaction, which, indeed, I have seen other gentlemen bestow upon their persons in a much greater degree, with much less reason for their excuse.

When he was completely equipt, and the time approached for our going, ' Alas!' he cried, ' what does all this signify? I am but a clown in better cloaths. Why was my father so neglectful of my education, or rather why was I so negligent to avail myself of the little he allowed me? What would I not give to redeem the time I have thrown away. But 'tis in vain: I have neither wit to recommend myself, nor address to disguise my want of it; I have nothing to plead in my favour, but common honour and honesty; and what cares that old hard-hearted fellow for qualities, which could not reconcile him to his own son-in-law? he will certainly look upon me with contempt. As for Constantia, gratitude, perhaps, might in time have disposed her heart towards me, and my zealous services might have induced her mother to overlook my deficiencies, but there is an end of that only chance I had for happiness, and I am a fool to thrust myself into a society, where I am sure to heap fresh fuel on my passion, and fresh misfortunes on my head.'

With these impressions, which I could only sooth but not dispel, Ned proceeded to the place of meeting with an aching heart and dejected countenance. We found the whole party assembled to receive us, and though my friend's embarrassment disabled him from uttering any one of the ready made speeches he had digested for the purpose, yet I saw nothing in Mr. Somerville's countenance or address, that

could augur otherwise than well for honest Ned;
Mrs. Goodison was as gracious as possible, and
Constantia's smile was benignity itself. Honest
Abrahams, who has all the hospitality as well as
virtues of his forefathers the patriarchs, received us
with open arms, and a face in which wide-mouthed
joy grinned most delectably. It was with pleasure I observed Mr. Somerville's grateful attentions
towards him and his good dame; they had nothing
of ostentation or artifice in them, but seemed the
genuine effusions of his heart; they convinced me
he was not a man innately morose, and that the resentment, so long fostered in his bosom, was effectually extirpated. Mrs. Abrahams, in her province,
had exerted herself to very good purpose, and spread
her board, if not elegantly, yet abundantly; Abrahams, on his part kept his wine and his tongue going
with incessant gaiety and good-humour, and whilst
he took every opportunity of drawing forth Ned's
honest heart and natural manners to the best advantage, I was happy in discovering that they did not
escape the intuition of Somerville, and that he made
faster progress towards his good opinion, than if he
had exhibited better breeding and less sincerity of
character.

In the course of the evening the old gentleman
told us he had determined upon taking his daughter
and Constantia into the country with him, where he
flattered himself Mrs. Goodison would recover her
health and spirits sooner than in town, and at the
same time gave us all in turn a pressing invitation to
his house. Abrahams and his wife excused themselves on the score of business; but Ned, who had
no such plea to make, or any disposition to invent
one, thankfully accepted the proposal.

The day succeeding and some few others, were
passed by Mrs. Goodison and Constantia at Mr.

Somerville's in the necessary preparations and arrangements previous to their leaving London; during this time Ned's diffidence and their occupations did not admit of any interview, and their departure was only announced to him by a note from the old gentleman, reminding him of his engagement; his spirits were by this time so much lowered from their late elevation, that he even doubted if he should accept the invitation; love however took care to settle this point in his own favour, and Ned arrived at the place of his destination rather as a victim under the power of a hopeless passion, than as a modern fine gentleman with the assuming airs of a conqueror. The charms of the beautiful Constantia, which had drawn her indolent admirer so much out of his character and so far from his home, now heightened by the happy reverse of the situation, and set off with all the aids of dress, dazzled him with their lustre; and though her change of fortune and appearance was not calculated to diminish his passion, it seemed to forbid his hopes: in sorrow, poverty and dependance, she had inspired him with the generous ambition of rescuing her from a situation so ill proportioned to her merits, and, though he had not actually made, he had very seriously meditated a proposal of marriage: He saw her now in a far different point of view, and comparing her with himself, her beauty, fortune and accomplishments with his own conscious deficiencies, he sunk into despair. This was not unobserved by Constantia; neither did she want the penetration to discern the cause of it. When he had dragged on his wretched existence for some days, he found the pain of it no longer supportable, and, ashamed of wearing a face of woe in the house of happiness, he took the hardy resolution of bidding farewell to Constantia and his hopes for ever.

Whilst he was meditating upon this painful subject one evening during a solitary walk, he was surprized to hear himself accosted by the very person, from whose chains he had determined to break loose; Constantia was unattended, the place was retired, the hour was solemn, and her looks were soft and full of compassion. What cannot love effect? it inspired him with resolution to speak; it did more, it supplied him with eloquence to express his feelings.

Constantia in few words gave him to understand that she rightly guessed the situation of his mind; this at once drew from him a confession of his love and his despair—of the former he spoke little and with no display; he neither sought to recommend his passion, or excite her pity; of his own defects he spoke more at large, and dwelt much upon his want of education; he reproached himself for the habitual indolence of his disposition, and then, for the first time raising his eyes from the ground, he turned them on Constantia, and after a pause exclaimed, ' Thank heaven! you are restored to a condition, which no longer subjects you to the possible sacrifice I had once the audacity to hint at. Conscious as I am of my own unworthiness at all times to aspire to such a proposal, let me do myself the justice to declare that my heart was open to you in the purest sense; that to have tendered an asylum to your beloved mother, without ensnaring your heart by the obligation, would still have been the pride of my life, and I as truly abhorred to exact, as you could disdain to grant an interested surrender of your hand: and now, lovely Constantia, when I am about to leave you in the bosom of prosperity, if I do not seem to part from you with all that unmixt felicity, which your good fortune ought to inspire, do not reproach me for my unhappy weakness; but recollect for once in your life, that your charms are irresistible and my soul only too susceptible of their power and too far plunged into despair, to admit of any happiness hereafter.'

At the conclusion of this speech Ned again fixed his eyes on the ground; after a short silence, ' I perceive,' replied Constantia, ' that my observations of late were rightly formed, and you have been torturing your mind with reflections very flattering to me, but not very just towards yourself : believe me, Sir, your opinion is as much too exalted in one case, as it is too humble in the other. As for me, having as yet seen little of the world but its miseries, and being indebted to the benevolence of human nature for supporting me under them, I shall ever look to that principle as a greater recommendation in the character of a companion for life, than the most brilliant talents or most elegant accomplishments : in the quiet walks of life I shall expect to find my enjoyments.' Here Ned started from his reverie, a gleam of joy rushed upon his heart, by an involuntary motion he had grasped one of her hands ; she perceived the tumult her words had created, and extricated her hand from his—' Permit me,' said she, ' to qualify my respect for a benevolent disposition by remarking to you, that without activity there can be no virtue : I will explain myself more particularly ; I will speak to you with the sincerity of a friend—You are blessed with excellent natural endowments, a good heart and a good understanding ; you have nothing to do but to shake off an indolent habit, and, having youth at your command, to employ the one and cultivate the other : the means of doing this it would be presumption in me to prescribe, but as my grandfather is a man well acquainted with the world and fully qualified to give advice, I should earnestly recommend to you not to take a hasty departure before you have consulted him, and I may

venture to promise you will never repent of any confidence you may repose in his friendship and discretion.'

Here Constantia put an end to the conference and
turned towards the house ; Ned stood fixed in deep
reflection, his mind sometimes brightening with
hope, sometimes relapsing into despair : his final determination, however, was to obey Constantia's advice and seek an interview with Mr. Somerville.

NUMBER XLVI.

THE next morning, as soon as Ned and Mr. Somerville met, the old gentleman took him into his
library, and when he was seated, ' Sir,' said he,
' I shall save you some embarrassment, if I begin
our conference by telling you that I am well apprised of your sentiments towards my Constantia;
I shall make the same haste to put you out of suspense, by assuring you that I am not unfriendly to
your wishes.'

This was an opening of such unexpected joy to
Ned, that his spirits had nearly sunk under the surprize ; he stared wildly without power of utterance,
scarce venturing to credit what he had heard; the
blood rushed into his cheeks, and Somerville, seeing
his disorder, proceeded : ' When I have said this on
my own part, understand, young gentleman, that I
only engage not to obstruct your success, I do not,
nay I cannot, undertake to ensure it : that must depend upon Constantia ; permit me to add, it must
depend upon yourself.' Here Ned, unable to sup-
press his transports, eagerly demanded what there

could be in his power to do, that might advance him
in the good opinion and esteem of Constantia; such
was his gratitude to the old gentleman for his kindness, that he could scarce refrain from throwing
himself at his feet, and he implored him instantly
to point out the happy means, which he would im-
plicitly embrace, were they ever so difficult, ever so
dangerous.

' There will be neither hardship nor hazard,' replied Mr. Somerville, ' in what I shall advise.
Great things may be accomplished in a short time
where the disposition is good and the understanding
apt: though your father neglected your education,
it is no reason you should neglect yourself; you
must shake off your indolence; and as the first step
necessary towards your future comfort is to put yourself at ease in point of fortune, you must make yourself master of your own estate; that I suspect can
only be done by extricating your affairs from the
hands they are in; but as this is a business, that
will require the assistance of an honest and able agent,
I shall recommend to you my own lawyer, on whose
integrity you may securely rely; he will soon re-
duce your affairs to such a system of regularity, that
you will find it an easy business, and when you
discover how many sources of future happiness it
opens to you, you will pursue it as an employment
of no less pleasure than advantage.'

To this good advice Ned promised the fullest and
most unreserved obedience; Mr. Somerville resum-
ed his subject and proceeded; ' When you have
thus laid the foundation in œconomy, what remains
to be done will be a task of pleasure: this will consist in furnishing your mind and enlarging your
experience, in short, Sir, rubbing off the rust of indolence and the prejudices of a narrow education:
now for this important undertaking I have a friend

in my eye, whose understanding, temper, morals and manners qualify him to render you most essential services; with this amiable and instructive companion I should in the first place recommend you to take a tour through the most interesting parts of your own country, and hereafter, as occasion shall serve, you may, or you may not, extend your travels into other countries : this is the best counsel I have to give you, and I tender it with all possible good wishes for your success.'

A plan, proposed with so much cordiality and holding forth such a reward for the accomplishment of its conditions, could not fail to be embraced with ardour by the late despairing lover of Constantia. The worthy lawyer was prepared for the undertaking, and Ned was all impatience to convince Mr. Somerville, that indolence was no longer his ruling defect. He gave instant orders for his journey, and then flew to Constantia, at whose feet he poured forth the humble, yet ardent, acknowledgments of a heart overflowing with gratitude and love : it seemed as if love's arrow, like *Ithuriel's* spear, possessed the magic powers of transformation with a touch : there was a spirit in his eyes, an energy in his motions, an illumination over his whole person, that gave his form and features a new cast : Constantia saw the sudden transformation with surprize, and as it evinced the flexibility of his nature and the influence of her own charms, she saw it also with delight : ' So soon !' was her only reply, when he announced his immediate departure, but those words were uttered with such a cadence, and accompanied by such a look, as to the eye and ear of love conveyed more meaning than volumes would contain, unaided by such expression—' Yes, adorable Constantia,' he exclaimed, ' I am now setting forth to give the earliest proof in my power of a ready and alert obedience to the dictates of my best adviser; these few moments, which your condescension indulges me with, are the only moments I shall not rigidly de- vote to the immediate duties of my task: inspired with the hope of returning less unworthy of your attention, I chearfully submit to banish myself from your sight for a time, content to cherish in my heart the lovely image there imprest, and flattering my- self I have the sanction of your good wishes for the success of my undertaking.' Constantia assured him he had her good wishes for every happiness in life, and, then yielding her hand to him, he tenderly pressed it to his lips and departed.

It would be an uninteresting detail to enumerate the arrangements, which Ned by the instructions of his friendly and judicious agent adopted on his re- turn to Poppy-hall. His affairs had indeed been much neglected, but they were not embarrassed, so that they were easily put into such order and regu- lation, as gave him full leisure for pursuing other objects of a more animating nature: with this view he returned to his friend Mr. Somerville, and was again blest with the presence of Constantia, to whom every day seemed to add new graces: he was wel- comed by all parties in the most affectionate man- ner; Mr. Somerville, upon conversing with his lawyer, received a very flattering report of Ned's activity and attention, nor was he displeased to hear from the same authority, that his estate and pro- perty far exceeded any amount, which the unpre- tending owner himself had ever hinted at.

It was now the latter end of April, and Ned had allowed himself only a few days to prepare for his tour, and to form an acquaintance with the amiable person, who at Mr. Somerville's request had en- gaged to accompany him; their plan was to em- ploy six months in this excursion through England

and part of Scotland, during which they were to
visit the chief towns and principal manufactories,
and Mr. Somerville had further contrived to lay out
their course, so as to fall in with the houses of some
of his friends by the way, where he had secured
them a welcome in such societies, as promised no
less profit than amusement to a young person in the
pursuit of experience. Measures had been taken to
provide equipage, servants, and all things requisite
for a travelling establishment, amongst which a few
well-selected books were not forgotten, and, thus at
length equipped, Ned with his companion, on the
first morning of the month of May, having taken
leave of Mr. Somerville and Mrs. Goodison, and received a tender adieu from his beloved Constantia,
stept reluctantly into his chaise, and left the finest
eyes in the creation to pay the tribute of a tear to
the sorrows of the scene.

From this period I had heard nothing of his proceedings till a few days ago, when I was favoured
by him with the following letter, dated from the
house of Mr. Somerville:

' DEAR SIR,
' I am just returned from a six months tour, in
the course of which I have visited a variety of places
and persons in company with a gentleman, from
whose pleasing society I have reaped the highest enjoyment, and, if I do not deceive myself, no small
degree of profit and instruction.
' Before I sate out upon this excursion, I had the
satisfaction of seeing my private affairs put in such
a train, and arranged upon so clear a system, that I
find myself in possession of a fund of occupation for
the rest of my days in superintending the concerns
of my estate, and interesting myself in the welfare and
prosperity of every person, who depends upon me.

' When I returned to this charming place, the reception I met with from Mr. Somerville was as flattering as can be conceived; the worthy mother of
my beloved Constantia was no less kind to me; but
in what words can I attempt to convey to you the
impression I felt on my heart, when I was welcomed
with smiles of approbation by the ever-adorable object of my affection? What transport did it give
me, when I found her anxious to enquire into every
circumstance that had occurred in the course of my
travels! none were too minute for her notice; she
seemed to take an interest in every thing that had
happened to me, and our conversations were renewed
time after time without weariness on her part, or any
prospect of exhausting our subject.

' At this time I had no other expectation but of a
second excursion with the conductor of the first,
and as that gentleman was in frequent conference
with Mr. Somerville, I took for granted they were
concerting the plan of a foreign tour; and though
my heart was every hour more and more fondly attached to Constantia, so that a separation from her
was painful to reflect on, yet I was resolved at all
events not to swerve from my engagements with her
grandfather, and therefore held myself in trembling
expectation of another summons to go forth: delightfully as the hours passed away in her society, I
dreaded lest any symptoms of self-indulgence should
lower me in her opinion, or create suspicions in Mr.
Somerville and Mrs. Goodison that I was in any
danger of relapsing into my former indolence: I
therefore seized the first opportunity of explaining
myself to those respectable friends, when Constantia
was not present, and addressing myself to Mr. Somerville, assured him that I was not disposed to
forget any part of his good advice, nor so much my
own enemy as to evade any one of those conditions

to the performance of which he had annexed the hope of so transcendant a reward: conscious that he could impose nothing upon me so hard to do, or so painful to suffer, which such a prize would not infinitely overbalance, I had no other backwardness or apprehension as to his commands, but what sprung from the conviction, that after all my efforts I must ever remain unworthy of Constantia.

' I shall never forget Mr. Somerville's reply, nor the action which accompanied it. My good friend, said he (leaning over the arm of the chair, and kindly taking me by the hand) it is more than enough for a man to have made one such fatal error in his life as I have done, one such unhappy sacrifice to the false opinions of the world; but though I have heartily repented of this error, I am not so far reformed, as to be without ambition in the choice of a husband for our Constantia; no, Sir, I am still as ambitious as ever, but I hope with better judgment and upon better principles; I will not bate an atom of virtue in the bargain I am to make; I insist upon the good qualities of the heart and temper to the last scruple; these are the essentials which I rigidly exact, and all these you possess: there are indeed other, many other, incidental articles, which you may, or you may not, superadd to the account; but I am contented to strike hands with you on the spot, though you shall never have set foot upon foreign soil.—What says my daughter to this?

' When I cast my eyes upon the countenance of the most benevolent of women, and saw it turned expressively upon me, smiling through tears, joy palpitated at my heart, whilst she delivered herself as follows:—I were of all beings most insensible, could I withhold my testimony to this gentleman's merits, or my entire assent to his alliance with my daughter; but as I have ever reposed perfect confidence in her, and, as far as I was enabled, always consulted her wishes, I should be glad this question might be fairly and candidly referred to her unbiassed judgment for decision : she is very young ; our friend here is neither old in years nor experience ; both parties have time before them ; should she be willing to hold off from the married state for a while, should she foresee advantages in our friend's undertaking a second tour with the same instructive associate, (whether into foreign countries or nearer home) let her be the judge of what is most likely to conduce to her future happiness in a husband, and as I am persuaded our friend here will practise no unfair measures for biassing her judgment, let him consult Constantia's wishes on the case, and as she determines so let him act, and so let us agree.

' With these instructions, which Mr. Somerville seconded, I hastened to Constantia, and without hesitation or disguise related to her what had passed and requested her decision. Judge (if it be possible to judge) of my transports, when that ingenuous, that angelic creature gave me a reply, that left no room to doubt that I was blest in the possession of her heart, and that she could not endure a second separation.

' I flew to Mr. Somerville ; I fell at the feet of Mrs. Goodison ; I interceded, implored, and was accepted. Nothing ever equalled the generosity of their behaviour. I am now to change my name to Somerville, at that worthy gentleman's express desire, and measures are already in train for that purpose. The same abilities, which I am indebted to for the good condition of my affairs, are employed in perfecting the marriage settlement, and the period now between me and happiness would by any other person but myself be termed a very short one.

' Thus am I on the very eve of being blest with

the loveliest, the divinest object upon earth, and
thus have I by the good counsel of my friends (in
which number I shall ever reckon you) broke the
shackles of that unmanly indolence, under which I
was sinking apace into irretrievable languor and in-
significance.   Henceforward I intreat you to regard
me as a new man, and believe that with my name I
have put off my infirmity.   We are in daily expectation of our friendly Abrahams, who is *an Is-
raelite indeed*: your company would round our circle
and complete the happiness of

> ' Your ever affectionate

> ' EDWARD.'

NUMBER XLVII.

PEOPLE have a custom of excusing the enormities of
their conduct by talking of their passions, as if they
were under the controul of a blind necessity, and
sinned because they could not help it.   Before any
man resorts to this kind of excuse, it behoves him
to examine the justice of it, and to be sure that these
passions, which he thus attempts to palliate, are
strictly natural, and do not spring either from the
neglect of education or the crime of self-indulgence.

Of our infancy, properly so called, we either remember nothing, or few things faintly and imper-
fectly; some passions however make their appearance in this stage of human life, and appear to be
born with us, others are born after us; some follow
us to the grave, others forsake us in the decline of
age.

The life of man is to be reviewed under three periods, infancy, youth, and manhood; the first includes that portion of time before reason shews itself; in the second it appears indeed, but being incompetent to the proper government of the creature, requires the aid, support, and correction of education; in the third it attains to its maturity.

Now as a person's responsibility bears respect to his reason, so do human punishments bear respect to his responsibility: Infants and boys are chastised by the hand of the parent or the master; rational adults are amenable to the laws, and what is termed mischief in the first case, becomes a crime in the other. It will not avail the man to plead loss of reason by temporary intoxication, nor can he excuse himself by the plea of any sudden impulse of passion. If a prisoner tells his judge that it is his nature to be cruel, that anger, lust, or malice are inherent in his constitution, no human tribunal will admit the defence: yet thus it is that all people deal with God and the world, when they attempt to palliate their enormities, by pleading the uncontroulable propensity of their natural desires, as if the Creator had set up a tyrant in their hearts, which they were necessitated to obey.

This miserable subterfuge is no less abject than impious; for what can be more degrading to a being, whose inherent attribute is free-agency and whose distinguishing faculty is reason, than to shelter himself from the dread of responsibility under the humiliating apology of mental slavery? It is as if he should say—' Excuse the irregularities of my conduct, for I am a brute and not a man; I follow instinct and renounce all claim to reason; my actions govern me, not I my actions;'—and yet the people, to whom I allude, generally set up this plea in excuse for those passions in particular, which have their origin in that stage of life, when the hu-

man mind is in the use and possession of reason;
an imposition so glaring that it convicts itself; notwithstanding this it is too often seen, that whilst the
sensualist is avowing the irresistible violence of his
propensities, vanity shall receive it not only as an
atonement for the basest attempts, but as an expected tribute to the tempting charms of beauty; nay,
such is the perversion of principle in some men,
that it shall pass with them as a recommendation
even of that sex, the purity of whose minds should
be their sovereign grace and ornament.

The passion of fear seems coeval with our nature; if they, who have our infancy in charge, suffer
this passion to fix and increase upon us; if they
augment our infant fears by invented terrors, and
present to our sight frightful objects to scare us; if
they practise on our natural and defenceless timidity
by blows and menaces, and crush us into absolute
subjection of spirit in our early years, a human
creature thus abused has enough to plead in excuse
for cowardice; and yet this, which is the strongest
defence we can make upon the impulse of passion,
is perhaps the only one we never resort to: In most
other passions we call that constitution, which is
only habit.

When we reflect upon the variety of passions, to
which the human mind is liable, it should seem as
if reason, which is expressly implanted in us for
their correction and controul, was greatly over-
matched by such a host of turbulent insurgents;
but upon a closer examination we may find that reason has many aids and allies, and though her anta-
gonists are also many and mighty, yet that they are
divided and distracted, whilst she can in all cases
turn one passion against another, so as to counter-
balance any power by its opposite, and make evil
instruments in her hands conducive to moral ends:

Avarice, for instance, will act as a counterpoise to lust and intemperance, whilst vanity on the other hand will check avarice; fear will keep a bad man honest, and pride will sometimes make a coward brave.

Observe the manners of *Palpatius* in company with his patron; assiduous, humble, obliging; for ever smiling, and so supple and obsequious, you would think he had no will of his own, and was born for the uses and occasions of others: Follow Palpatius to his house, see him with his wife and children, hear him dictate to his servants and the needy dependants, who make suit through him to his principal, you will find all things reversed; the sycophant turns out a tyrant, and he is only indebted to his hypocrisy for keeping his insolence out of sight.

Procax is one of the most dissolute men living; he is handsome, impudent, and insinuating, qualifications that ensure his success with the ladies: He professed the most vehement passion for Fulvia; but Fulvia was on the point of marrying Vetulus, a rich old man, who wanted an heir, and till that event took place she held out against Procax upon motives of convenience only: Fulvia soon became the wife of Vetulus; she had no longer any repugnance to be the mistress of Procax; but the same man, who had pleaded the irresistible violence of his desires before marriage, now pretended conscience, and drew back from her advances; nay he did more, he put Vetulus upon his guard, and Fulvia's virtue was too closely watched to be in any future danger: What sudden change was this in Procax? Vetulus had no heirs, and Procax had a contingent interest in the entail of his estate.

Splendida, in one of her morning airings, was solicited for charity by a poor woman with an infant in her arms.—' It is not for myself, madam,' said the

D 2

wretched creature, ' it is for my husband, who lies
under that hedge tormented with a fever, and dying
for want of relief.'—Splendida directed her eyes towards the spot, and saw a sickly object stretched
upon the ground, clad in the tattered regimental of
a foot soldier: Her heart was touched, and she
drew out her purse, which was full of guineas: The
blood rushed into the beggar's meagre visage at the
sight; Splendida turned over the gold; her hand de-
layed for a moment, and the impulse was lost; un-
happily for the suppliant, Splendida was alone and
without a witness: She put her hand once more into her pocket, and taking out a solitary shilling,
dropped it into the shrivelled palm that was stretched out to receive it, and drove on. Splendida returned home, drest herself, and went to a certain
great lady's assembly; a subscription was put about
for the benefit of a celebrated actress; the lady condescended to receive subscriptions in person, and
delivered a ticket to each contributor: Splendida
drew forth the same purse, and wrapping twenty
guineas in a paper, put them into the hand of the
noble beggar: The room rang with applauses of her
charity—' I give it,' says she, ' to her virtues, rather than to her talents; I bestow it on the wife
and mother, not upon the actress.' Splendida on
her return home took out her accompt-book, and
set down twenty-one pounds one shilling to the article of charity; the shilling indeed Heaven audited
on the score of alms, the pounds were posted to the
account of vanity.

NUMBER XLVIII.

————

An toti morimur?
SENECA IN TROAD.

I BELIEVE there are few people, who have not at some time or other felt a propensity to humour themselves in that kind of melancholy, which arises, in the mind upon revisiting the scene of former happiness, and contemplating the change that time has wrought in its appearance by the mournful comparison of present with past impressions.

In this train of thought I was the other day carried almost imperceptibly to the country seat of a deceased friend, whose loss I must ever lament. I had not been there since his death, and there was a dreariness in the scene as I approached, that might have almost tempted me to believe even things inanimate partook of my sensations. The traces of my friend, whose solicitude for order and seemliness reached to every thing about him, were no longer to be seen: The cottages and little gardens of his poor neighbours, which used to be so trim and neat, whilst his eye was over them, seemed to be falling into neglect; the lawn before his house was now become a solitude; no labourers at their work; no domestics at their sports and exercises: I looked around for my old acquaintance, that used to be grazing up and down, upon their pensions of pasturage; they had probably been food for hounds long ago; Nature had lost her smile of hospitality and benevolence; methought I never saw any thing more disconsolate.

As I entered the house, an aged woman, whom I
had long remembered as one of the family, met me
in the passage, and, looking me in the face, cried
out, ' Is it you, Sir?'—and burst into tears: She
followed me into the common sitting-room, and as
she was opening the shutters, observed to me—
' That it did not look as it used to do, when my
lord was living.' It was true: I had already made
the remark in silence :—' How the face of a friend,'
said I within myself, ' enlivens all things about
him! What hours of placid delight have I passed
within these walls! Have I ever heard a word here
fall from his lips, that I have wished him to recall?
Has the reputation of the absent ever bled by a stab
of his giving? Has the sensibility of any person
present suffered for an expression of his? Once, and
only once, in this very spot, I drew from him the
circumstantial detail of an unfortunate period in his
life: It was a recital so manly and ingenuous, so
void of colouring, so disdainful of complaint and so
untainted by asperity, that it carried conviction to
my mind, and I can scarce conceive a degree of prejudice that could have held out against it; but I
could perceive that the greatest event in a man's
history may turn by springs so subtle and concealed,
that they can never be laid open for public exculpa-
tion, and that in the process of all human trials
there may be things too small for the fingers of the
law to feel; motives, which produce the good or
ill fortunes of men and govern their actions, but
which cannot guide the judgments, or even come
under the contemplation of those who are appointed
to decide upon them.'

I soon quitted this apartment, and entered one
which I contemplated with more satisfaction, and
even with a degree of veneration ; for it was the
chamber, in which I had seen my friend yield up the

last breath of life. Few men had endured greater persecution in the world; none could leave it in greater peace and charity : If forgiveness of injuries constitutes a merit, our enemies surely are those to whom we are most beholden. How awful is the last scene of a man's life, who has filled a dubious and important part on the stage of the world!— ' Of a truth,' thought I, ' thou art happily removed out of an unfriendly world; if thou hadst deceived my good opinion, it had been an injury to my nature : But though the living man can wear a mask and carry on deceit, the dying Christian cannot counterfeit : Sudden death may smite the hypocrite, the sensualist, the impostor, and they may die in their shame; but slow and gradual dissolution, a lingering death of agony and decay, will strip the human heart before it seizes it; it will lay it naked, before it stops it. There is no trifling with some solemnities; no prevaricating with God, when we are on the very threshold of his presence : Many worldly friendships dissolve away with his breath to whom they were pledged; but thy last moments, my friend, were so employed as to seal my affection to thy memory closer than it was ever attached to thy person; and I have it now to say, there was a a man, whom I have loved and served, and who has not deceived or betrayed me.'

And what must I now think of popularity, when I reflect upon those who had it, and upon this man, who had it not? Fallacious test!—Contemptible pursuit! How often, since the exile of Aristides, has integrity been thy victim and villany thine idol? Worship it then, thou filthy idolater, and take the proper wages of thy servility; be the dupe of cunning, and the stalking-horse of hypocrisy.

What a contrast to the death I have now been reviewing, occurs to my mind, when I reflect upon the dreadful consummation of the once popular *Antitheus*! I remember him in the height of his fame, the hero of his party; no man so caressed, followed and applauded: He was a little loose, his friends would own, in his moral character, but then he was the honestest fellow in the world; it was not to be denied, that he was rather free in his notions, but then he was the best creature living. I have seen men of the gravest characters wink at his sallies, because he was so pleasant and so well bred, it was impossible to be angry with him. Every thing went well with him, and *Antitheus* seemed to be at the summit of human prosperity, when he was suddenly seized with the most alarming symptoms: He was at his country house, and (which had rarely happened to him) he at that time chanced to be alone; wife or family he had none, and out of the multitude of his friends no one happened to be near him at the moment of this attack.

A neighbouring physician was called out of bed in the night to come to him with all haste in this extremity: He found him sitting up in his bed supported by pillows, his countenance full of horror, his breath struggling as in the article of death, his pulse intermitting, and at times beating with such rapidity as could hardly be counted. *Antitheus* dismissed the attendants he had about him, and eagerly demanded of the physician, if he thought him in danger: the physician answered that he must fairly tell him he was in imminent danger—'How so! how so! do you think me dying?' He was sorry to say the symptoms indicated death—'Impossible! you must not let me die; I dare not die: O doctor! save me if you can.'—Your situation, Sir, is such, said the physician, that it is not in mine, or any other man's art, to save you; and I think I should not do my duty if I gave you any false hopes in these moments, which, if I am not mistaken, will not more than suffice for any worldly or other concerns, which you may have upon your mind to settle.—' My mind is full of horror,' cried the dying man, ' and I am incapable of preparing it for death.'—He now fell into an agony, accompanied with a shower of tears; a cordial was administered, and he revived in a degree; when turning to the physician, who had his fingers on his pulse, he eagerly demanded of him, if he did not see that blood upon the feet-curtains of his bed. There was none to be seen the physician assured him; it was nothing but a vapour of his fancy.—' I see it plainly,' said Antitheus, ' in the shape of a human hand: I have been visited with a tremendous apparition. As I was lying sleepless in my bed this night, I took up a letter of a deceased friend, to dissipate certain thoughts that made me uneasy. I believed him to be a great philosopher, and was converted to his opinions: Persuaded by his arguments and my own experience that the disorderly affairs of this evil world could not be administered by any wise, just or provident Being, I had brought myself to think no such Being could exist, and that a life produced by chance must terminate in annihilation: This is the reasoning of that letter, and such were the thoughts I was revolving in my mind, when the apparition of my dead friend presented itself before me; and unfolding the curtains of my bed, stood at my feet, looking earnestly upon me for a considerable space of time. My heart sunk within me; for his face was ghastly, full of horror, with an expression of such anguish as I can never describe: His eyes were fixed upon me, and at length with a mournful motion of his head—' Alas, alas !' he cried, ' we are in a fatal error'—and taking hold of the curtains with his hand, shook them violently and disappeared.—This I protest to you, I both saw and heard, and look! where the print of his hand is left in blood upon the curtains.'

Antitheus survived the relation of this vision very few hours, and died delirious in great agonies.

What a forsaken and disconsolate creature is a man without religion !

Reader, whosoever thou art, deceive not thyself; let not passion, or prosperity, or wit, or wantonness, seduce thy reason to an attempt against the truth. If thou hast the faculties of a man, thou wilt never bring thyself to a fixed persuasion that there is no God : Struggle how thou wilt against the notion, there will be a moment when the glaring conviction will burst upon thy mind. Now mark what follows—If there is a God, the government of the world is in that God ; and this once admitted, the necessity of a future state follows of consequence. Ask thyself then, what can be the purposes of that future state; what, but those of justice and retribution, to reward the good and to punish the evil? Our present life then is a life of probation, a state of trial and of discipline, preparatory to that future state. Now see what is fallen upon thee, and look well to thyself for the consequences: Thou hast let the idea of a God into thy mind, because indeed thou couldst not keep it out, and religion rushes through the breach. It is natural religion hitherto, and no more : But no matter ; there is enough even in natural religion to make thee tremble. Whither wilt thou now resort for comfort, whither fly for refuge from the wrath to come?—Behold the asylum is open, Christianity is thy salvation and redemption : That, which natural religion hath shadowed out to thee in terrors, Christianity will reveal in glory : It will clear up thy doubts, disperse thy fears, and turn thy hopes into certainty. Thy reasonings about a future state, which are but reasonings, it will not only verify by divine authorities, but by positive proof, by visible example, attested by witnesses, confirmed by the evidence of the senses, and uncontradicted by the history of ages. Now thou wilt know to thy comfort, that there is a Mediator gone before thee, who will help out thy imperfect atonement, when thou art brought to judgment in a future state. Thou wilt indeed be told for certain, that this life is a state of probation, and that thou shalt be brought to account for thine actions; but thou wilt be taught an easy lesson of salvation; thou wilt be cheared with the mercies of thy God, and comforted with the assurance of pardon, if thou wilt heartily turn to repentance: Thou wilt find that all this system of religion is conformable to those natural notions, which reason suggested to thee before, with this advantage, that it makes them clearer, purifies, refines, enlarges them; shuts out every dismal prospect, opens all that is delightful, and *points a road to Heaven through paths of peace and pleasantness.*

NUMBER XLIX.

As I was turning over a parcel of old papers some time ago, I discovered an original letter from Mr. Caswell, the mathematician, to the learned Dr. Bentley, when he was living in Bishop Stillingfleet's family, inclosing an account of an apparition taken from the mouth of a clergyman who saw it. In this account there are some curious particulars, and I shall therefore copy the whole narrative without any omission except of the name of the deceased person who is supposed to have *appeared*, for reasons that will be obvious.

' To the Rev. Mr. Richard Bentley, at my Lord
    Bishop of Worcester's house in Park Street, in
    Westminster, London.

    ' SIR,

    ' When I was in London, April last, I fully intended to have waited upon you again, as I said, but a cold and lameness seized me next day; the cold took away my voice, and the other my power of walking, so I presently took coach for Oxford. I am much your debtor, and in particular for your good intentions in relation to Mr. D. though that, as it has proved, would not have turned to my advantage: however, I am obliged to you upon that and other accounts, and if I had opportunity to shew it, you should find how much I am your faithful servant.

    ' I have sent you inclosed a relation of an apparition; the story I had from two persons, who each had it from the author, and yet their accounts somewhat varied, and passing through more mouths has varied much more; therefore I got a friend to bring me to the author at a chamber, where I wrote it down from the author's mouth; after which I read it to him, and gave him another copy; he said he could swear to the truth of it, as far as he is concerned: he is the Curate of Warblington, Batchelour of Arts of Trinity College in Oxford, about six years standing in the University; I hear no ill report of his behaviour here: he is now gone to his Curacy; he has promised to send up the hands of the tenant and his man, who is a smith by trade, and the farmer's men, as far as they are concerned.

Mr. Brereton, the Rector, would have him say nothing of the story, for that he can get no tenant,
though he has offered the house for ten pounds a
year less. Mr. P. the former incumbent, whom
the apparition represented, was a man of a very ill
report, supposed to have got children of his maid,
and to have murthered them; but I advised the
Curate to say nothing himself of this last part of
P. but leave that to the parishioners, who knew him.
Those who knew this P. say he had exactly such a
gown, and that he used to whistle.

Your's,

' J. Caswell.'

I desire you not to suffer any copy of this to be
taken, lest some Mercury news-teller should print
it, till the Curate has sent up the testimony of
others and self.

H. H. Dec. 15, 1695.

NARRATIVE.

' At Warblington, near Havant in Hampshire,
within six miles of Portsmouth, in the parsonage
house dwelt Thomas Perce the tenant, with his wife
and a child, a man-servant Thomas . . . . and a
maid-servant. About the beginning of August,
Anno 1695, on a Monday, about nine or ten at
night, all being gone to bed, except the maid with
the child, the maid being in the kitchen, and having
raked up the fire, took a candle in one hand, and
the child in the other arm, and turning about saw
one in a black gown walking through the room,
and thence out of the door into the orchard: upon
this the maid, hasting up stairs, having recovered
but two steps, cried out; on which the master and
mistress ran down, found the candle in her hand,
she grasping the child about its neck with the other
arm; she told them the reason of her crying out;

she would not that night tarry in the house, but removed to another belonging to one Henry Salter,
farmer; where she cried out all the night from the
terror she was in, and she could not be persuaded to
go any more to the house upon any terms.

'On the morrow, (i. e. Tuesday) the tenant's
wife came to me, lodging then at Havant, to desire
my advice, and have consult with some friends about
it; I told her I thought it was a flam, and that they
had a mind to abuse Mr. Brereton the Rector, whose
house it was; she desired me to come up; I told
her I would come up and sit up or lie there, as she
pleased; for then as to all stories of ghosts and
apparitions I was an infidel: I went thither and
sate up the Tuesday night with the tenant and his
man-servant: about twelve or one o'clock I searched
all the rooms in the house to see if any body were
hid there to impose upon me: at last we came into
a lumber-room, there I smiling told the tenant that
was with me, that I would call for the apparition,
if there was any, and oblige him to come: the
tenant then seemed to be afraid, but I told him I
would defend him from harm! and then I repeated
Barbara, celarent Darii, &c. jestingly; on this the
tenant's countenance changed, so that he was ready
to drop down with fear: then I told him I perceived he
was afraid, and I would prevent its coming, and
repeated *Baralipton*, &c. then he recovered his spirits
pretty well and we left the room and went down
into the kitchen, where we were before, and sate up
there the remaining part of the night and had no
manner of disturbance.

'Thursday night the tenant and I lay together in
one room and the man in another room, and he saw
something walk along in a black gown and place
itself against a window, and there stood for some
time, and then walked off. Friday morning the

man relating this, I asked him why he did not call
me, and I told him I thought that was a trick or
flam; he told me the reason why he did not call me
was, that he was not able to speak or move. Friday night we lay as before, and Saturday night,
and had no disturbance either of the nights.

' Sunday night I lay by myself in one room (not
that where the man saw the apparition) and the
tenant and his man in one bed in another room;
and betwixt twelve and two the man heard something walk in their room at the bed's foot, and
whistling very well; at last it came to the bed's
side, drew the curtain and looked on them; after
some time it moved off; then the man called to me,
desired me to come, for that there was something
in the room went about whistling: I asked him
whether he had any light or could strike one, he
told me no; then I leapt out of bed, and, not staying
to put on my clothes, went out of my room and
along a gallery to the door, which I found locked
or bolted; I desired him to unlock the door, for
that I could not get in; then he got out of bed and
opened the door, which was near, and went immediately to bed again; I went in three or four steps,
and, it being a moonshine night, I saw the apparition move from the bed side, and clap up against
the wall that divided their room and mine: I went
and stood directly against it within my arm's length
of it, and asked it in the name of God what it was,
that made it come disturbing of us; I stood some
time expecting an answer, and receiving none, and
thinking it might be some fellow hid in the room to
fright me, *I put out my arm to feel it, and my hand*
seemingly went through the body of it, and felt no
manner of substance, till it came to the wall; then
I drew back my hand, and still it was in the same
place : till now I had not the least fear, and even

now had very little; then I adjured it to tell me what it was: when I had said those words, it, keeping its back against the wall, moved gently along towards the door: I followed it, and it, going out at the door, turned its back towards me: it went a little along the gallery; I followed it a little into the gallery, and it disappeared, where there was no corner for it to turn, and before it came to the end of the gallery, where was the stairs. Then I found myself very cold from my feet as high as my middle, though I was not in great fear; I went into the bed betwixt the tenant and his man, and they complained of my being exceeding cold. The tenant's man leaned over his master in the bed, and saw me stretch out my hand towards the apparition, and heard me speak the words; the tenant also heard the words. The apparition seemed to have a morning gown of a darkish colour, no hat nor cap, short black hair, a thin meagre visage of a pale swarthy colour, seemed to be of about forty-five or fifty years old; the eyes half shut, the arms hanging down; the hands visible beneath the sleeve; of a middle stature. I related this description to Mr. John Lardner, rector of Havant, and to Major Battin of Langstone in Havant parish; they both said the description agreed very well to Mr. P. a former rector of the place, who has been dead above twenty years: upon this the tenant and his wife left the house, which has remained void since.

   ' The Monday after last Michaelmas-day, a man of Chodson in Warwickshire having been at Havant fair, passed by the aforesaid parsonage-house about nine or ten at night, and saw a light in most of the rooms of the house; his pathway being close by the house, he, wondering at the light, looked into the kitchen window, and saw only a light, but turning himself to go away, he saw the appearance of a man in a long gown; he made haste away; the apparition followed him over a piece of glebe land of several acres, to a lane, which he crossed, and over a little meadow, then over another lane to some pales, which belong to farmer Henry Salter my landlord, near a barn, in which were some of the farmer's men and some others; this man went into the barn, told them how he was frighted and followed from the parsonage-house by an apparition, which they might see standing against the pales, if they went out; they went out, and saw it scratch against the pales, and make a hideous noise; it stood there some time and then disappeared; their description agreed with what I saw. This last account I had from the man himself, whom it followed, and also from the farmer's men.

'THO. WILKINS, Curate of W.'
Dec. 11, 1695, *Oxon.*

I shall make no remark upon this genuine account, except as to the passage which I have put in italics: if Mr. Wilkins was thoroughly possest of himself at that moment, as he deposes, and is strictly correct in his fact, the narrative is established.

NUMBER L.

To the Observer.

SIR,

I AM a plain man without pretensions, and lead a retired life in the country: the sports of the season, a small farm, which I hold in my own hands, and a pretty good kitchen garden, in which I take

amusement, with the help of a few English books,
have hitherto made my life, though it is that of a
bachelor, pass off with more than tolerable comfort.
By this account of my time you will perceive that
most of my enjoyments depend upon the weather;
and though the wear-and-tear of age may have
made me more sensible to the seasons than I have
been, yet I cannot help thinking that our climate in
England is as much altered for the worse, as my
constitution may be. I do not pretend to reason
upon natural causes, but speak upon observation
only; for by an exact journal of my time (which I
keep more for a check upon my actions than for
any importance which appertains to them), I can
find that I am obliged to my books for helping me
through more rainy hours in the course of years last
past, than I have been accustomed to be, or indeed
than I could wish; for you must know I never
read, when I can amuse myself out of doors.

My studies are but trifling, for I am no scholar,
but in bad weather and dark evenings they have
served to fill up time; a very little discouragement
however suffices to put me out of conceit with my
books, and I have thoughts of laying them totally
on the shelf, as soon as ever I can provide some
harmless substitute in their place: this, you see, is
not so easy for me to do, being a solitary man, and
one that hates drinking, especially by myself; add
to this, that I smoke no tobacco, and have more
reasons than I chuse to explain against engaging in
the nuptial state: my housekeeper, it is true, is a
decent conversable woman, and plays a good game
at all-fours; and I had begun to fill up an hour in
her company, till I was surprized unawares by a
neighbour, who is a wag, and has never ceased
jeering me upon it ever since: I took next to
making nets for my currant bushes, but alas! I have

worked myself out of all employ, and am got
weary of the trade: I have thought of making
fishing-rods; but I have a neighbour so tenacious
of his trout, that I should only breed a quarrel, and
fish in troubled waters, were I to attempt it. To
make short of my story, Sir, I have been obliged,
after many efforts to go back to my books, though
I have lost all the little relish I had for them ever
since I have been honoured with the visits of a
learned gentleman, who is lately settled in my
neighbourhood. He must be a prodigious scholar,
for I believe in my conscience he knows every thing
that ever was written, and every body that ever
writes. He has taken a world of kind pains, I
must confess, to set me right in a thousand things,
that I was ignorant enough to be pleased with : he
is a fine spoken man, and in spite of my stupidity
has the patience to convince me of the faults and
blunders of every author in his turn. When he
shews them to me, I see them as clear as day, and
never take up the book again; he has now gone
pretty nearly through my whole nest of shelves,
pointing out as he proceeds, what I, like a fool,
never saw before, nor ever should have seen but for
him. I used to like a *Spectator* now and then, and
generally sought out for *Clio*, which, I was told,
were Mr. Addison's papers; but I have been in a
gross mistake, to lose my time with a man that
cannot write common English ; for my friend has
proved this to me out of a fine book, three times as
big as the *Spectator*, and, which is more, this great
book is made by a foreign gentleman, who writes
and speaks clear another language from Mr. Addison ; surely he must be a dunce indeed, who is to be
taught his mother tongue by a stranger ! I was apt
to be tickled with some of our English poets, Dryden and Pope and Milton, and one Gray, that turns

out to be a very contemptible fellow truly, for he
has shewn me all their secret histories in print,
written by a learned man greater than them all put
together, and now I would not give a rush for one
of them; I could find in my heart to send *Bell* and
all his books to the devil. As for all the writers
now living, my neighbour, who by the way has a
hand in reviewing their works, assures me he can
make nothing of them, and indeed I wonder that a
man of his genius will have any thing to say to
them. It was my custom to read a chapter or two
in the Bible on a Sunday night; but there I am
wrong again; I shall not enter upon the subject
here, but it won't do, that I am convinced of, Sir;
it positively will not do.

The reason of my writing to you at all is only to
let you know, that I received a volume of your
Observer by the coach; my friend has cast his eye
over it, and I have returned it by the waggon,
which he says is the fittest conveyance for waste
paper. I am, Sir,

Your humble servant,
RUSTICUS.

I shall give no other answer to my correspondent
but to lament his loss of so innocent a resource as
reading, which I suspect his new acquirements will
hardly compensate. I still think that half an hour
passed with Mr. Addison over a *Spectator*, notwithstanding all his false grammar, or even with one of
the poets, notwithstanding their infirmities, might
be as well employed as in weaving nets for the currant bushes, or playing at all-fours with his housekeeper. No man has a right to complain of the
critic, whose sagacity discovers inaccuracies in a
favourite author, and some readers may probably
be edified by such discoveries; but the bulk of

them, like my correspondent Rusticus, will get nothing but disgust by the information : every man's work is fair game for the critic ; but let the critic beware that his own production is not open to retaliation. As for our late ingenious biographer of the poets, when I compare his life of Savage with that of Gray, I must own he has exalted the low, and brought down the lofty ; with what justice he has done this the world must judge. On the part of our authors now living, whom the learned gentleman in the letter condemns in the lump, I have only this to observe, that the worse they fare now, the better they will succeed with posterity ; for the critics love the sport too well to hunt any but those who can stand a good chace ; and authors are the only objects in nature, which are magnified by distance and diminished by approach : let the illustrious dead change places with the illustrious living, and they shall escape no better than they have done who make room for them ; the more merit they bring amongst us, the heavier the tax they shall pay or it.

Let us suppose for a moment that Shakspeare was now an untried poet, and opened his career with any one of his best plays : the next morning ushers into the world the following, or something like the following critique.

' Last night was presented, for the first time, a tragedy called *Othello, or the Moor of Venice*, avowedly the production of *Mr. William Shakspeare*, the actor. This gentleman's reputation in his profession is of the *mediocre* sort, and we predict that his present tragedy will not add much to it in any way. —*Mediocribus esse poetis*—the reader can supply the rest—*verb. sap.* As we profess ourselves to be friendly to the players in general, we shall reserve our fuller critique of this piece, till after its third night; for *we hold it very stuff of the conscience* (to use Mr. Shakspeare's own words) not to war against the poet's purse; though we might apply the author's quaint conceit to himself—

' Who steals *his* purse, steals trash; 'tis something; nothing.

In this last reply we agree with Mr. Shakspeare that *'tis nothing*, and our philosophy tells us *ex nihilo nihil fit*.

' For the plot of this tragedy the most we can say is, that it is certainly of the *moving* sort, for it is here and there and every where; a kind of theatrical *hocus-pocus*; a creature of the pye-ball breed, like Jacob's muttons, between a black ram and a white ewe. It brought to our mind the children's game of—*I love my love with an A*—with this difference only, that the young lady in this play loves her love with a B, *because he is black—Risum teneatis ?*

' There is one *Iago*, a bloody-minded fellow, who stabs men in the dark behind their backs; now this is a thing we hold to be most vile and ever-to-be abhorred. Othello smothers his white wife in bed; our readers may think this a shabby kind of an action for a general of his high calling; but we beg leave to observe that it shews some spirit at least in Othello to attack the enemy in her *strong quarters* at once. There was an incident of a *pocket-handkerchief*, which *Othello* called out for most lustily, and we were rather sorry that his lady could not produce it, as we might then have seen one *handkerchief* at least employed in the tragedy. There were some *vernacular* phrases, which caught our ear, such as where the black damns his wife twice in a breath—*Oh damn her, damn her !*—which we thought savoured more of the language spoken *at* the doors, than *within* the doors of the theatre; but

when we recollect that the author used to amuse a
leisure hour with calling up gentlemen's coaches
after the play was over, before he was promoted to
take a part in it, we could readily account for old
habits. Though we have seen many gentlemen and
ladies kill themselves on the stage, yet we must
give the author credit for the new way in which his
hero puts himself out of the world: Othello having
smothered his wife, and being taken up by the officers of the state, prepares to dispatch himself and
escape from the hands of justice ; to bring this
about, he begins a story about his killing a man in
Aleppo, which he illustrates *par example* by stabbing
himself, and so winds up his story and his life in
the same moment. The author made his appearance in the person of one *Brabantio*, an old man,
who makes his first entry from a window; this occasioned some risibility in the audience : the part is
of an inferior kind, and Mr. Shakspeare was more
indebted to the exertions of his brethren, than to
his own, for carrying his play through. Upon the
whole, we do not think the passion of jealousy, on
which the plot turns, so proper for tragedy as comedy, and we would recommend to the author, if
his piece survives its nine nights, to cut it down to
a farce, and serve it up to the public *cum micá salis*
in that shape. After this specimen of Mr. William
Shakspeare's tragic powers, we cannot encourage
him to pursue his attempts upon Melpomene ; for
there is a good old proverb, which we would advise
him to bear in mind—*ne sutor ultra crepidam*—If he
applies to his friend *Ben,* he will turn it into English for him.'

NUMBER LI.

Ulcera animi sananda magis quam corporis.

EX SENTENT.

Canst thou not minister to a mind diseas'd?

MACBETH.

It seems as if most of the antient writers of history thought no events worth recording to posterity but accounts of battles and sieges and the overthrow of empires ; as if men were to be celebrated only in proportion to the devastation they had made of the human species. As my respect, on the contrary, is directed chiefly to those peaceable characters, who have been the benefactors of mankind, it is with pleasure I discovered an anecdote of an antient king of Egypt of this description, named Osymanduas : This good prince, amongst other praiseworthy actions, has the credit of making the first public library in that learned nation, before books were collected at Athens by Pisistratus : Osymanduas made no scruple to convert one of the chief temples to this generous use, and gave it in charge to the priests belonging to it to digest and arrange his collection ; when this was done, he laid it open to the public, and by a very apposite and ingenious device, which he caused to be inscribed upon the front of the edifice, invited all his subjects to enter in and partake of his benefaction : He considered it as the duty of a good king to provide against the mental as well as bodily ailments of his people ; it appeared to him that books were the best medicines for the mind of man, and consequently that a collec-

tion of books, such as his library contained, might
well be entitled—a magazine or warehouse of medicines for the mind; with this idea he directed the
following words to be engraved over the door of
his library in conspicuous characters—Ψυχῆς ἰατρεῖον.
There is a beautiful simplicity in the thought,
which seems to give an insight into the benevolent
design of the donor; and as I hold it a more noble
office to preserve the mind in health, than to keep
the body after death from corruption, I cannot hesitate to give Osymanduas more credit for this benefaction of a library, than if he had been founder of
the pyramids.

As the distempers of the mind may be figura-
tively classed under the several characters of those
maladies, which are incidental to the body, so the
several descriptions of books may very well be
sorted into the various *genera* of medicines, which
practice has applied to those respective distempers.
A library, thus pharmaceutically disposed, would
have the appearance of a dispensatory, and might
be properly enough so called; and when I recollect
how many of our eminent collectors of books have
been of the medical faculty, I cannot but think it probable that those great benefactors to literature, Rat-
cliffe, Mead, Sloane, Hunter, and others, have had
this very idea of Osymanduas in their minds, when
they founded their libraries. If therefore it should
be thought agreeable to the will of the donors,
and a proper mark of respect to their memories, so
to arrange their collections, now in the repositories
of Oxford and the British Museum, it will be necessary to find out a different set of titles, and instead of sorting them as they now are into the compartments of *The Historians*; *The Poets*; *The Di-
vines*, it will be right to set up new inscriptions in
their places, and intitle them, *The Alteratives*; *The*

Stimulatives; *The Narcotics*. I need not point out
to the learned keepers of these libraries how to proceed in an arrangement, to which their own judgments are so fully competent; nothing more will
be required of them, but to ascertain the particular
species of disease, which the mind of the patient is
affected with, and send him forthwith to the proper
class of authors for his cure.

For instance; if the complaint arises from cold
humours and a want of free perspiration by a stop-
page and constipation of the pores of the mind, by
which the feelings are rendered inert, and deprived
of that proper emanation and expansion, which the
health of the soul requires; let such a one be shut
into the warm bath of *the Sudorifics*, which I need
not explain to be *the Satyrists*, and they will soon
open his pores and disperse all obstructions. If
the mental disease be of the inflammatory and fe-
verish sort, attended with fits and paroxysms of
anger, envy, revenge, and other atrabilious symptoms, which cannot be mistaken, it will be proper
to turn the patient into the cell of the moralists,
who will naturally be found under the title of *The
Coolers and Sedatives*: On the contrary, where the
complaint is of the lethargic nature, in which irri-
tation is necessary, the controversialists will furnish
him a remedy: In short, we need only say, that
when the several authors are properly arranged,
every case may find its cure. The comic writers
will act as carminatives to dispel the vapours;
books of travels as cathartics to procure a motion;
memoirs and novels will operate as provocatives,
politics as corrosives, and panegyrics as emetics.
Two compartments should be kept apart and specially distinguished, viz. the sacred writings under
the title *Restoratives*, and the works of the infidels
under the denominations of deadly poisons: The

former will be sovereign in all galloping consumptions of dissipation, and the latter will be resorted to by none but suicides and desperadoes.

I should now dismiss the subject, but that I had forgotten to speak of the essayists, who from their miscellaneous properties certainly come under the class of compounds, and cannot therefore be so precisely specified ; as they are applicable to chronic diseases rather than acute ones, they may very well stand in the list of correctors, which taken in a regular course and under proper regimen are found very efficacious in all cases, where the constitution is impaired by excess and bad habits of living : They seem most to resemble those medicinal springs, which are impregnated with a variety of properties, and when critically analyzed are found to contain salt, nitre, steel, sulphur, chalk and other calcareous particles : When the more respectable names of *Bath*, *Spa*, *Pyrmont*, *Seltzer*, and others, are disposed of, I am not without hope these humbler essays, which my candid readers are now in the course of taking, may be found to have the wholesome properties of *Tunbridge waters*.

It is supposed that this library of the venerable *Osymanduas* descended to the Ptolemies, augmented probably by the intermediate monarchs, and ultimately brought to perfection by the learned and munificent Philadelphus, son of Ptolemy Lagus, so well known for his Greek translation of the Hebrew Septuagint.

Little attention was paid to literature by the Romans in the early and more martial ages : I read of no collections antecedent to those made by Æmilius Paulus and Lucullus, the latter of whom, being a man of great magnificence, allowed the learned men of his time to have free access to his library, but neither in his life-time, nor at his death, made it public property. Cornelius Sylla before his dictatorship plundered Athens of a great collection of books, which had been accumulating from the time of the tyranny, and these he brought to Rome, but did not build or endow any library for public use. This was at last undertaken by Julius Cæsar upon an imperial scale not long before his death, and the learned M. Varro was employed to collect and arrange the books for the foundation of an ample library; its completion, which was interrupted by the death of Julius and the civil wars subsequent thereto, was left for Augustus, who assigned a fund out of the Dalmatian booty for this purpose, which he put into the hands of the celebrated Asinius Pollio, who therewith founded a temple to liberty on Mount Aventine, and with the help of Sylla's and Varro's collections in addition to his own purchases, opened the first public library in Rome in an apartment annexed to the temple above mentioned. Two others were afterwards instituted by the same emperor, which he called the Octavian and Palatine Libraries; the first, so named in honour of his sister, was placed in the temple of Juno; the latter, as its title specifies, was in the imperial palace: These libraries were royally endowed with establishments of Greek and Latin librarians, of which C. Julius Hyginus the grammarian was one,

The emperor Tiberius added another library to the palace, and attached his new building to that front which looked towards the *Via sacra*, in which quarter he himself resided. Vespasian endowed a public library in the temple of Peace. Trajan founded the famous Ulpian library in his new forum, from whence it was at last removed to the *Collis Viminalis* to furnish the baths of Dioclesian. The Capitoline library is supposed to have been founded by Domitian, and was consumed, together

with the noble edifice to which it was attached,
by a stroke of lightning in the time of Commodus.
The emperor Hadrian enriched his favourite villa
with a superb collection of books, and lodged them
in a temple dedicated to Hercules. These were in
succeeding times so multiplied by the munificence
and emulation of the several emperors, that in the
reign of Constantine, Rome contained no less than
twenty-nine public libraries, of which the principal
were the Palatine and the Ulpian.

Though books were then collected at an im-
mense expence, several private citizens of fortune
made considerable libraries. Tyrannio the grammarian even in the time of Sylla was possessed of
three thousand volumes: Epaphroditus, a grammarian also, had in later times collected thirty thousand of the most select and valuable books; but
Sammonicus Serenus bequeathed to the emperor
Gordian a library containing no less than sixty-two
thousand volumes. It was not always a love of literature that tempted people to these expences, for
Seneca complains of the vanity of the age in furnishing their banquetting rooms with books, not
for use, but for shew, and in a mere spirit of pro-
fusion. Their baths, both hot and cold, were always supplied with books to fill up an idle hour
amongst the other recreations of the place; in like
manner their country houses and even public offices
were provided for the use and amusement of their
guests or clients.

The Roman libraries in point of disposition much
resembled the present fashion observed in our public ones, for the books were not placed against the
walls, but brought into the area of the room in
separate cells and compartments, where they were
lodged in presses: The intervals between these
compartments were richly ornamented with inlaid

plates of glass and ivory, and marble basso-relievos.
In these compartments, which were furnished with
desks and couches for the accommodation of readers, it was usual to place the statues of learned
men, one in each; and this we may observe is one
of the few elegancies, which Rome was not indebted to Greece for, the first idea having been
started by the accomplished Pollio, who in his library on Mount Aventine set up the statue of his
illustrious contemporary Varro, even whilst he was
living: It was usual also to ornament the press,
where any considerable author's works were contained, with his figure in brass or plaister of a
small size.

There is one more circumstance attending these
public libraries, which ought not to be omitted, as
it marks the liberal spirit of their institution: It
was usual to appropriate an adjoining building for
the use and accommodation of students, where
every thing was furnished at the emperor's cost:
they were lodged, dieted and attended by servants
specially appointed, and supplied with every thing,
under the eye of the chief librarian, that could be
wanting, whilst they were engaged in their studies,
and had occasion to consult the books: This establishment was kept up in a very princely stile at
Alexandria in particular, where a college was endowed and a special fund appointed for its support, with a president, and proper officers under
him, for the entertainment of learned strangers,
who resorted thither from various parts to consult
those invaluable collections, which that famous library contained in all branches of science.

NUMBER LII.

Singula lætus
Exquiritque, auditque, virum monumenta priorum.

VIRGIL.

OF all our dealers in second-hand wares, few bring their goods to so bad a market, as those humble wits who retail other peoples' worn-out jokes. A man's good sayings are so personally his own, and depend so much upon manner and circumstances, that they make a poor figure in other people's mouths, and suffer even more by printing than they do by repeating: It is also a very difficult thing to pen a witticism; for by the time we have adjusted all the descriptive arrangements of this man said, and t'other man replied, we have miserably blunted the edge of the repartee. These difficulties however have been happily overcome by Mr. Joseph Miller and other facetious compilers, whose works are in general circulation, and may be heard of in most clubs and companies where gentlemen meet, who love to say a good thing without the trouble of inventing it. We are also in a fair train of knowing every thing that a late celebrated author said, as well as wrote, without an exception even of his most secret ejaculations. We may judge how valuable these diaries will be to posterity, when we reflect how much we should now be edified, had any of the antients given us as minute a *collectanea* of their illustrious contemporaries.

We have, it is true, a few of Cicero's table-jokes; but how delightful would it be to know what he said, when nobody heard him! How piously he reproached himself when he laid in bed too late in a morning, or eat too heartily at Hortensius's or Cæsar's table. We are told indeed that Cato the Censor loved his jest, but we should have been doubly glad to have partaken of it: what a pity it is that nobody thought it worth their while to record some pleasanter specimen than Macrobius has given us of his retort upon Q. Albidius, a glutton and a spendthrift, when his house was on fire—' What he could not eat, he has burnt,' said Cato; where the point of the jest lies in the allusion to a particular kind of sacrifice, and the good humour of it with himself. It was better said by P. Syrus the actor, when he saw one Mucius, a malevolent fellow, in a very melancholy mood—' Either some ill fortune has befallen Mucius, or some good has happened to one of his acquaintance.'

A man's fame shall be recorded to posterity by the trifling merit of a jest, when the great things he has done would else have been buried in oblivion: Who would now have known that L. Mallius was once the best painter in Rome, if it was not for his repartee to Servilius Geminus? ' You paint better than you model,' says Geminus, pointing to Mallius's children, who were crooked and ill-favoured. —' Like enough,' replied the artist; ' I paint in the daylight, but I model, as you call it, in the dark.'

Cicero, it is well known, was a great joker, and some of his good sayings have reached us; it does not appear as if his wit had been of the malicious sort, and yet Pompey, whose temper could not stand a jest, was so galled by him, that he is reported to have said with great bitterness—' Oh! that Cicero would go over to my enemies, for then he would be afraid of me.'—If Cicero forgave this sarcasm, I should call him not only a better-tempered, but a braver man than Pompey.

But of all the antient wits, Augustus seems to have had most point, and he was as remarkable for taking a jest, as for giving it. A country fellow came to Rome, who was so like the emperor, that all the city ran after him; Augustus heard of it, and ordering the man into his presence—'Harkye, friend!' says he, 'when was your mother in Rome?'—'Never, an please you!' replied the countryman, 'but my father has been here many a time and oft.' The anecdote of the old soldier is still more to his credit: he solicited the emperor to defend him in a suit; Augustus sent his own advocate into court; the soldier was dissatisfied, and said to the emperor—'I did not fight for you by proxy at Actium'—Augustus felt the reproof, and condescended to his request in person. When Pacuvius Taurus greedily solicited a largess from the emperor, and to urge him to the greater liberality added, that all the world would have it, that he had made him a very bountiful donation—'But you know better,' said Augustus, 'than to believe the world,—and dismissed the sycophant without his errand. I shall mention one more case, where, by a very courtly evasion, he parried the solicitation of his captain of the guard, who had been cashiered, and was petitioning the emperor to allow him his pay; telling him that he did not ask that indulgence for the sake of the money which might accrue to him, but that he might have it to say he had resigned his commission, and not been cashiered—'If that be all your reason,' says the emperor, 'tell the world that you have received it, and I will not deny that I have paid it.'

Vatinius, who was noted to a proverb as a common slanderer, and particularly obnoxious for his scurrility against Cicero, was pelted by the populace in the amphitheatre, whilst he was giving them the Gladiators : he complained to the Ædiles of the insult, and got an edict forbidding the people to cast any thing into the area but apples. An arch fellow brought a furious large fir-apple to the famous law-yer Cascellius, and demanded his opinion upon the edict.—' I am of opinion,' says Cascellius, ' that your fir-apple is literally and legally an apple, with this proviso however, that you intend to throw it at Natinius's head.'

As there is some danger in making too free with *old jokes*, I shall hold my hand for the present ; but if these should succeed in being acceptable to my readers, I shall not be afraid of meeting Mr. Joseph Miller and his modern witticisms with my antients. In that case I shall not despair of being to lay be-fore the public a veritable Roman newspaper, com-pounded of events in the days of Julius Cæsar : by what happy chance I traced this valuable relic, and with what pains I possessed myself of it, may be matter of future explanation: I have the satisfaction however to premise to the reader, that it is written with great freedom, and as well sprinkled with pri-vate anecdotes as any of the present day, whose agreeable familiarity is so charming to every body but the parties concerned : it has also a good dash of the dramatic ; and as some fastidious people have been inclined to treat our intelligencers and review-ers with a degree of neglect bordering upon con-tempt, I shall have pleasure in shewing that they have classical authority for all their quirks and con-ceits, and that they are all written in the true quaint spirit of criticism : it is to be lamented that the Roman theatre furnishes no ladies to match the heroines of our stage ; but I can produce some en-comiums upon Laberius, Roscius, and the famous

Publius Syrus, which would not be unapplicable to some of our present capital actors: I am sorry to be obliged to confess, that they were not in the habit of speaking epilogues in those days; but I have a substitute in a prologue written and spoken by Decimus Laberius, which I am tempted to throw out as a lure to my newspaper; but I must first explain upon what occasion it was composed.

This Laberius was a Roman knight of good family, and a man withal of high spirit and pretensions, but unfortunately he had a talent for the drama: he read his own plays better than any man then living could act them, for neither Garrick nor Henderson was yet born. P. Clodius, the fine gentleman and rake of the age, had the indecorum to press Laberius to come forward on the public stage, and take the principal character in one of his own plays: Laberius was indignant, and Clodius proceeded to menaces:—' Do your worst,' says the Roman knight, ' you can but send me to Dyracchium and back again'—proudly intimating that he would suffer the like banishment with Cicero, rather than consent to his demand; for acting was not then the amusemeut of people of fashion, and private theatres were not thought of. Julius Cæsar was no less captivated with Laberius's talents than Clodius had been, and being a man not apt to be discouraged by common difficulties, took up the same solicitation, and assailed our Roman knight, who was now sixty years of age, and felt his powers in their decline: conscious of this decline no less than of his own dignity, he resisted the degrading request; he interceded, he implored of Cæsar to excuse him: it was to no purpose, Cæsar had made it his point, and his point he would carry: the word of Cæsar was law, and Laberius, driven out of all his defences, was obliged to submit and com-

ply. Cæsar makes a grand spectacle for all Rome;
bills are given out for a play of Laberius, and the
principal part is announced to be performed by the
author himself: the theatre is thronged with spectators; all Rome is present, and Decimus Laberius
presents himself on the stage, and addresses the audience in the following prologue:

PROLOGUE BY DECIMUS LABERIUS.

' O strong Necessity ! of whose swift course
So many feel, so few escape the force,
Whither, ah ! whither, in thy prone career,
Hast thou decreed this dying frame to bear ?
Me in my better days nor foe, nor friend,
Nor threat, nor bribe, nor vanity, cou'd bend ;
Now lur'd by flattery in my weaker age,
I sink my knighthood and ascend the stage.
Yet muse not therefore——How shall man gainsay
Him, whom the Deities themselves obey ?
Sixty long years I've liv'd without disgrace
A Roman knight; let dignity give place !
I'm Cæsar's actor now, and compass more
In one short hour, than all my life before.
' O Fortune! fickle source of good and ill,
If here to place me 'twas thy sovereign will,
Why, when I'd youth and faculties to please
So great a master and such guests as these,
Why not compel me then, malicious power !
To the hard task of this degrading hour ?
Where now, in what profound abyss of shame,
Dost thou conspire with Fate to sink my name?
Whence are my hopes ? What voice can age supply
To charm the ear ; what grace to please the eye?
Where is the action, energy, and art,
The look, that guides its passion to the heart ?
Age creeps like ivy o'er my wither'd trunk,
Its bloom all blasted, and its vigour shrunk ;
A tomb, where nothing but a name remains
To tell the world whose ashes it contains.'

The original is so superiorly beautiful, that to

prevent a bathos I shall insert it after the translation.

> *Necessitas, cujus cursus transversi impetum*
> *Voluerunt multi effugere, pauci potuerunt,*
> *Quo me detrusit pæne extremis sensibus?*
> *Quem nulla ambitio, nulla unquam largitio,*
> *Nullus timor, vis nulla, nulla auctoritas*
> *Movere potuit in juventa de statu;*
> *Ecce in senecta ut facile labefecit loco*
> *Viri excellentis mente clemente edita*
> *Submissa placidè blandiloquens oratio!*
> *Etenim ipsi Dii negare cui nihil potuerunt,*
> *Hominem me denegare quis posset pati?*
> *Ergo bis tricenis annis actis sine nota*
> *Eques Romanus lare egressus meo*
> *Domum revertas mimus: Nimirum hoc die*
> *Uno plus vixi mihi quam vivendum fuit.*
> *Fortuna, immoderata in bono æque atque in malo,*
> *Si tibi erat libitum literarum laudibus*
> *Floris cacumen nostræ famæ frangere,*
> *Cur cum vigebam membris præviridantibus,*
> *Satisfacere populo et tali cum poteram viro,*
> *Non flexibilem me concurvasti ut carperes?*
> *Nunc me quo dejicis? quid ad scenam affero?*
> *Decorem formæ, an dignitatem corporis,*
> *Animi virtutem, an vocis jucundæ sonum?*
> *Ut hedera serpens vires arboreas necat,*
> *Ita me vetustas amplexa annorum enecat:*
> *Sepulchri similis nihil nisi nomen retines.*

The play which this pathetic prologue was attached
to was a comedy, in which Laberius took the character of a slave, and in the course of the plot (as
usual) was beaten by his master: in this condition,
having marked his habit with counterfeited stripes,
he runs upon the stage, and cries out amain—*Porro,
Quirites! libertatem perdimus*—' In good faith, Countrymen, there is an end of freedom.' The indignant
spectators sent up a shout; it was in the language of
our present playhouse bills, ' a burst of applause; a

most violent burst of applause from a most crowded
and brilliant house, overflowing in all parts.' Laberius, not yet content with this atonement to the
manes of his knighthood, subjoins the following
pointed allusion : *Necesse est multos timeat, quem
multi timent*—' The man, whom many fear, must
needs fear many.' All eyes were now turned upon
Cæsar, and the degraded Laberius enjoyed a full
revenge.

We may naturally suppose this conduct lost him
the favour of Cæsar, who immediately took up
Publius Syrus, a Syrian slave, who had been ma-
numitted for his ingenious talents, and was acting
in the country theatres with much applause: Cæsar
fetched him out of his obscurity, as we bring up an
actress from Bath or York, and pitted him against
Laberius.   It was the triumph of youth and vigour
over age and decay, and Cæsar, with malicious ci-
vility, said to Laberius, *Favente tibi me victus es,
Laberi, a Syro*—' You are surpassed by Syrus in
spite of my support.'   As Laberius was going out
of the theatre, he was met by Syrus, who was inconsiderate enough to let an expression escape him,
which was very disrespectful to his veteran competitor : Laberius felt the unbecoming insult, and,
turning to Syrus, gave him this extempory answer——

> ' To stand the first is not the lot of all;
> 'Tis now your turn to mount, and mine to fall:
> 'Tis slippery ground; beware you keep your feet;
> For public favor is a public cheat.'

> ' *Non possunt primi esse omnes omni in tempore;
> Summum ad gradum cum claritatis veneris,
> Consistes ægre; et quam descendas, decides :
> Cecidi ego: Cadet qui sequitur.   Laus est publica.*'

I need not remind the learned reader in what
credit the sayings of this Publius Syrus have been
justly held by all the *literati* from Seneca to Scaliger,
who turned them into Greek; and it is for the honour of the fraternity of the stage, that both he and
Sophron, whose moral sentences were found under
Plato's pillow when he died, were actors by profession.

I shall now only add that my Newspaper contains a very interesting description of two young
actors, Hylas and Pylades, who became great favourites with Augustus, when he was emperor, and
made their first appearance at the time this journal
was written. If the Reader shall find any allusion
to two very promising young performers, now living, whose initials correspond with the above, I can
promise him that our contemporaries will not suffer
by the comparison. I may venture to say in the
words of Doctor Young—

> The Roman wou'd not blush at the mistake.

NUMBER LIII.

THERE is no period of ancient history would afford
a more useful study to a young prince, than an accurate delineation of the whole life of Tiberius:
This ought to be done with great care and ability,
for it is a character extremely difficult to develope,
and one that by a continued chain of incidents furnishes a lesson in every link of its connexion highly
interesting to all pupils, but most to those who are
on the road to empire. To trace the conduct of

Tiberius from his first appearance in history to his death, is as if we should begin with the last acts of Augustus, and read his story backwards to its commencement in the civil wars; each narration would then begin with honour, and conclude with infamy. If Augustus had never attained to empire, he would have had a most disgraceful page in history; on the other hand, had Tiberius died with Germanicus, he would have merited a very glorious one: It should seem therefore that he was by nature a better man than his predecessor. The cautious timid character of Augustus kept him under constant awe of those he governed, and he was diligent to secure to himself the opinions of mankind; but there are rents and fissures enough in the veil, which adulation has thrown over him, through which to spy out the impurities and meannesses of his natural disposition. Tiberius seems on his part also to have had a jealous holding and respect towards Germanicus, which had an influence over the early part of his reign; but it was a self-restraint, founded in emulation, not in fear. It is hinted that Augustus had in mind to restore the commonwealth, and give back her liberties to Rome; and these may very possibly have been his meditations; but they never arose in his mind till he found his life in the last stage of decay, when, having no heir of his own body, he would willingly have had the empire cease with him, and left posterity to draw the conclusion, that no successor could be found fit to take it after him; this I can readily believe he would have done in his last moments if he could, and even before his last moments if he dared; but the shock, which such a revolution might possibly have occasioned, alarmed his fears, and he was too tenacious of power to quit it upon any other motives than those of absolute conviction that he could hold it no longer. This is so much in character, that I think it very probable he might have tried it upon Tiberius in his long death-bed conversation with him at Nola—*Revocatum ex itinere Tiberium diu secreto sermone detinuit, neque post ulli majori negotio animum accommodavit.* *(Suetonius.)* This passage is very curious, and some important conjectures may fairly be grounded upon it. Suetonius says that the conference was *long,* and also that it was *private;* and he adds that Augustus, after his conversation with his successor, never turned his thoughts to any important business, or, in other words, any matter of state whatever. The *secrecy* of this conference very much favours my conjecture, that he made an attempt to dissuade Tiberius from holding on the empire, and the *length* of time it took up corroborates the probability of that conjecture; and I further incline to think it likely that it might make serious impressions on Tiberius's mind, as to the measure proposed; for I can never believe that the repugnance, with which Tiberius took the charge of the government upon him, was wholly feigned, though historians agree in giving it that turn; his long and voluntary exile in the island of Rhodes, where he seemed for a time to have renounced all desire of succeeding to the empire, might be a reason with Augustus for making this experiment upon a man of his cold and sequestered habits. At all events I think it highly natural to suppose, that Augustus would not have closetted him in this manner, if it were only for the purpose of giving him lessons and instructions in the arts of government; for in that case his vanity, which made him act a part for applause even in his expiring moments, would have opened his doors to his family and attendants, that they might have been present to record his sayings; and we should have had as many fine maxims in his dying speech, as Socrates uttered

in his prison, or Seneca in his bath : Add to this,
that he certainly bore no good-will to Tiberius,
who was not a successor to his mind, nor could he
wish to elevate the Claudian family to the throne :
It is not likely however that he altogether succeeded
with Tiberius, or brought him to make any absolute
promise of abdication; for in that case he would not
have failed to have taken credit with the people
about him, for having been the means of restoring
the liberties of his country, and he would have made
as great a parade of patriotism, as would have become a Cato or a Solon ; but the author above
quoted says he took no further account of public
business, and therefore we may conclude the conference, if it took that turn, did not come to any satisfactory conclusion on the point.

Tiberius on his accession found the empire in a
critical situation, for besides the movements which
Clemens on one part and Scribonius Libo on another
were making, the Pannonian and German armies
were in absolute revolt. This was no time for
making any change in the constitution of the imperial power, had he been so disposed; as he was a
man of deep measures, he held himself on the reserve
with the senate, and suffered them to solicit his ac-
ceptance of the sovereign power upon their knees :
He wished to have assessors in the government; he
would take his share, and whatever department in
the state they should recommend to his charge, he
would readily undertake. Had he persisted in refusing the empire, or had he attempted to throw the
constitution back to its first principles of freedom,
the mutinous legions would have forced the sove-
reignty upon Germanicus; but by this suggestion
of a partition he artfully sounded the temper of the
senate, where there were some leading men of very
doubtful characters, whom Augustus had marked

out in his last illness; from two of these, Asinius Gallus and L. Aruntius, Tiberius's proposal drew an answer, in which they demanded of him to declare what particular department of the state he would chuse to have committed to him. This was opening enough for one of his penetration, and he drew his conclusions upon the spot, evading for the time the snare that was laid for him.

The servile and excessive adulation of the senate soon convinced him, that the Roman spirit had suffered a total change under the reign of Augustus, and that the state might indeed be thrown into convulsions by any attempt at a change in favour of freedom, but that slavery and submission under a despotic master was their determined choice, and if the alternative was to lie between himself and any other, there was little room for hesitation: Who more fit than the adopted heir of Augustus, and a descendant of the Claudian house, which ranked so high in the Patrician nobility, and so superior in pretensions of ancestry and merit to the Julian and Octavian gentry, from whom his predecessors were ignobly descended?

When the German and Pannonian mutinies were appeased, there seems to have been a period of repose, when he might have new modelled the constitution, had he been so disposed; but this I take to be appearance only, for those mutinies had been quelled by Germanicus and Drusus, and both these princes were in the adoption; and the latter of a very turbulent and ambitious spirit.

For the space of two complete years Tiberius never stirred out of the doors of his palace, devoting his whole time to the affairs of government. In this period he certainly did many excellent things; and though his manners were not calculated for popularity, yet his reputation through the empire was universal; he regulated all domestic matters with consummate prudence, and on some occasions with a liberal and courteous spirit: In the distant provinces, where wars and disturbances were more frequent, public measures were more indebted for their success to the good policy of his instructions, than to the courage and activity of his generals, though Germanicus was of the number.

The death of that most amiable and excellent prince, which was imputed to the machinations of Cneius Piso, involved Tiberius in some degree in the same suspicion; but as Tacitus in his account of the event, gives admission to an idle story of sorceries and incantations practised by Piso for compassing the death of Germanicus, and states no circumstance that can give any reasonable ground for belief that he actually poisoned him, I am not inclined to give credit to the transaction, even in respect to Piso's being guilty of the murder, much less with regard to Tiberius. Tacitus indeed hints at secret orders supposed by some to have been given by the emperor to Piso; but this, which at best is mere matter of report, does not go to the affair of the poisoning, but only to some private intimations, in which the empress was chief mover, for mortifying the pride of Agrippina. It is not to be supposed, when Piso openly returned to Rome, and stood a public trial, that these orders, had any such existed, could have been so totally suppressed, that neither the guilty person should avail himself of them, nor any one member of so great and numerous a family produce them in vindication of him when yet living, or of his memory after death; and this in no period of time, not even when the Claudian family were superseded in the empire, and anecdotes were industriously collected to blacken the character of Tiberius.

The death of Drusus followed that of Germanicus, and the same groundless suspicions were levelled at the emperor; but these are rejected by Tacitus with contempt, and the words he uses, which are very strong, are a proper answer to both imputations— *Neque quisquam scriptor tam infensus exstitit, ut Tiberio objectaret, cum omnia conquirerent, intenderentque.*

It would have been most happy for the memory of Tiberius had his life been terminated at this fatal period; henceforward he seems to have been surrendered to desperation and disgust; he retired to the Campania, and devolved the government upon his minister Sejanus; there were times, in which some marks of his former spirit appeared, but they were short and transient emanations; the basest of mankind had possession of his soul, and whether he was drugged by Sejanus and his agents, or that his brain was affected by a revulsion of that scrophulous humour, which broke out with such violence in his face and body, it seems highly natural to conjecture, that he was never in his sound mind during his secession in the island of Capreæ. A number of circumstances might be adduced in support of this conjecture; it is sufficient to instance his extraordinary letter to the senate; can words be found more expressive of a distracted and desperate state of mind than the following? *Quid scribam vobis, Patres Conscripti, aut quomodo scribam, aut quib omnio non scribam hoc tempore, Dii me deæque pejus perdant, quam perire quotidie sentio, si scio.*

I beg leave now to repeat what I advanced in the outset of this paper, and which alone led me to the subject of it, that a detail comprizing all the great and interesting events within the life of Tiberius, with reasonings and remarks judiciously interspersed, as these occurrences arise in the course of the narration, would compound such a body of useful precepts and instructions, as would apply to every species of example, which a prince should be taught either to imitate or avoid; and these lessons would carry the greater force and recommendation with them, and have an advantage over all fabulous morals, by being incorporated with a real history of the most interesting sort.

NUMBER LIV.

However disposed we may be to execrate the bloody act of the regicides, yet we must admit the errors and misconduct of Charles's unhappy reign to be such as cannot be palliated; in our pity for his fate we must not forget the history of his failings, nor, whilst we are sympathising in the pathos of of the tragedy, overlook its moral.

Four successive parliaments, improvidently dissolved, were sufficient warnings for the fifth to fall upon expedients for securing to themselves a more permanent duration, by laying some restraints upon a prerogative so wantonly exerted.

Let us call to mind the inauspicious commencement of this monarch's reign; before the ceremony of his coronation had taken place, he espoused a sister of France, and set a catholic princess on the throne of a protestant kingdom, scarce cool from the ferment of religious jealousies, recently emancipated from the yoke of Rome, and of course intolerant through terror, if not by principle: The most obnoxious man in the kingdom was Montague, author of the proscribed tract, intitled *Apello Cæsarem*, and him Charles enrolled in his list of royal chaplains: By throwing himself incontinently into the hands of Buckingham, he shewed his people

they were to expect a reign of favouritism, and the
choice of the minister marked the character of the
monarch : He levied musters for the Palatinate of
twelve thousand men, exacted contributions for coat
and conduct-money, declared martial law in the
kingdom, and furnished his brother of France with a
squadron of ships for the unpopular reduction of
Rochelle, and the mariners refused the service :
These measures stirred the parliament then sitting
to move for a redress of grievances, before they provided for his debts, and their remonstrances provoked him upon the instant to dissolve them.

Every one of these proceedings took place before
his coronation, and form the melancholy prelude to
his misguided government.

A second parliament was called together, and to
intimidate them from resuming their redress of grievances, and divert their attempts from the person of
his favourite, he haughtily informs them, that he cannot suffer an enquiry even on the meanest of his servants. What was to be expected from such a me-
nacing declaration ? They, disdaining *illam ofculari,
quâ sunt oppressi, manum*, proceed to impeach Buckingham ; the king commits the managers of that
process to the Tower, and resorting to his prerogative,
dissolves his second parliament as suddenly, and
more angrily, than his first.

A third parliament meets, and in the interim new
grievances of a more awakening sort had supplied
them with an ample field for complaint and remon-
strance ; in the intermission of their fittings, he had
exacted a loan, which they interpreted a tax without
parliament, and of course a flagrant violation of the
constitution ; this he enforced with so high a hand,
that several gentleman of name in their counties had
been committed to close imprisonment for refusing
payment ; ship-money also at this time began to be

questioned as an intolerable grievance, and being
one of the resources for enabling the crown to govern without a parliament, it was considered by
many as a violation of their rights, an inequitable
and oppressive tax, which ought to be resisted, and
accordingly it was resisted : This parliament therefore, after a short and inefficient sitting, shared the
sudden fate of its predecessors.

The same precipitancy, greater blindness, a more
confirmed habit of obstinacy, and a heightened degree of aggravation marked this period of intermission
from parliaments, for now the leading members of
the late house were sent to close imprisonment in the
Tower, and informations were lodged against them
in the Star-Chamber.

The troubles in Scotland made it necessary for
the king once more to have resort to a parliament ;
they met for the fourth time on the thirteenth of
April 1640, and the fifth day of the following month
sent them back to their constituents to tell those
grievances in the ears of the people, which their
sovereign disdained to listen to.——Ill - counselled
sovereign ! but will that word apologize for conduct so intemperate ? It cannot : A mind, so flex-
ible towards evil counsel, can possess no requisites
for government : What hope now remained for
moderate measures, when the people's representa-
tives should again assemble ? In this fatal moment
the fuel was prepared and the match lighted, to
give life to the flames of civil war ; already Scotland had set those sparks into a blaze ; the king,
unable to extinguish the conflagration by his own
power and resources, for the fifth and last time convenes his parliament ; but it was now too late for any
confidence or mutual harmony to subsist between
the crown and commons ; on the third of Novem-
ber following their last dissolution, the new-elected

members take possession of their seats, and the house soon resounds with resolutions for the impeachment of the minister Strafford and the primate Laud: The humble monarch confirms the fatal bill of attainder, and sends Strafford to the scaffold ; he ratifies the act for securing parliament against future dissolution, and subscribes to his own death-warrant with the same pen.

The proceedings of this famous parliament are of a mixt nature ; in many we discern the true spirit of patriotism, and not a few seem dictated by revenge and violence : The Courts of High Commission and Star-Chamber are abolished, and posterity applauds their deliverers ; the city-crosses are pulled down, the bishops sent to the Tower, and their whole order menaced with expulsion from parliament, and here we discover the first dawnings of fanatic phrensy : An incurable breach is made in the constitution ; its branches are dissevered, and the axe of rebellion is laid to the root of the tree : The royal standard is set up; the father of his people becomes the general of a party, and the land is floated with the blood of its late peaceable inhabitants : Great characters start forth in the concussion, great virtues and great vices : Equal courage and superior conduct at length prevail for the leaders of the people ; a fanatic champion carries all before him ; the sovereign surrenders himself weakly, capitulates feebly, negociates deceitfully, and dies heroically.

And this is the reign, this is the exit of a king! Let kings ponder it, for it is a lesson, humbling perhaps to their pride of station, but pointedly addressed to their instruction.

If there is a trust in life, which calls upon the conscience of the man who undertakes it more strongly than any other, it is that of the education of an heir-

apparent to a crown: The training such a pupil is
a task indeed; how to open his mind to a proper
knowledge of mankind, without letting in that
knowledge which inclines to evil; how to hold off
flattery and yet admit familiarity; how to give the
lights of information, and shut out the false colours
of seduction, demands a judgment for distinguishing
and an authority for controuling, which few go-
vernors in that delicate situation ever possess, or can
long retain: To educate a prince, born to reign over
an enlightened people, upon the narrow scale of
secret and sequestered tuition, would be an abuse of
common sense; to let him loose upon the world is
no less hazardous in the other extreme, and each
would probably devote him to an inglorious destiny: That he should know the leading characters
in the country he is to govern, be familiar with its
history, its constitution, manners, laws and liberties, and correctly comprehend the duties and dis-
tinctions of his own hereditary office, are points
that no one will dispute: That he should travel
through his kingdom I can hardly doubt, but whether those excursions should reach into other states,
politically connected with, or opposed to, his own,
is more than I will presume to lay down as a general
rule, being aware that it must depend upon personal
circumstances: splendor he may be indulged in,
but excess in that, as in every thing else, must be
avoided, for the mischiefs cannot be numbered,
which it will entail upon him; excess in expence
will subject him to obligations of a degrading sort;
excess in courtesy will lay him open to the forward
and assuming, raise mountains of expectation about
him, and all of them undermined by disappointment, ready charged for explosion, when the hand
of presumption shall set fire to the train: Excess
in pleasure will lower him in character, destroy

health, respect, and that becoming dignity of mind, that conscious rectitude, which is to direct and support him, when he becomes the dispenser of justice to his subjects, the protector and defender of their religion, the model of their imitation, and the sovereign arbiter of life and death in the execution of every legal condemnation : To court popularity is both derogatory and dangerous, nor should he, who is destined to rule over the whole, condescend to put himself in the league of a party : To be a protector of learning and a patron of the arts, is worthy of a prince, but let him beware how he sinks himself into a pedant or a virtuoso : It is a mean talent, which excels in trifles ; the fine arts are more likely to flourish under a prince, whose ignorance of them is qualified by general and impartial good-will towards their professors, than by one, who is himself a dabbler ; for such will always have their favourites, and favouritism never fails to irritate the minds of men of genius concerned in the same studies, and turns the spirit of emulation into the gall of acrimony.

Above all things let it be his inviolable maxim to distinguish strongly and pointedly in his attentions between men of virtuous morals and men of vicious : There is nothing so glorious and at the same time nothing so easy ; if his countenance is turned to men of principle and character, if he bestows his smile upon the worthy only, he need be at little pains to frown upon the profligate, all such vermin will crawl out of his path, and shrink away from his presence : Glittering talents will be no passport for dissolute morals, and ambition will then be retained in no other cause, but that of virtue ; men will not chuse crooked passages and bye alleys to preferment, when the broad highway of honesty is laid open and strait before them. A prince, though he gives a good example in his own person, what does he profit the world, if he draws it back again by the bad example of those whom he employs and favours ? Better might it be for a nation, to see a libertine on its throne, surrounded by virtuous counsellors, then to contemplate a virtuous sovereign, delegating his authority to unprincipled and licentious servants.

The king, who declares his resolution of countenancing the virtuous only amongst his subjects, speaks the language of an honest man : if he makes good his declaration, he performs the functions of one, and earns the blessings of a righteous king; a life of glory in this world, and an immortality of happiness in the world to come.

NUMBER LV.

Non erat his locus.

THERE is a certain delicacy in some men's nature, which though not absolutely to be termed a moral attribute, is nevertheless so grateful to society at large, and so recommendatory of those who possess it, that even the best and worthiest characters cannot be truly pleasing without it : I know not how to describe it better than by saying it consists in a happy discernment of ' times and seasons.'

Though this engaging talent cannot positively be called a virtue, yet it seems to be the result of many virtuous and refined endowments of the mind, which produces it ; for when we see any man so tenderly considerate of our feelings, as to put aside his own for our accommodation and repose, and to consult opportunities with a respectful attention to our ease and leisure, it is natural to us to think favourably of such a disposition, and although much of his discernment may be the effect of a good judgment and proper knowledge of the world, yet there must be a great proportion of sensibility, candour, diffidence, and natural modesty in the composition of a faculty so conciliating and so graceful. A man may have many good qualities, and yet if he is unacquainted with the world, he will rarely be found to understand those apt and happy moments, of which I am now speaking; for it is a knowledge not to be gained without a nice and accurate observation of mankind, and even when that observation has given it, men, who are wanting in the natural good qualities above described, may indeed avail themselves of such occasions to serve a purpose of their own, but without a good heart no man will apply his experience to general practice.

But as it is not upon theories that I wish to employ these papers, I shall now devote the remainder of my attention to such rules and observations as occur to me upon the subject of *the times and seasons*.

Men, who in the fashionable phrase *live out of the world*, have a certain awkwardness about them, which is for ever putting them out of their place in society, whenever they are occasionally drawn into it. If it is their studies which have sequestered them from the world, they contract an air of pedantry, which can hardly be endured in any mixed company without exposing the object of it to ridicule; for the very essence of this contracted habit consists in an utter ignorance *of times and seasons*. Most of that class of men who are occupied in the education of youth, and not a few of the young men themselves, who are educated by them, are of this description : We meet with many of Jack Lizard's cast in the Spectator, who will learnedly maintain *there is no heat in fire*. There is a disputatious precision in these people, which lets nothing pass in free conversation, that is not mathematically true; they will confute a jest by syllogism, canvass a merry tale by cross-examination and dates, work every common calculation by X *the unknown quantity*, and in the festive sallies of imagination convict the witty speaker of false grammar, and nonsuit all the merriment of the table.

The man of form and ceremony, who has shaped his manners to the model of what is commonly called *The Old Court*, is another grand defaulter against *times and seasons:* His entrances and exits are to be performed with a stated regularity; he measures his devoirs with an exactitude that bespeaks him a correct interpreter of *The Red Book*; pays his compliments with a minuteness, that leaves no one of your family unnamed, enquires after the health of your child who is dead, and desires to be kindly remembered to your wife, from whom you are divorced; Nature formed him in strait lines, habit has stiffened him into an unrelenting rigidity and no familiarity can bend him out of the upright. The uneducated squire of rustic manners forms a contrast to this character, but he is altogether as great an intruder upon *times and seasons*, and his total want of form operates to the annoyance of society as effectually as the other's excess. There cannot be in human nature a more terrible thing than vulgar familiarity ; a low-bred fellow, who affects to put himself at his ease amongst his superiors and be pleasant company to them, is a nuisance to society ; there is nothing so ill understood by the world in general as familiarity : if it was not for the terror, which men have of the very troublesome consequences of condescension to their inferiors, there would not be a hundredth part of that pride and holding-back amongst the higher ranks, of which the low are so apt to complain. How few men do we meet with, who when the heart is open and the channel free, know how to keep their course within the buoys and marks, that true good-manners have set up for all men to steer by! Jokes out of season, unpleasant truths touched upon incautiously, *plump questions* (as they are called) put without any preface or refinement, manual caresses compounded of hugs and flaps and squeezes, more resembling the gambols of a bear than the actions of a gentleman, are sure to follow upon the overflowing ebullitions of a vulgar familiarity broke loose from all restraints. It is a painful necessity men of sensibility are under, when they find themselves compelled to draw back from the eager advances of an honest heart, only because the shock of its good-humour is too violent to be endured; it is very wounding to a social nature to check festivity in any degree, but there is nothing sinks the spirits so effectually as boisterous mirth, nobody so apt to overact his character as a jolly fellow, and stunned with the vociferation of his own tongue to forget that every other man is silent and suffering: In short, it is a very difficult thing to be properly happy and well pleased with the company we are in, and none but men of good education, great discernment, and nice feelings know how to be familiar. These rural gentry are great dealers in long stories of their own uninteresting atchievements, they require of you to attend to the narrative of their paltry squabbles and bickerings with their neighbours; they are extremely eloquent upon the laws against poachers, upon turnpike roads and new enclosures, and all these topics they will thrust in by the neck and shoulders to the exclusion of all others.

Plain-speaking, if we consider it simply as a mark
of truth and honesty, is doubtless a very meritorious
quality, but experience teaches that it is too frequently under bad management, and obtruded on
society out of *time and season* in such a manner as to
be highly inconvenient and offensive. People are
not always in a fit humour to be told of their faults,
and these plain-speaking friends sometimes perform
their office so clumsily, that we are inclined to suspect they are more interested to bring us to present
shame than future reformation: It is a common
observation with them, when things turn out amiss,
to put us in mind how they dissuaded us from such
and such an undertaking, that they foresaw what
would happen, and that the event is neither more
nor less than they expected and predicted. These
retorts, cast in our teeth in the very moment of vexation, are what few tempers, when galled with disappointment, can patiently put up with; they may
possibly be the result of zeal and sincerity, but they
are so void of contrivance, and there is so little delicacy in the timing of them, that it is a very rare
case indeed, when they happen to be well understood,
and kindly taken. The same want of sensibility towards human infirmities, that will not spare us in
the moments of vexation, will make no allowances
for the mind's debility in the hours of grief and
sorrow: If a friend of this sort surprises us in the
weakness of the soul, when death perhaps has robbed us of some beloved object, it is not to contribute
a tear, but to read us a lecture, that he comes; when
the heart is agonised, the temper is irritable, and as
a moraliser of this sort is almost sure to find his ad-
monitions take the contrary effect from what he in-
tended, he is apt to mistake an occasional impatience in us for a natural one, and leaves us with the
impression that we are men, who are ill prepared

against the common vicissitudes of life, and endowed with a very small share of fortitude and resignation; this early misconception of our character, in the course of time leads him to another, for he no sooner finds us recovered to a proper temper of mind, than he calls to mind our former impatience, and comparing it with our present tranquillity concludes upon appearances, that we are men of light and trivial natures, subject indeed to fits and starts of passion, but incapable of retention, and as he has then a fine subject for displaying his powers of plain-speaking, he reminds us of our former inattention to his good advice, and takes credit for having told us over and over again that we ought not to give way to violent sorrow, and that we could not change the course of things by our complaining of them. Thus for want of calculating *times and seasons* he begins to think despisingly of us, and we in spite of all his sincerity grow tired of him and dread his company.

Before I quit this subject I must also have a word with the valetudinarians, and I wish from my heart I could cure them of their *complaints*,—that species I mean which comes under my notice as an *Observer*, without intruding upon the more important province of the physician. Now as this island of our's is most happily supplied with a large and learned body of professors under every medical description and character, whether operative or deliberative, and all these stand ready at the call and devoted to the service of the sick or maimed, whether it be on foot, on horseback, or on wheels, to resort to them in their distresses, it cannot be for want of help that the valetudinarian states his case to all companies so promiscuously. Let the whole family of death be arrayed on one side, and the whole army of physic, regulars and irregulars, be drawn out on the other, and I will venture to say that for every possible disease in the ranks of the besieger, there shall be a champion in the garrison ready to turn out and give him battle: Let all who are upon the sick list in the community be laid out between the camps, and let the respective combatants fight it out over the bodies, but let the forces of life and health have no share in the fray: Why should their peace be disturbed, or their society contaminated by the infectious communication? It is as much out of *time and place* for a man to be giving the diary of his disease in company, who are met for social purposes, as it is for a doctor to be talking politics or scandal in a sick man's chamber; yet so it is that each party are for ever out of character; the chatterer disgusts his patient by an inattention to his complaints, and the valetudinarian disgusts his company by the enumeration of them, and both are equally out of season.

Every man's observation may furnish him with instances not here enumerated, but if what I have said shall seem to merit more consideration than I have been able to give it in the compass of this paper, my readers may improve upon the hint, and society cannot fail to profit by their reflections.

NUMBER LVI.

————————

———————— Ω τρισάλθιοι
Αιταντες οἱ φυσῶντες ἐφ᾿ ἑαυτοῖς μέχα,
Ἀυτοὶ γὰρ ὐκ ἴσασιν ἀνθρώπȣ φύσιν.

MENANDER. Gubernatoribus.

Oh wretched mortals! by false pride betray'd,
Ye know not of what nature man is made."

Though I think our nation can never be accused
of want of charity, yet I have observed with much
concern a poor unhappy set of men amongst us,
whose case is not commiserated as it ought to be ;
—and as I would gladly contribute any thing in my
power towards their relief, the best proof I can give
them of my good will is by endeavouring to convince them of a certain truth, which all the world
except themselves has discovered long ago, viz.
' That a proud man is the most contemptible being
in nature.' Now if these proud men to whom I address myself, and for whose miserable situation I
have such compassion, shall once find a friend to
convince them, that they are truly ' the most contemptible beings in nature,' it can never be supposed
they will persist to entertain a companion in their
bosoms, who affords them so little pleasure, and yet
involves them in so much disgrace. I must consider them therefore as mistaken rather than obstinate,
and treat them accordingly ; for how can I suppose
there would be such an absurdity in the world as a
proud man, if the poor creature was not behind hand
with the rest of mankind in a discovery that concerns himself so materially ? I admit indeed that
pride is a very foolish thing, but I contend that wise

men are sometimes surprized into very foolish things,
and if a little friendly hint can rescue them, it would
be an ill-natured action to with-hold the information: ' If you are proud, you are a fool'—says an
old Greek author called Sotades—'Αν' ἀλαζονῆς, τῶτ'
ἀνοίας ἐστὶ φρύαγμα—but I hope a little plain English,
without the help of Sotades, will serve to open the
eyes of a plain Englishman, and prevent him from
strutting about the world merely to make sport for
his neighbours ; for I declare in truth, that so far
from being annoyed and made splenetic as some folks
are, when I fall into company with a proud fellow
creature, I feel no other impulse than of pity, with
now and then a small propensity to titter, for it
would be downright rudeness to laugh in a man's
face on such an occasion ; and it hurts me to see an
honest gentleman, who may have many more natural
good qualities than he himself is aware of, run about
from house to house only to make sport for the scof-
fers, and take a world of pains, and put on an air of
gravity and importance, for no better purpose than
to provoke ridicule and contempt—' Why is earth
and ashes proud ?' says the Son of Sirach ; ' Pride
was not made for men.'

As I am determined to put these poor men upon
their guard in all points, I shall remind them of another error they are in, which sadly aggravates their
misfortunes, and which arises from a circumstance
of a mere local nature, viz. ' That England is the
worst country a proud man can exhibit himself
in.'—I do really wish they would well consider the
land they live in ; if they do not know, they ought
to be told, that we are a free people ; that freedom
tends to make us independent of one another, fear-
less in our persons, warm in our resentments, bold
of tongue, and vindictive against insult ; England is
the place upon earth, where a proud stomach finds

the least to feed upon; indeed it is the only stomach, that can here complain of its entertainment : if the proud man thinks it will be sufficient to pay his fine of affability to his neighbours once in seven years upon a parliamentary canvass, he is cruelly mistaken; the common people in this country have such a share of intuition, understand their own strength so well, and scrutinize into the weaknesses of their superiors so acutely, that they are neither to be deceived nor intimidated ; and on that account, (as the proud man's character is compounded of the impostor and the bully) they are the very worst people he can deal with. A man may strut in Spain, vapour in France, or kick and cuff the vulgar as he likes in Russia ; he may sit erect in his palanquin in India without dropping his eyes upon the earth he moves over ; but if he carries his head in the air here, and expects the croud to make way for him, he will soon run foul of somebody that will make him repent of his stateliness. Pride then, it seems, not only exposes a man to contempt, but puts him in danger ; it is also a very expensive frolic, if he keeps it up as it should be kept, for what signifies his being proud, if there is not somebody always present to exercise his pride upon ? He must therefore of necessity have a set of humble cousins and toad-eaters about him, and as such cattle cannot be had for nothing in this country, he must pay them according to the value of their services; common trash may be had at a common price, but clever fellows know their own consequence, and will stand out upon terms : If Nebuchadnezzar had not had ' all people, nations and languages' at his command, he might have called till he was hoarse before any one would have come to worship his ' image in the plain of Dura;' let the proud man take notice withal that Nebuchadnezzar's *image* was made of *gold,* and

if he expects to be worshipped by all people after
this fashion, and casts himself in the same mould,
he must also cast himself in the same metal. Now
if I am right in my assertion, that sycophants bear
a higher price in England than elsewhere (and, if
scarcity makes things dear, I trust they do), let the
proud man consider if it be worth his while to pay
dear for bad company, when he may have good-
fellowship at an easy rate: Here then is another instance of his bad policy, and sure it is a sorrowful
thing to be poor and proud.

That I may thoroughly do my duty to an order
of men, to whose service I dedicate this short essay,
I must not omit to mention, that it behoves a proud
man in all places and on all occasions to preserve
an air of gloominess and melancholy, and never to
suffer so vulgar an expression as mirth or laughter
to disarrange the decorum of his features: other
men will be apt to make merry with his humour,
but he must never be made merry by their's: In
this respect he is truly to be pitied, for if once he
grows sociable he is undone. On the contrary, he
must for ever remain in the very predicament of the
proud man described in the fragment of Euripides's Ixion—Φιλοις ἄμικτός καὶ πάσηπόλει—Urbi atque
amicis pariter insociabilis: He must have no friend,
for that would be to admit an equal; he must take
no advice, for that would be to acknowledge a superior: Such society as he can find in his own
thoughts, and such wisdom as he was sent into the
world with, such he must go on with: as wit is not
absolutely annexed to pedigree in this country, and
arts and sciences sometimes condescend to throw
their beams upon the low-born and the humble, it is
not possible for the proud man to descend amongst
them for information and society; if truth does not
hang within his reach, he will never dive into a well

to fetch it up: His errors, like some arguments, move *in a circle*; for his pride begets ignorance, and his ignorance begets pride; and thus in the end he has more reasons for being *melancholy* than Master Stephen had, not only becaufe it is *gentleman-like*, but because he can't help it, and don't know how to be merry.

I might enumerate many more properties of this contemptible character, but these are enough, and a proud man is so dull a fellow at best, that I shall gladly take my leave of him; I confess also that I am not able to treat the subject in any other than a vague and desultory manner, for I know not how to define it myself, and at the same time am not reconciled to any other definition of pride, which I have met in Mr. Locke's essay or elsewhere. It is called a passion, and yet it has not the essentials of a passion; for I can bring to mind nothing under that description, which has not reference either to God, to our fellow-creatures, or to ourselves. The sensual passions for instance, of whatever sort, have their end in selfish gratification; the generous attributes, such as valour, friendship, public spirit, munificence, and contempt of danger, have respect to our fellow-creatures; they look for their account in an honourable fame, in the enjoyment of present praise, and in the anticipation of that which posterity shall bestow; whilst the less ostentatious and purer virtues of self-denial, resignation, humility, piety, forbearance, and many others, are addressed to God alone, they offer no gratification to self, they seek for no applause from man. But in which of these three general classes shall we discover the passion of pride? I have indeed sometimes seen it under the cloak of religion, but nothing can be more opposite to the practice of it: It is in vain to enquire for it amongst the generous and social attributes, for its place is no where to be found in so-

ciety; and I am equally at a loss to think how that
can be called a selfish gratification, which brings
nothing home to a man's heart but mortification,
contempt, abhorrence, secret discontent and public
ridicule. It is composed of contraries, and founded
in absurdity; for at the same time that it cannot
subsist without the world's respect, it is so constituted as never to obtain it. Anger is proverbially
termed a short madness, but pride methinks is a per-
petual one; if I had been inclined to use a softer
word, I would have called it folly; I do confess I
have often seen it in that more venial character, and
therefore not to decide upon the point too hastily,
I shall leave the proud man to make his choice between folly and madness, and take out his commission from which party he sees fit.

Good heaven! how pleasant, how complacent to
itself and others is an humble disposition! To a
soul so tempered how delightfully life passes in
brotherly love and simplicity of manners! Every eye
bestows the chearing look of approbation upon the
humble man; every brow frowns contempt upon
the proud. Let me therefore advise every gentleman, when he finds himself inclined to take up the
character of pride, to consider well whether he can
be quite proud enough for all purposes of life: whether his pride reaches to that pitch as to meet universal contempt with indifference; whether it will
bear him out against mortification, when he finds
himself excluded from society, and understands
that he is ridiculed by every body in it; whether it
is convenient to him always to walk with a stiff
back and a stern countenance; and lastly, whether
he is perfectly sure, that he has that strength and
self-support in his own human nature, as may defy
the power and set at nought the favour of God, *who
resisteth the proud, but giveth grace to the humble.*

There is yet another little easy process, which I
would recommend to him as a kind of probationary
rehearsal before he performs in public: I am persuaded it will not be amiss if he first runs over a
few of his airs and graces by himself in his own
closet: Let him examine himself from head to foot
in his glass, and if he finds himself no handsomer,
no stronger, no taller than the rest of his fellow-
creatures, he may venture without risque to conclude that he like them is a man, and nothing more :
Having settled this point, and taken place in the
human creation, he may next proceed to consider
what that place ought to be; for this purpose he
may consult his pedigree and his rent-roll, and if
upon a careful perusal of these documents he shall
find, (as most likely he will) that he is not decidedly
the noblest and the richest man in the world, perhaps he will see no good cause, why he should strut
over the face of it, as if it was his own : I would
then have him go back to his glass, and set his features in order for the very proudest and most arro-
gant look he can put on; let him knit his brow,
stretch his nostrils, and bite his lips with all the
dignity he can summon; and after this, when he
has reversed the experiment by softening them into
a mild complacent look, with as much benignity
as he can find in his heart to bestow upon them,
let him ask himself honestly and fairly, which character best becomes him, and whether he does not
look more like a man with some humanity than
without it: I would in the next place have him
call his understanding to a short audit, and upon
casting up the sum total of his wit, learning, talents,
and accomplishments, compute the balance between
others and himself, and if it shall turn out that his
stock of all these is not the prodigious thing it
ought to be, and even greater than all other men's,

he will do well to husband it with a little frugal
humility: The last thing he must do, (and if he
does nothing else I should hope it would be sufficient)
is to take down his Bible from the shelf, and look
out for the parable of the Pharisee and Publican;
it is a short story and soon read, but the moral is so
much to his purpose, that he may depend upon it,
if that does not correct his pride, his pride is incor-
rigible, and all the *Observers* in the world will be
but waste paper in his service.

NUMBER LVII.

Μακάριος ὅστις οὐσίαν καὶ νοῦν ἔχει·
Χρῆται γὰρ οὗτος εἰς ἅ δεῖ ταύτη καλῶς·
Οὕτω μαθεῖν δεῖ πάντα καὶ πλοῦτον φέρειν.
Ἀσχημοσύνης γὰρ γίνετ᾽ ἐνίοις αἴτιος.

MENANDER. CIRCULATORE.

> Abundance is a blessing to the wise;
> The use of riches in discretion lies:
> Learn this, ye men of wealth—a heavy purse
> In a fool's pocket is a heavy curse.

THERE are so many striking advantages in the possession of wealth, that the inheritance of a great estate, devolving upon a man in the vigour of mind
and body, appears to the eye of speculation as a lot
of singular felicity.

There are some countries, where no subject can
properly be said to be independent; but in a constitution so happily tempered as our's, that blessing
seems peculiarly annexed to affluence. The English landed gentleman, who can set his foot upon
his own soil, and say to all the world—*This is my*

freehold; the law defends my right: Touch it who dare !
—is surely as independent as any man within the
rules of society can be, so long as he encumbers
himself by no exceedings of expence beyond the
compass of his income : If a great estate therefore
gives a man independence, it gives him that, which
all, who do not possess it, seem to sigh for.

When I consider the numberless indulgencies,
which are the concomitants of a great fortune, and
the facility it affords to the gratification of every generous passion, I am mortified to find how few,
who are possessed of these advantages, avail themselves of their situation to any worthy purposes :
That happy temper, which can preserve a medium
between dissipation and avarice, is not often to be
found, and where I meet one man, who can lauda-
bly acquit himself under the test of prosperity, I
could instance numbers, who deport themselves
with honour under the visitation of adversity. Man
must be in a certain degree the artificer of his own
happiness ; the tools and materials may be put into his hands by the bounty of Providence, but the
workmanship must be his own.

I lately took a journey into a distant county, upon
a visit to a gentleman of fortune, whom I shall call
Attalus. I had never seen him since his accession
to a very considerable estate ; and as I have met
with few acquaintance in life of more pleasant qualities, or a more social temper than Attalus, before
this great property unexpectedly devolved upon
him, I flattered myself that fortune had in this instance bestowed her favours upon one who deserved
them ; and that I should find in Attalus's society
the pleasing gratification of seeing all those maxims, which I had hitherto revolved in my mind as
matter of speculation only, now brought forth into

actual practice; for amongst all my observations
upon human affairs, few have given me greater
and more frequent disappointment, than the almost
general abuse of riches. Those rules of liberal œconomy, which would make wealth a blessing to its
owner and to all he were connected with, seem
so obvious to me, who have no other interest in the
subject than what meditation affords, that I am apt
to wonder how men can make such false estimates
of the true enjoyments of life, and wander out of
the way of happiness, to which the heart and understanding seem to point the road too plainly to admit
of a mistake.

With these sanguine expectations I pursued my
journey towards the magnificent seat of Attalus, and
in my approach it was with pleasure I remarked
the beauty of the country about it; I recollected
how much he used to be devoted to rural exercises,
and I found him situated in the very spot most favo-
rable to his beloved amusements; the soil was clean,
the hills easy, and the downs were chequered with
thick copses, that seemed the finest nurseries in nature for a sportsman's game: When I entered upon
his ornamented demesne, nothing could be more
enchanting than the scenery; the ground was finely
shaped into hill and vale; the horizon every where
bold and romantic, and the hand of art had evidently improved the workmanship of nature with
consummate taste; upon the broken declivity
stately groves of beech were happily disposed; the
lawn was of the finest verdure gently sloping from
the house; a rapid river of the purest transparency
ran through it, and fell over a rocky channel into a
noble lake within view of the mansion; behind this
upon the northern and eastern flanks I could discern the tops of very stately trees, that sheltered a

spacious enclosure of pleasure-ground and gardens, with all the delicious accompaniments of hot-houses and conservatories.

It was a scene to seize the imagination with rapture; a poet's language would have run spontaneously into metre at the sight of it: 'What a subject,' said I within myself, 'is here present for those ingenious bards, who have the happy talent of describing nature in her fairest forms! Oh! that I could plant the delightful author of *The Task* in this very spot! perhaps whilst his eye—*in a fine phrensy rolling*—glanced over this enchanting prospect, he might burst forth into the following, or something like the following, rhapsody—'

> Blest above men, if he perceives and feels
> The blessings he is heir to, He! to whom
> His provident forefathers have bequeathed
> In this fair district of their native isle
> A free inheritance, compact and clear.
> How sweet the vivifying dawn to him,
> Who with a fond paternal eye can trace
> Beloved scenes, where rivers, groves and lawns
> Rise at the touch of the Orphean hand,
> And Nature, like a docile child, repays
> Her kind disposer's care! Master and friend
> Of all that blooms or breathes within the verge
> Of this wide-stretcht horizon, he surveys
> His upland pastures white with fleecy flocks,
> Rich meadows dappled o'er with grazing herds,
> And vallies waving thick with golden grain.
>   Where can the world display a fairer scene?
> And what has Nature for the sons of men
> Better provided than this happy isle;
> Mark! how she's girded by her watery zone,
> Whilst all the neighb'ring continent is trench'd
> And furrow'd with the ghastly seams of war:
> Barriers and forts and arm'd battalions stand
> On the fierce confines of each rival state,
> Jealous to guard, or eager to invade;
> Between their hostile camps a field of blood,
> Behind them desolation void and drear,

Where at the summons of the surly drum
The rising and the setting sun reflects
Nought but the gleam of arms, now here, now there
Flashing amain, as the bright phalanx moves:
Wasteful and wide the blank in Nature's map,
And far far distant where the scene begins
Of human habitation, thinly group'd
Over the meagre earth; for there no youth,
No sturdy peasant, who with limbs and strength
Might fill the gaps of battle, dares approach ;
Old age instead, with weak and trembling hand
Feebly solicits the indignant soil
For a precarious meal, poor at the best.

   Oh, Albion ! oh, blest isle, on whose white cliffs
Peace builds her halcyon nest, thou, who embrac'd
By the uxorious ocean sit'st secure,
Smiling and gay and crown'd with every wreath,
That Art can fashion or rich Commerce waft
To deck thee like a bride, compare these scenes
With pity not with scorn, and let thy heart,
Not wanton with prosperity, but warm
With grateful adoration, send up praise
To the great Giver—thence thy blessings come.

   The soft luxurious nations will complain
Of thy rude wintry clime, and chide the winds
That ruffle their fine forms ; trembling they view
The boisterous barrier that defends thy coast,
Nor dare to pass it till their pilot bird,
The winter-sleeping swallow, points the way ;
But envy not their suns, and sigh not thou
For the clear azure of their cloudless skies ;
The same strong blast, that beds the knotted oak
Firm in his clay-bound cradle, nerves the arm
Of the stout hind, who fells him to the ground.
These are the manly offspring of our isle ;
Their's are the pure delights of rural life,
Freedom their birth-right and their dwelling peace;
The vine, that mantles o'er their cottage roof,
Gives them a shade no tyrant dares to spoil.

   Mark ! how the sturdy peasant breasts the storm,
The white snow sleeting o'er his brawny chest ;
He heeds it not, but carols as he goes
Some jocund measure or love-ditty, soon
In sprightlier key and happier accent sung
To the kind wench at home, whose ruddy cheeks

Shall thaw the icy winter on his lips,
And melt his frozen features into joy.
But who, that ever heard the hunter's shout,
When the shrill fox-hound doubles on the scent,
Which of you, sons and fathers of the chace,
Which of your hardy, bold, adventurous band
Will pine and murmur for Italian skies?
Hark! from the covert-side your game is view'd!
Music, which none but British dryads hear,
Shouts, which no foreign echoes can repeat,
Ring thro' the hollow-wood and sweep the vale.
Now, now, ye joyous sportsmen, ye, whose hearts
Are unison'd to the extatic cry
Of the full pack, now give your steeds the rein!
Your's is the day—mine was, and is no more:
Yet ever as I hear you in the wind,
Tho' chill'd and hovering o'er my winter hearth,
Forth, like some Greenwich veteran, if chance
The conqu'ring name of *Rodney* meets his ear,
Forth I must come to share the glad'ning sound,
To shew my scars and boast of former feats.
　　They say our clime's inconstant, changeful—True!
It gives the lie to all astrology,
Makes the diviner mad and almost mocks
Philosophy itself; Cameleon-like
Our sky puts on all colours, blushing now,
Now louring like a froward pettish child;
This hour a zephyr, and the next a storm,
Angry and pleas'd by fits—Yet take our clime,
Take it for all in all and day by day,
Thro' all the varying seasons of the year,
For the mind's vigour and the body's strength,
Where is its rival?—Beauty is its own:
Not the voluptuous region of the Nile,
Not aromatic India's spicy breath,
Nor evening breeze from Tagus, Rhone or Loire
Can tinge the maiden cheek with bloom so fresh.
Here too, if exercise and temperance call,
Health shall obey their summons; every fount,
Each rilling stream conveys it to our lips;
In every zephyr we inhale her breath;
The shepherd tracks her in the morning dew,
As o'er the grassy down or to the heath
Streaming with fragrance he conducts his flock.
But oh! defend me from the baneful east,

Screen me, ye groves! ye interposing hills,
Rise up and cover me! Agues and rheums,
All Holland's marshes strike me in the gale;
Like Egypt's blight his breath is all alive:
His very dew is poison, honey-sweet,
Teeming with putrefaction; in his fog
The locust and the caterpillar swarm,
And vegetable nature falls before them:
Open, all quarters else, and blow upon me,
But bar that gate, O regent of the winds!
It gives the food that melancholy doats on,
The quick'ner that provokes the slanderer's spleen,
Makes green the eye of Jealousy and feeds
The swelling gorge of Envy till it bursts:
'Tis now the poet's unpropitious hour;
The student trims his midnight lamp in vain,
And beauty fades upon the painter's eye:
Hang up thy pallet, *Romney!* and convene
The gay companions of thy social board;
Apelles' self would throw his pencil by,
And swear the skies conspir'd against his art.

But what must Europe's softer climes endure,
Thy coast, Calabria! or the neighbouring isle,
Of antient Ceres once the fruitful seat?
Where is the bloom of Enna's flowery field,
Mellifluous Hybla, and the golden vale
Of rich Panormus, when the fell *Siroc,*
Hot from the furnace of the Libyan sands,
Breathes all it's plagues upon them? Hapless isle
Why must I call to mind thy past renown?
Is it this desolating blast alone,
That strips thy verdure? Is it in the gulph
Of yawning earthquakes that thy glory sinks?
Or hath the flood that thund'ring Ætna pours
From her convuls'd and flaming entrails whelm'd
In one wide ruin every noble spark
Of pristine virtue, genius, wisdom, wit?
Ah no! the elements are not in fault;
Nature is still the same: 'Tis not the blast
From Afric's burning sands, it is the breath
Of Spain's despotic master lays thee low;
'Tis not alone the quaking earth that reels
Under thy tottering cities, 'tis the fall
Of freedom, 'tis the pit which slavery digs,
That buries every virtue; 'tis the flood

Of superstition, the insatiate fires
Of persecuting zealots that devour thee;
These are the Titans who disturb thy peace,
This is thy grave, O Sicily! the hell
Deeper than that, which heathen poets feign'd
Under thy burning mountain, that engulphs
Each grace and every muse, arts, arms and all
That elegance inspires or fame records.

   Return, ye victims of caprice and spleen,
Ye summer friends, daughters more fitly call'd
Than sons of Albion, to your native shores
Return, self-exiles as you are, and face
This only tyrant which our isle endures,
This hoary-headed terror of the year,
Stern Winter—What, tho' in his icy chains
Imprison'd for a time e'en Father Thames
Checks his imperial current, and beholds
His wealthy navigation in arrest,
Yet soon, like Perseus on his winged steed,
Forth from the horns of the celestial Ram
Spring, his deliverer, comes—down, down at once
The frighted monster dives into the earth,
Or bursts asunder with a hideous crash,
As thro' his stubborn ribs th' all-conqu'ring sun
Drives his refulgent spear: the ransom'd floods,
As at a signal, rise and clap their hands;
The mountains shout for joy; the laughing hours
Dance o'er the eastern hills, and in the lap
Of marriageable earth their odours fling,
Wreaths of each vernal flowret, whilst the choir
Of feather'd songsters make the groves resound
With Nature's hymenæals—all is joy.

   Hail, bounteous Spring! primæval season, hail!
Nature's glad herald! who to all the tribes
That link creation's scale, from lordly man
To the small insect, that eludes his sight,
Proclaims that universal law of life,
The first great blessing of the new-born world,
' Increase and multiply!'—No sooner heard
By sultry climes, than strait the rebel sun
Mounts his bright throne, and o'er the withering earth
Scatters his bold Titanian fires around,
And cancels Heaven's high edict; Nature feels
Quick growth and quick decay; the verdant scene
Glitters awhile and vanishes at once.

Not such the tints that Albion's landscape wears,
Her mantle dipt in never-fading green,
Keeps fresh its vernal honours thro' the year;
Soft dew-drops nurse her rose's maiden bloom,
And genial showers refresh her vivid lawn.
Thro' other lands indignant of delay
Spring travels homeward with a stranger's haste;
Here he reposes, dwells upon the scene
Enamour'd, native here prolongs his stay,
And when his fiery successor at length
Warns him from hence, with ling'ring step and slow,
And many a stream of falling tears he parts,
Like one, whom surly creditors arrest
In a fond consort's arms and force him thence.
    But now, my Muse, to humbler themes descend!
'Tis not for me to paint the various gifts
Which freedom, science, art, or fav'ring Heav'n
Shower on my native isle; quench'd are the fires,
Which young ambition kindled in my breast;
Morning and noon of life's short day are past,
And what remains for me ere night comes on,
But one still hour perchance of glimmering eve
For sober contemplation? Come, my Muse,
Come then! and as from some high mountain's top
The careful shepherd counts his straggling flock,
So will we take one patient last survey
Of this unquiet, babbling, anxious world;
We'll scan it with a calm but curious eye;
Silence and solitude are all our own;
Their's is the tumult, their's the throng; my soul
Is fitted to the task—for, oh fair truth!
Yet I am thine, on thy perennial base
I will inscribe my monumental verse;
And tho' my heart with kindred ardor beats
To every brave compatriot, yet no ties,
Tho' dignified with friendship's specious name,
Shall shackle my free mind, nor any space
Less than the world's wide compass bound my love.
    No more; for now the hospitable gates
Of wealthy Attalus invite their guest;
I paus'd and look'd, and yielding to the wish
That fortune had bequeath'd me such a lot,
A momentary sigh surpriz'd my heart:
Flocks, herds, and fields of golden grain, of these
I envied not the owner; but I saw

The curling smoke from cottages ascend,
And heard the merry din of childish sports;
I saw the peasant stooping to his plough
And whistling time away; I met a form,
Fair as a fabled nymph; Nature had spread
Her toilette, Health her handmaid dealt the bloom,
Simplicity attir'd her; by the copse
Skirting the horn-beam row, where violets bud
And the first primrose opens to the spring,
With her fond lover arm in arm she walk'd,
Not with the stealthy step and harlot leer
Of guilty assignation, nor unnerv'd
By midnight feast or revel, but in prime
Of youth and health and beauty's genuine glow:
I mark'd the conscious look of honest truth,
That greets the passenger with eye direct,
Nor fears nor meditates surprize; my heart
Yearn'd at the sight, and as they pass'd I cried—
' Why was it not my fortune to have said
' Go, and be happy?'—On a rising slope
Full to the south the stately mansion stands,
Where dwells the master of this rich domain;
Plain and of chaste proportion the device,
Not libell'd and bedawb'd with tawdry frize
Or lac'd pilaster, patch'd with refuse scraps,
Like that fraternal pile on Thames's bank,
Which draws its title not its taste from Greece.
    Happy! if there in rural peace he dwells,
Untortur'd by ambition, and enjoys
An eye for nature and a heart for man.

NUMBER LVIII.

Οὐκ ἔσαμαι πλυτεῖν ἔτ' εὔχομαι, ἀλλὰ μοι εἴη
Ζῆν ἀπὸ τῶν ὀλίγων μηδὲν ἔχοντι κακόν.

THEOGNIS.

' I ask not wealth; let me enjoy
An humble lot without annoy !'

Upon my arrival at the house I was shewn into a
small room in the base-story, which the owner of
this fine place usually occupied, and in which he
now received me : here I had been but a very few
minutes before he proposed to shew me the house,
and for that purpose conducted me up stairs to the
grand apartment, and from thence made the entire
tour, without excepting any one of the bed-cham-
bers, offices or even closets in the house : I cannot
say my friend Attalus consulted times and seasons
in chusing so early a moment after my arrival for
parading me about in this manner; some of the
apartments were certainly very splendid; a great
deal of rich furniture and many fine pictures solicited
my notice, but the fatigue of so ill-timed a peram-
bulation disabled me from expressing that degree of
admiration, which seemed to be expected on this
occasion, and which on any other I should have
been forward to bestow: I was sorry for this, because I believe he enjoyed little other pleasure in
the possession of his house, besides this of shewing
it; but it happened to my host, as it does too frequently to the owners of fine places, that he missed

the tribute of flattery by too great eagerness in ex-
acting it.

It appeared to me that Attalus was no longer the
gay lively man he was formerly; there was a gloom
upon his countenance and an inquietude in his manner, which seemed to lay him under a constraint
that he could not naturally get rid of: time hung
heavy on our hands till the hour of dinner, and it
was not without regret I perceived he had arranged
his family meals upon the fashionable system of
London hours, and at the distance of two hundred
miles from the capital had by choice adopted those
very habits, which nothing but the general custom
of late assemblies and long sittings in Parliament
can excuse upon the plea of necessity: it was now
the midst of summer, which made the absurdity of
such a disposition of our time more glaring, for
whilst the best hours of the afternoon were devoted
to the table, all exercise and enjoyment out of doors
were either to be given up, or taken only in the
meridian heat of the day. I discovered a further
bad consequence of these habits upon society and
good-fellowship, for such of the neighbouring gentry, who had not copied his example, were deterred
from making him any visits, not presuming to disturb him at unsuitable hours, and yet not able,
without a total disarrangement of their own comforts, to make their time conform to his. Attalus
himself, I must acknowledge, both saw and confessed the bad system he was upon, he found himself grown unpopular amongst his country neighbours on this very score, and was piqued by their
neglect of him: ' it was a villainous custom,' he
observed, ' and destructive both of health and pleasure; but all people of fashion dined at five, and
what could he do? he must live as other great families lived; if indeed he was a mere private gen-

tleman, he might do as he liked best.' If it be so, thought I, this man's great fortune is an incumbrance to him: if it robs him of health and pleasure, what does it give him, nay what can it give him, in compensation for the loss of such blessings? if fashion takes away from Attalus the liberty of doing what he best likes, and is best for him, I must have been mistaken in supposing independence was the result of affluence; I suspect there are not all the advantages in his condition which I supposed there were—I will examine this more narrowly.

The next morning, after a late breakfast, the consequence I had foreseen ensued, for we were advanced into the hottest hours of the day, when Attalus, being impatient to shew me the beauties of his park and grounds, gave orders for the equipages and horses to be made ready, and we were to set out upon the survey in a burning sun. When the train was in waiting at the door, we sallied forth, but here a discussion began, in which so many things required a new arrangement, that a long stop was put to our march, whilst the scrutinizing eye of Attalus was employed in a minute examination of every thing appertaining to the cavalry and carriages; the horses were wrong harnessed, they were to be changed from the off-side to the near-side, saddles were to be altered, and both groom and coachman were heartily recommended to repeated damnation for their stupidity and inattention— 'Never any man was so plagued with rascally servants as I am,' cried Attalus; 'they are the curse and vexation of my life; I wish I could live without them; no man can be happy, who has to do with them.'—Is it so? (said I within myself) then I have the advantage over you in that respect, for I have but one man and one horse, and both are always ready at a moment's warning.

I mounted a phaeton with Attalus and we set forward in a broiling day: my conductor immediately began to vent his angry humour upon the wrong object, and plied his thong at such a furious rate upon his unoffending horses, that the high mettled animals so resented the unjust correction, that after struggling and kicking under the lash for some time, one of them reared across the pole of the chaise and snapped it: this produced a storm of passion more violent than the first, and though it was evident the servant had put the horses on their proper sides at first, the fault was charged upon him with vehement imprecations, and this produced a second halt longer and more disagreeable than our setting out had been: our purpose however was not to be defeated and we must positively proceed; Attalus was not in a humour to submit with patience to disappointments, so that having ordered two of his servants to dismount, we took their horses and set off upon our tour; the beauties of nature were before us, but that serenity of mind, which should ever accompany the contemplation of those beauties, was wanting; Attalus was one of fortune's spoilt children, and his temper, grown irritable by indulgence and humoursome by prosperity, had lost its relish for simplicity, and was wholly given up to a silly passion for ostentation and parade; he immediately began to harangue upon the many evil qualities of servants, a topic at the best unedifying and commonly most disgusting to the hearers; he bewailed his own ill-fortune in that respect very bitterly, and so much of the way passed off before this philippic was concluded, that I began to think I had been carried out for no better purpose than to hear a declamation in the open air: I brought him at last to a stop, by observing, he had a paradise about him, and that it was a pity his vexations did

not suffer him to enjoy it—Upon this hint he seemed
to recollect himself, and proceeded to expatiate upon
his own improvements, pointing out to me what he
had done, and what he had more in mind to do, if
his overseer had obeyed his instructions, and proper
people had been found to execute his designs.

I took notice of a group of neat cottages, which
had a very picturesque and pleasing appearance, for
they were deliciously situated, and had all the air, as
I observed, of happy habitations—' No matter for
that,' replied Attalus, 'down they must all come,
for they are cruelly in my eye, and I purpose to
throw all that hill into wilderness with plantations
of pine, where you see the rock and broken ground,
which will be a bold and striking contrast to the ornamented grounds about it—I am surprized,' added
he, ' you can see any beauty in those paltry huts.'
—Before I could make reply, an old peasant had
approached us, and humbly enquired of Attalus,
when he was to be dislodged from his cottage—' I
have ordered the workmen to take it down next
week,' said he, ' the season is favourable for your
removal, and you must seek out elsewhere.' The
decree was heard without an effort to reply; a
sigh was all the plea the poor man offered, and with
that sigh he sent a look to heaven that in its passage
rent my heart : I determined to be gone next morning.

We proceeded in our circuit till we were crossed
by a high enclosure, which aukwardly enough se-
parated a pasture of about three acres, in which was
a brick-kiln too conspicuously placed not to annoy
the sight, and at that very moment too furiously
employed in the act of duty, not to be excessively
offensive to the smell ; we found ourselves involved
in columns of thick smoke, which were not of the
most grateful odour in the world; I confess I was

not a little surprized at the location of this flaming
nuisance, and as we were making our way through
the smothering cloud, remarked to Attalus that ornament must give place to use—'I brought you
hither,' says he, 'purposely to shew you how I am
treated by a surly obstinate fellow in my neighbourhood, who has not another foot of land in the world,
but this cursed patch of ground, and which the ras-
cal keeps on purpose to spite me, though I have
bidden three times the value of it: indeed it is in-
dispensably necessary to me, as you may well believe by the annoyance it produces in his hands; I
have tried all means to get it from him, rough and
smooth, and if a prosecution would have laid against
it, I would have driven him out of it by the expences
of a suit; but all to no purpose; I am so tormented
by the fellow's obstinacy, and my comforts are so
sacrificed by the nuisance, that I have no longer
any enjoyment in my place; nay I have stopped
most of my works and discharged my labourers,
for what signifies carrying on improvements, when
I can no longer live in my house with that cursed
brick-kiln for ever in my eye, and with little intermission in my nostrils also?'

A new theme of discontent was now started,
which the unhappy Attalus pursued with heavy
complaints as we travelled down a stream of smoke,
which seemed as if maliciously to pursue us, determined not to quit it's execrator, till he left off his
execrations; at last they both ceased in the same
moment and parted by consent. As soon as Attalus desisted from his invectives I took up my reflections, and if a wish could have purchased his
possessions, encumbered with the vexations of their
owner, I would not have taken them at the price.
Down sunk the vision of prosperity; swifter than
the shifting of a play-house scene vanished all the
enchanting prospect; a naked lodge in a warren

with content had been more enviable in my eye
than his palace haunted with disgust; I saw Attalus, the veriest darling of fortune, sickening and
furfeited with prosperity; peevish with his servants,
unsociable to his neighbours, a slave to fashions,
which he obeyed and disapproved, unfeeling to the
poor, tired with the splendor of a magnificent house,
and possessing an extensive territory, yet sighing
after a small nook of land, the want of which poisoned all his comforts.—And what then are riches?
said I within myself. The disturbers of human
happiness; the corrupters of human nature. I remember this Attalus in his youth; I knew him in-
timately at school and college; he was of a joyous,
social temper; placid, accommodating, full of resource; always in good humour with himself and
the world, and he had a heart as liberal and com-
passionate as it was sincere and open; this great
estate was then out of sight; it must be this estate
then, which has wrought the unhappy change in
his manners and disposition; and if riches operate
thus upon a nature like his, where is the wonder if
we meet so many wretches, who derive their wants
from their abundance?

How beautiful is the maxim of *Menander!*—
Ψυχὴν ἔχειν δεῖ πλουσιαν—enrich your mind! 'Riches,'
says the same elegant and moral dramatist, 'are no
better than an actor's wardrobe,' the paltry tinsel,
that enables him to glitter for a few minutes in a
counterfeited character—

> To fret and strut his hour upon the stage,
> And then be heard no more.

In another place he says, 'they transform a man
into a different kind of being from what he was
originally'—

Εἰς ἕτερον ἦθος, ἀκ ἐν ᾧ' τὸ πρόσθεν ἦν·

and then concludes with that Attic simplicity, so neatly turned and elegantly expressed as to distance all translation.

Κρεῖττον γάρ ἐστω, αν σκοπῇ τὶς κατὰ λόγον,
Μὴ πολλ' ἀηδῶς, ὀλίγα δ' ἡδέως ἔχειν.

> Better to choose, if you would choose the best,
> A chearful poverty, than wealth unblest.

NUMBER LIX.

Omnes eodem cogimur ; omnium
Versatur urna serius ocius
Sors exitura.

HORAT. CARM.

> All to the same last home are bound;
> Time's never-weary wheel runs round;
> And life at longest or at shortest date
> Snaps like a thread betwixt the shears of Fate.

I REMEMBER to have been told of a certain humourist, who set up a very singular doctrine upon the subject of death, asserting that he had discovered it to be not a necessary and inevitable event, but an act of choice and volition; he maintained that he had certain powers and resources within himself sufficient to support him in his resolution of holding out against the summons of death, till he became weary of life; and he pledged himself to his friends, that he would in his own person give experimental proof of his hypothesis.

What particular address death made use of, when this ingenious gentleman was prevailed upon to step out of the world, I cannot take upon myself to say ; but certain it is, that in some weak moment he was over persuaded to lay his head calmly on the pillow and surrender up his breath.

Though an event, so contrary to the promise he had given, must have been a staggering circumstance to many, who were interested in the success of his experiment, yet I see good reason to suspect that his hypothesis is not totally discredited, and that he has yet some surviving disciples, who are acting such a part in this world as nobody would act but upon a strong presumption, that they shall not be compelled to go out of it, and enter upon another.

Mortality, it must be owned, hath means of providing for the event of death, though none have yet been discovered of preventing it : Religion and virtue are the great physicians of the soul : patience and resignation are the nursing-mothers of the human heart in sickness and in sorrow ; conscience can smooth the pillow under an aching head, and Christian hope administers a cordial even in our last moments, that lulls the agonies of death : But where is the need of these had this discovery been established ? Why call in physicians and resort to cordials, if we can hold danger at a distance without their help ? I am to presume therefore, that every human being, who makes his own will his master, and goes all lengths in gratifying his guilty passions without restraint, must rely upon his own will for keeping him out of all danger of future trouble, or he would never commit himself so confidentially and entirely to a master, which can give him no security in return for his blind obedience and devotion : All persons of this description I accordingly set down in the lump as converts to the doctrine of the learned gentleman, who advanced the

interesting discovery above-mentioned, but who unluckily missed some step in the proof, that was to
have established it.

To what lengths of credulity they may really go
is hard to say, but some such hopes as these must
buoy them up, because I cannot think that any
man would be wilfully wicked, fraudulent, perfi-
dious, avaricious, cruel, or whatever else is detest-
able in the eye of God, if he saw death, his messenger, at the door; and I am even unwilling to
believe, that he would be wantonly guilty, was he
only convinced, that when death shall come to the
door, he must be obliged to admit him : for if this
be so, and if admission may not be denied, then
hath death a kind of visitorial power over us,
which makes him not a guest to be invited at our
pleasure, but a lord and master of the house, to
enter it as his own, and (which is worst of all)
without giving notice to us to provide for his entertainment.   What man is such a fool in common
life, as to take up his abode in a tenement, of
which he is sure to be dispossessed, and yet neglect
to prepare himself against a surprise, which he is
subject to every moment of the day and night ? We
are not apt to overlook our own interests and safety
in worldly concerns, and therefore when the soul is
given up to sin, I must suspect some error in the
brain.

What shall I say to persuade the inconsiderate
that they exist upon the precarious sufferance of
every moment, that passes over them in succession?
How shall I warn a giddy fool not to play his an-
tick tricks and caper on the very utmost edge of a
precipice ? Who will guide the reeling drunkard
in his path, and teach him to avoid the grave-
stones of his fellow-sots, set up by death as marks
and signals to apprise him of his danger ? If the

voice of nature, deposing to the evidence of life's deceitful tenure from the beginning of things to the moment present, will neither gain audience nor belief, what can the moralist expect?

Which of all those headlong voluptuaries, who seem in such haste to get to the end of life, is possessed of the art of prolonging it at pleasure? To whom has the secret been imparted? Either they are deceived by a vain hope of evading death, or there is something in a life of dissipation not worth preserving. I am astonished at the stupidity of any man, who can deny himself the gratification of conscious integrity: The proud man must be a consummate blockhead to take such wearisome pains for a little extorted flattery of the most servile sort, and overlook the ready means of gaining general respect upon the noblest terms: Is it not an abuse of language and an insult to common sense for a silly fellow to announce himself to the world as a man of pleasure, when there is not an action in his life, but leaves a sting behind it to belie the character he professes? Can one fellow-creature find amusement in tormenting another? Is it possible there can be a recreation in malice, when it slanders the innocent; in fraud, when it cheats the unsuspecting; in perfidy, when is betrays a benefactor? If any being, who does me wrong, will justify himself against the wrong by confessing, that he takes delight in injury, I will own to one instance of human depravity, which till that shall happen I will persist to hope is not in existence: The fact is that all men have that respect for justice, that they attempt to shelter their very worst actions under its defence; and even those contemptible pilferers of reputation, who would be as much unknown by their names as they are by the concealmen. of them, qualify (I am persuaded) the dirty deed they are about by some convenient phantom of offence in the character they assault; even their hands cannot be raised to strike without prefacing the blow by saying to themselves—This man deserves to die.—Foolish wretches, what computation must they make of life, who devote so great a portion of it to miseries and reproaches of their own creating!

Let a rational creature for once talk common sense to himself, and if no better words than the following occur to his thoughts, let him make use of them: he is heartily welcome to the loan.

'I know there is a period in approach, when I must encounter an enemy to my life, whose power is irresistible: This is a very serious thing for me to reflect upon, and knowing it to be a truth infallible, I am out of hope, that I can so far forget the terms of my existence, as totally to expel it from my thoughts: If I could foresee the precise hour, when this enemy will come, I would provide against it as well as I am able, and fortify my mind to receive him with such complacency as I could muster: But of this hour I have, alas! no foresight; it may be this moment, or the next, or years may intervene before it comes to pass: It behoves me then to be upon my guard: He may approach in terrors, that agonize me to think of; he may seize my soul in the commission of some dreadful act, and transport it to a place whose horrors have no termination: I will not then commit that dreadful act, because I will not expose myself to that dreadful punishment: It is in my own choice to refrain from it, and I am not such a desperate fool to make choice of misery: If I act with this precaution, will he still appear in this shape of terror! Certainly he will not, nor can he in justice transport me to a place of punishment, when I

have committed nothing to deserve it : Whither
then will he convey me ? To the mansions of everlasting happiness : Where are my fears ? What is
now become of his terrors ? He is my passport, my
conductor, my friend : I will welcome him with
embraces : I will smile upon him with gratitude,
and accompany him with exultation.'

NUMBER LX.

I WOULD wish no man to deceive himself with opinions, which he has not thoroughly reflected upon
in his solitary hours : Till he has communed with
his own heart in his chamber, it will be dangerous
to commit himself to its impulses amidst the dis-
tractions of society : In solitude he will hear another voice than he has been used to hear in the colloquial scenes of life ; for conscience, though mute
as the antient chorus in the bustle of the drama,
will be found a powerful speaker in soliloquy.   If
I could believe that any man in these times had seriously and deliberately reasoned himself into an
absolute contempt of things sacred, I should expect
that such a being should uniformly act up to his
principles in all situations, and, having thrown
aside all the restraints of religion, should discharge
from his mind all those fears, apprehensions, and
solicitudes, that have any connection with the dread
of futurity.   But, without knowing what passes in
the private thoughts of men, who profess these
daring notions, I cannot help observing, that, if
noisy clamour be a mark of cowardice, they also

have the symptoms strongly upon them of belying their own conscience : They are bold in the crowd, and loudest in the revels of the feast ; there they can echo the insult, dash the ridicule in the very face of Heaven, and stun their consciences in the roar of the carousal.

Let me picture to myself a man of this description surprised into unexpected solitude after the revels of an evening, where he has been the wit of the company, at the expence of decency and religion ; here his triumphs are over ; the plaudits of his comrades no longer encourage him ; the lights of the feast are extinguished, and he is surrendered to darkness and reflection : Place him in the midst of a desart heath, a lonesome traveller in some dark tempestuous night, and let the elements subscribe their terrors to encounter this redoubted champion—

> Who durst defy the Omnipotent.

If consistency be the test of a man's sincerity, he ought now to hold the same language of defiance, and with undaunted spirit cry out to the elements— ' Do your worst, ye blind tools of chance ! Since there can be neither intelligence nor direction in your rage, I set you at nought. You may indeed subject me to some bodily inconvenience, but you can raise no terrors in my mind, for I have said you have no master : There is no hand to point the lightning, and the stroke of its flash is directed to no aim : If it smites the oak, it perishes ; if it penetrates my breast, it annihilates my existence, and there is no soul within me to resume it. What have I to fear ? The worst you threaten is a momentary extinction without pain or struggle ; and as I only wait on earth till I am weary of life, the most you can do is to forestall me in the natural

rights of suicide. I have lived in this world as the
only world I have to live in, and have done all
things therein as a man, who acts without account
to an Hereafter. The moral offices, as they are
called, I have sometimes regarded as a system of
worldly wisdom, and where they have not crossed
my purposes, or thwarted my pleasures, I have occasionally thought fit to comply with them : My
proper pride in some instances, and self-interest in
others, have dissuaded me from the open violation
of a trust, for it is inconvenient to be detected ;
and though I acknowledge no remonstrances from
within upon the score of infamy, I do not like the
clamours of the crowd. As for those mercenary
inducements, which a pretended revelation holds
forth as lures for patience under wrongs and tame
resignation to misfortune, I regard them as derogatory to my nature ; they sink the very character
of virtue by meanly tendering a reversionary happiness as the bribe for practising it: the doctrine
therefore of a future life, in which the obedient are
to expect rewards, and the disobedient are threat-
ened with punishments, confutes itself by its own
internal weakness, and is a system so sordid in its
principle, that it can only be calculated to dupe us
into mental slavery, and frighten us out of that
generous privilege, which is our universal birth-
right, the privilege of dismissing ourselves out of
existence, when we are tired with its conditions.'

Had I fabricated this language for infidelity with
the purpose of stamping greater detestation upon its
audacity, I had rather bear the blame of having
overcharged the character, than to be able (as I
now am) to point out a recent publication, which
openly avows this shameless doctrine: But as I do
not wish to help any anonymous blasphemer into
notice, let the toleration of the times be his shelter,

and their contempt his answer! In the mean time I
will take leave to oppose to it a short passage from
a tract, lately translated into English, intitled Philosophical and Critical Enquiries concerning Christianity, by Mr. Bonnet of Geneva; a work well deserving an attentive perusal:

'Here I invite that reader, who can elevate his
mind to the contemplation of the ways of Providence, to meditate with me on the admirable me-
thods of divine wisdom in the establishment of
Christianity; a religion, the universality of which
was to comprehend all ages, all places, nations,
ranks, and situations in life; a religion, which
made no distinction between the crowned head and
that of the lowest subject; formed to disengage the
heart from terrestrial things, to ennoble, to refine,
to sublime the thoughts and affections of man; to
render him conscious of the dignity of his nature,
the importance of his end, to carry his hopes even
to eternity, and thus associate him with superior
intelligences; a religion, which gave every thing to
the spirit and nothing to the flesh; which called its
disciples to the greatest sacrifices, because men who
are taught to fear God alone, can undergo the se-
verest trials; a religion in short (to conclude my
weak conceptions on so sublime a subject) which
was the perfection or completion of natural law,
the science of the truly wise, the refuge of the humble, the consolation of the wretched; so majestic
in its simplicity, so sublime in its doctrine, so great
in its object, so astonishing in its effects. I have
endeavoured (says this excellent author in his conclusions) to explore the inmost recesses of my heart,
and having discovered no secret motive there, which
should induce me to reject a religion so well calculated to supply the defects of my reason, to comfort me under affliction and to advance the perfec-

tion of my nature, I receive this religion as the greatest blessing Heaven in its goodness could confer upon mankind; and I should still receive it with gratitude, were I to consider it only as the very best and most perfect system of practical philosophy.

BONNET.

That man, hurried away by the impetuosity of his passions, is capable of strange and monstrous irregularities I am not to learn; even vanity and the mean ambition of being eccentric may draw out very wild expressions from him in his unguarded hours; but that any creature should be deliberately blasphemous, and reason himself (if I may so express it) into irrationality, surpasses my conception, and is a species of desperation for which I have no name.

If the voice of universal nature, the experience of all ages, the light of reason and the immediate evidence of my senses cannot awaken me to a dependence upon my God, a reverence for his religion and an humble opinion of myself, what a lost creature am I !

Where can we meet a more touching description of God's omnipresence and providence than in the 139th psalm? And how can I better conclude this paper than by the following humble attempt at a translation of that most beautiful address to the Creator of mankind.

PSALM CXXXIX.

1. O Lord, who by thy mighty power
Hast search'd me out in every part,
Thou know'st each thought at every hour,
Or e'er it rises to my heart.

2. In whatsoever path I stray,
Where'er I make my bed at night,
No maze can so conceal my way,
But I stand open to thy sight.

3. Nor can my tongue pronounce a word,
   How secretly soe'er 'twere said,
   But in thine ear it shall be heard,
   And by thy judgment shall be weigh'd.

4. In every particle I see
   The fashion of thy plastic hand :
5 Knowledge too excellent for me,
   Me, wretched man, to understand.

6 Whither, ah! whither then can I
   From thine all present spirit go ?
7 To Heav'n ? 'tis there thou'rt thron'd on high :
   To Hell ? 'tis there thou rul'st below.

8 Lend me, O Morning, lend me wings!
   On the first beam of op'ning day
   To the last wave, that ocean flings
   On the world's shore, I'll flit away.

9 Ah fool! if there I meant to hide,
   For thou, my God, shalt reach me there ;
   Ev'n there thy hand shall be my guide,
   Thy right hand hold me in its care.

10 Again, if calling out for night,
   I bid it shroud me from thine eyes,
   Thy presence makes a burst of light,
   And darkness to the centre hies.

11 Nay, darkness cannot intervene
   Betwixt the universe and Thee;
   Light or no light, there's nought I ween,
   God self-illumin'd cannot see.

12 Thine is each atom of my frame ;
   Thy fingers strung my inmost reins,
   E'en in the womb, or e'er I came
   To life, and caus'd a mother's pains.

13 Oh! what a fearful work is man!
   A wonder of creative art!
   My God, how marvellous thy plan!
   'Tis character'd upon my heart.

14 My very bones, tho' deep conceal'd
   And buried in this living clay,

Are to thy searching sight reveal'd
As clear as in the face of day.

15 That eye, which thro' creation darts,
My substance, yet imperfect, scan'd,
And in thy books my embryo parts
Were written and their uses plan'd.

16 Ere Time to shape and fashion drew
These ductile members one by one,
Into man's image ere they grew,
Thy great prospective work was done.

17 O God! how gracious, how divine,
How dear thy counsels to my soul!
Myriads to myriads cou'd I join,
They'd fail to number up the whole.

18 I might as well go tell the sand,
And count it over grain by grain:
No; in thy presence let me stand,
And waking with my God remain.

19 Wilt thou not, Lord, avenge the good?
Shall not blasphemers be destroy'd?
Depart from me, ye men of blood,
Hence murderer, and my sight avoid!

20 Loud are their hostile voices heard
To take thy sacred name in vain:
21 Am I not griev'd? Doth not each word
Wring my afflicted heart with pain?

Doth not my zealous soul return
Hatred for hatred to thy foes?
22 Yea, Lord! I feel my bosom burn,
As tho' against my peace they rose.

23 Try me, dread Power! and search my heart;
Lay all its movements in thy view;
Explore it to its inmost part,
Nor spare it, if 'tis found untrue.

24 If devious from thy paths I stray,
And wickedness be found with me,
Oh! lead me back the better way
To everlasting life and Thee.

NUMBER LXI.

The deistical writers, who would fain persuade us that the world was in possession of as pure a system of morality before the introduction of Christianity as since, affect to make a great display of the virtues of many eminent heathens, particularly of the philosophers, Socrates, Plato, and some others.

When they set up these characters as examples of perfection, which human nature with the aids of revelation either has not attained to, or not exceeded, they put us upon an invidious task, which no man would voluntarily engage in, and challenge us to discuss a question, which, if thoroughly agitated, cannot fail to strip the illustrious dead of more than half the honours which the voice of ages has agreed to give them.

It is therefore to be wished that they had held the argument to its general terms, and shewn us where that system of ethics is to be found, which they are prepared to bring into comparison with the moral doctrines of Christ. This I take to be the fair ground whereon the controversy should have been decided, and here it would infallibly have been brought to issue; but they knew their weapons better than to trust them in so close a conflict.

The maxims of some heathen philosophers, and the moral writings of Plato, Cicero, and Seneca, contain many noble truths, worthy to be held in veneration by posterity; and if the deist can from these produce a system of morality as pure and perfect as that which claims its origin from divine revelation, he will prove that God gave to man a faculty of distinguishing between right and wrong with such correctness, that his own immediate revelation added no lights to those, which the powers of reason had already discovered. Let us grant therefore for a moment, that Christ's religion revealed to the world no new truths in morality, nor removed any old errors, and what triumph accrues to the deist by the admission? The most he gains is to bring reason to a level with revelation, as to its moral doctrines; in so doing he dignifies man's nature, and shews how excellent a faculty God gave his creatures in their original formation, to guide their judgments and controul their actions; but will this diminish the importance of revealed religion? Certainly not, unless he can prove one or both of the following positions; viz.

First, That the moral tenets of Christianity either fall short of, or run counter to, the moral tenets of natural religion; or,

Secondly, That Christ's mission was nugatory and superfluous, because the world was already in possesion of as good a system of morality as he imparted to mankind.

As to the first, I believe it has never been attempted by any heathen or deistical advocate to convict the Gospel system of false morality, or to allege that it is short and defective in any one particular duty, when compared with that system which the world was possest of without its aid. No man, I believe, has controverted its truths, though many have disputed its discoveries: No man has been hardy enough to say of any of its doctrines—*This we ought not to practise*; though many have been vain enough to cry out—*All this we knew before.*— Let us leave this position therefore for the present, and pass to the next viz. Whether Christ's mission was nugatory and superfluous, because the world already knew as much morality as he taught them.

This will at once be answered, if the Gospel assertion be established, that life and immortality were brought to light. We need not adduce any other of the mysteries of revelation; we may safely rest the question here, and say with the apostle to the Gentile world—*Behold! I shew you a mystery: We shall not all sleep, but we shall all be changed; in a moment, in the twinkling of an eye, at the last trump (for the trumpet shall sound) and the dead shall be raised incorruptible, and we shall be changed.* Mark to how short an issue the argument is now brought! Either the apostle is not warranted in calling this a *mystery,* or the deist is not warranted in calling Christ's mission nugatory and superfluous.

It now rests with the deist to produce from the writings and opinions of mankind antecedent to Christianity, such a revelation of things to come, as can fully anticipate the Gospel revelation, or else to admit with the apostle that *a mystery was shewn;* and if the importance of this *mystery* be admitted, as it surely must, the importance of Christ's mission can no longer be disputed; and though revelation shall have added nothing to the heathen system of morality, still it does not follow that it was superfluous and nugatory.

Let the deist resort to the heathen Elysium and the realms of Pluto in search of evidences, to set in competition with the Christian revelation of a future state; let him call in Socrates, Plato, and as many more as he can collect in his cause; it is but lost labour to follow the various tracks of reason through the pathless ocean of conjecture, always wandering, though with different degrees of deviation. What does it avail, though Seneca had taught as good morality as Christ himself preached from the Mount? How does it affect revealed religion, though Tully's Offices were found superior to Saint Paul's Epistles? Let the deist indulge himself in declaiming on the virtues of the heathen heroes and philosophers; let him ransack the annals of the Christian world, and present us with legions of crusaders drenched in human blood, furious fanatics rushing on each other's throats for the distinction of a word, massacring whole nations and laying nature waste for a metaphysical quibble, it touches not religion; let him array a host of persecuting Inquisitors with all their torturing engines, the picture indeed is terrible, but who will say it is the picture of Christianity?

When we consider the ages which have elapsed since the introduction of Christianity, and the events attending its propagation, how wonderful is the history we contemplate! We see a mighty light spreading over all mankind from one spark kindled in an obscure corner of the earth: An humble persecuted teacher preaches a religion of peace, of forgiveness of injuries, of submission to temporal authorities, of meekness, piety, brotherly love and universal benevolence; he is tried, condemned, and executed for his doctrines; he rises from the tomb, and, breaking down the doors of death, sets open to all mankind the evidence of a life to come, and at the same time points out the sure path to everlasting happiness in that future state: A few unlettered disciples, his adherents and survivors, take up his doctrines, and going forth amongst the provinces of the Roman empire, then in its zenith, preach a religion to the Gentiles, directly striking at the foundation of the most splendid fabric Superstition ever reared on earth: These Gentiles are not a rude and barbarous race, but men of illuminated minds, acute philosophers, eloquent orators, powerful reasoners, eminent in arts and sciences, and armed with sovereign power: What an undertaking for the teachers of Christianity! What a conflict for a religion, holding forth no temporal allurements! On the contrary, promising nothing but mortification in this world, and referring all hope of a reward for present sufferings to the unseen glories of a life to come.

The next scene which this review presents to us, shews the followers of Christianity suffering under persecution by the heathen, whom their numbers had alarmed, and who began to tremble for their gods: In the revolution of ages the church becomes triumphant, and, made wanton by prosperity, degenerates from its primitive simplicity, and running into idle controversies and metaphysical schisms, persecutes its seceding brethren with unremitting fury; whilst the Popes, thundering out anathemas and hurling torches from their throne, seem the vicegerents of the furies rather than of the author of a religion of peace: the present time affords a different view; the temper of the church grown milder, though its zeal less fervent; men of different communions begin to draw nearer to each other; as refinement of manners becomes more general, toleration spreads; we are no longer slaves to the laws of religion, but converts to the reason of it; and being allowed to examine the evidence and foundation of the faith that is in us, we discover that Christianity is a religion of charity, toleration, reason and peace, enjoining us to ' have compassion one of another, love as brethren, be pitiful, be courteous, not rendering railing for railing, but contrariwise blessing; knowing that we are thereunto called, that we should inherit a blessing.'

NUMBER LXII.

DARK and erroneous as the minds of men in general were before the appearance of Christ, no friend
to Revelation ever meant to say, that all the gross
and glaring absurdities of the heathen system, as
vulgarly professed, were universally adopted, and
that no thinking man amongst them entertained
better conceptions of God's nature and attributes,
juster notions of his superintendence and providence,
purer maxims of morality, and more elevated expectations of a future state, than are to be found in the
extravagant accounts of their established theology.
No thinking man could seriously subscribe his belief to such fabulous and chimerical legends; and
indeed it appears that opinions were permitted to
pass without censure, very irreconcileable to the
popular faith, and great latitude given to speculation in their reasonings upon natural religion ; and
what can be more gratifying to philanthropy, than
to trace these efforts of right reason, which redound
to the honour of man's nature, and exhibit to our
view the human understanding, unassisted by the
lights of revelation and supported only by its natural powers, emerging from the darkness of idolatry, and breaking forth into the following description of the Supreme Being, which is faithfully translated from the fragment of an antient Greek tragic
poet?—

  ' Let not mortal corruption mix with your idea
of God, nor think of him as of a corporeal being,
such as thyself; he is inscrutable to man, now ap-

pearing like fire, implacable in his anger; now in thick darkness, now in the flood of waters; now he puts on the terrors of a ravening beast, of the thunder, the winds, the lightning, of conflagrations, of clouds: him the seas obey, the savage rocks, the springs of fresh water, and the rivers that flow along their winding channels; the earth herself stands in awe of him; the high tops of the mountains, the wide expanse of the cærulean ocean tremble at the frown of their Lord and Ruler.'

This is a strain in the sublime stile of the Psalmist, and similar ideas of the Supreme Being may be collected from the remains of various heathen writers.

Antiphanes, the Socratic philosopher, says, ' That God is the resemblance of nothing upon earth, so that no conception can be derived from any effigy or likeness of the Author of the universe.'

Xenophon observes, ' That a Being, who controuls and governs all things, must needs be great and powerful, but being by his nature invisible, no man can discern what form or shape he is of.'

Thales, being asked to define the Deity, replied that ' He was without beginning and without end.' Being further interrogated, ' If the actions of men could escape the intelligence of God?' he answered, ' No, nor even their thoughts.'

Philemon, the comic poet, introduces the following question and answer in a dialogue: ' Tell me, I beseech you, what is your conception of God?— As of a Being, who, seeing all things, is himself unseen.'

Menander says, that ' God, the lord and father of all things, is alone worthy of our humble adoration, being at once the maker and the giver of all blessings.'

Melanippidas, a writer also of comedy, introduces

this solemn invocation to the Supreme Being, ' Hear me, O Father, whom the whole world regards with wonder and adores! to whom the immortal soul of man is precious.'

Euripides in a strain of great sublimity exclaims, ' Thee I invoke, the self-created Being, who framed all nature in thy ethereal mould, whom light and darkness and the whole multitude of the starry train encircle in eternal chorus.'

Sophocles also, in a fragment of one of his tragedies, asserts the unity of the Supreme Being; ' Of a truth there is one, and only one God, the maker of heaven and earth, the sea and all which it contains.'

These selections, to which however many others might be added, will serve to shew what enlightened ideas were entertained by some of the nature of God. I will next adduce a few passages to shew what just conceptions some had formed of God's providence and justice, of the distribution of good and evil in this life, and of the expectation of a future retribution in the life to come.

Ariston, the dramatic poet, hath bequeathed us the following part of a dialogue—

' Take heart; be patient! God will not fail to help the good, and especially those, who are as excellent as yourself; where would be the encouragement to persist in righteousness, unless those, who do well, are eminently to be rewarded for their well-doing?

' I would it were as you say! but I too often see men, who square their actions to the rules of rectitude, oppressed with misfortunes; whilst they, who have nothing at heart but their own selfish interest and advantage, enjoy prosperity unknown to us.

' For the present moment it may be so, but we must look beyond the present moment and await the issue, when this earth shall be dissolved: for to think that chance governs the affairs of this life, is a notion as false as it is evil, and is the plea, which vicious men set up for vicious morals : but be thou sure that the good works of the righteous shall meet a reward, and the iniquities of the unrighteous a punishment; for nothing can come to pass in this world, but by the will and permission of God.'

Epicharmus, the oldest of the comic poets, says, in one of the few fragments which remain of his writings, ' If your life hath been holy, you need have no dread of death, for the spirit of the blest shall exist for ever in heaven.'

Euripides has the following passage, ' If any mortal flatters himself that the sin which he commits, can escape the notice of an avenging Deity, he indulges a vain hope, deceiving himself in a false presumption of impunity, because the divine justice suspends for a time the punishment of his evil actions; but hearken to me, ye who say there is no God, and by that wicked infidelity enhance your crimes, There is, there is a God! let the evil doer then account the present hour only as gain, for he is doomed to everlasting punishment in the life to come.'

The Sibylline verses hold the same language, but these I have taken notice of in a former paper.

I reserve myself for one more extract, which I shall recommend to the reader as the finest, which can be instanced from any heathen writer, exhibiting the most elevated conceptions of the being and superintendance of one, supreme, all-seeing, ineffable God, and of the existence of a future state of rewards and punishments, by the just distribution of which to the good and evil, all the seeming irregularities of moral justice in this life shall hereafter be set strait ; and this, if I mistake not, is the summary of all that natural religion can attain to.

The following is a close translation of this famous fragment—

'Thinkest thou, O Niceratus, that those departed spirits, who are satiated with the luxuries of life, shall escape as from an oblivious God? the eye of justice is wakeful and all-seeing; and we may truly pronounce that there are two several roads conducting us to the grave; one proper to the just, the other to the unjust; for if just and unjust fare alike, and the grave shall cover both to all eternity—Hence! get thee hence at once! destroy, lay waste, defraud, confound at pleasure! but deceive not thyself; there is a judgment after death, which God, the lord of all things, will exact, whose tremendous name is not to be uttered by my lips, and he it is, who limits the appointed date of the transgressor.'

It is curious to discover sentiments of this venerable sort in the fragment of a Greek comedy, yet certain it is that it has either *Philemon* or *Diphilus* for its author, both writers of the New Comedy and contemporaries. Justin, Clemens, and Eusebius have all quoted it, the former from *Philemon*, both the latter from *Diphilus*: Grotius and Le Clerc follow the authority of Justin, and insert it in their collection of *Philemon's* fragments; Hertelius, upon the joint authorities of Clemens and Eusebius gives it to *Diphilus*, and publishes it as such in his valuable and rare remains of the Greek comic writers. I conceive there are now no *data*, upon which criticism can decide for either of these two claimants, and the honour must accordingly remain suspended between them.

Sentences of this sort are certainly very precious reliques, and their preservation is owing to a happy custom, which the Greeks had of marking the margins of their books opposite to any passage which particularly struck them, and this mark was generally the letter χ, the initial of χρησὸν, (useful) and the collection afterwards made of these distinguished passages they called χρησομάθειαν.

It would be a curious and amusing collation of moral and religious sentences, extracted from heathen writers, with corresponding texts, selected from the holy scriptures : Grotius hath done something towards it in his preface to the *Collectanea* of Stobæus ; but the quotations already given will suffice to shew, in a general point of view, what had been the advances of human reason before God enlightened the world by his special revelation.

NUMBER LXIII.

IF the deist, who contends for the all-sufficiency of natural religion, shall think that in these passages, which I have quoted in the preceding number, he has discovered fresh resources on the part of human reason as opposed to divine revelation, he will find himself involved in a very false conclusion. Though it were in my power to have collected every moral and religious sentence, which has fallen from the pens of the heathen writers antecedent to Christianity, and although it should thereby appear that the morality of the gospel had been the morality of right reason in all ages of the world, he would still remain as much unfurnished as ever for establishing his favourite position, that the scriptures reveal nothing more than man's understanding had discovered without their aid. We may therefore console ourselves without scruple in discovering that the heathen world was not immersed in total darkness, and the candid mind, however interested for Christianity, may be gratified with the reflection that the human understanding was not so wholly enslaved, but that in certain instances it could surmount the prejudices of system, and, casting off the shackles of idolatry, argue up to that supreme of all things, which the historian Tacitus emphatically defines, *summum illud et æternum neque mutabile neque interiturum.*

Now when the mind is settled in the proof of One Supreme Being, there are two several modes of reasoning, by which natural religion may deduce the probability of a future state : one of these results from an examination of the human soul, the other from reflecting on the unequal distribution of happiness in the present life.

Every man, who is capable of examining his own faculties, must discern a certain power within him, which is neither coeval with, nor dependent upon his body and its members ; I mean that power of reflection, which we universally agree to seat in the soul : it is not coeval with the body, because we were not in the use and exercise of it, when we were infants ; it is not dependent on it, because it is not subject to the changes which the body undergoes in its passage from the womb to the grave ; for instance, it is not destroyed, or even impaired, by amputation of the limbs or members, it does not evaporate by the continual flux and exhalation of the corporeal humours, is not disturbed by motion of the limbs, nor deprived of its powers by their inaction ; it is not necessarily involved in the sickness and infirmity of the body, for whilst that is decaying and dissolving away by an incurable disease, the intellectual faculties shall in many cases remain perfect and unimpaired : why then should it be supposed the soul of a man is to die with his body, and accompany it into the oblivious grave, when it did not make its entrance with it into life, nor partook of its decay, its fluctuations, changes, and casualties?

If these obvious reflections upon the nature and properties of the soul lead to the persuasion of a future state, the same train of reasoning will naturally discover that the condition of the soul in that future state must be determined by the merits or demerits of its antecedent life. It has never been the notion of heathen or of deist, that both the good and the evil shall enter upon equal and undistinguished felicity or punishment; no reasoning man could ever conceive that the soul of Nero and the soul of Antoninus in a future state partook of the same common lot; and thus it follows upon the evidence of reason, that the soul of man shall be rewarded or punished hereafter according to his good or evil conduct here; and this consequence is the more obvious, because it does not appear in the moral government of the world, that any such just and regular distribution of rewards and punishments obtains on this side the grave; a circumstance no otherwise to be reconciled to our suitable conceptions of divine justice, than by referring things to the final decision of a judgment to come.

Though all these discoveries are open to reason, let no man conclude that what the reason of a few discovered were either communicated to, or acknowledged by all: No; the world was dark and grossly ignorant, some indeed have argued well and clearly; others confusedly, and the bulk of mankind not at all; the being of a God, and the unity of that Supreme Being, struck conviction to the hearts of those, who employed their reason coolly and dispassionately in such sublime enquiries; but where

was the multitude meanwhile? Bewildered with a
mob of deities, whom their own fables had endowed with human attributes, passions and infirmities; whom their own superstition had deified
and enrolled amongst the immortals, till the sacred
history of Olympus became no less impure than
the journals of a brothel: Many there were, no
doubt, who saw the monstrous absurdity of such a
system, yet not every one, who discerned error,
could discover truth; the immortality of the soul, a
doctrine so harmonious to man's nature, was decried by system and opposed by subtilty; the question of a future state was hung up in doubt, or
bandied between conflicting disputants through all
the quirks and evasions of sophistry and logic:
Philosophy, so called, was split into a variety of
sects, and the hypothesis of each enthusiastic founder
became the standing creed of his school, which it
was an inviolable point of honour never to desert:
In this confusion of systems men chose for themselves, not according to conviction, but by the impulse of passion, or from motives of convenience;
the voluptuary was interested to dismiss the gods
to their repose, that his might not be interrupted
by them; and all, who wished to have their range
of sensuality in this world without fear or controul, readily enlisted under the banners of Epi-
curus, till his followers outnumbered all the rest;
this was the court-creed under the worst of the Roman emperors, and the whole body of the nation,
with few exceptions, adopted it; for what could be
more natural, than for the desperate to bury conscience in the grave of atheism, or rush into annihilation by the point of the poniard, when they were
weary of existence and discarded by fortune? With
some it was the standard principle of their sect to
doubt, with others to argue every thing; and when

we recollect that Cicero himself was of the *New Academy*, we have a clue to unravel all the seeming contradictions of his moral and metaphysical sentiments, amidst the confusion of which we are never to expect his real opinion, but within the pale of his own particular school, and that school professed controversy upon every point. I will instance one passage, which would have done honour to his sentiments, had he spoke his own language as well as that of the Platonists, whom he is here personating— *Nec vero Deus, qui intelligitur a nobis, alio modo intelligi potest, quam mens soluta quædam et libera, segregata ab omni concretione mortali, omnia sentiens et movens.* Whilst the purest truths were thrown out only as themes for sophistry to cavil at, the mass of mankind resembled a chaos, in which if some few sparks of light glimmered, they only served to cast the general horror into darker shades.

It must not however be forgotten, that there was a peculiar people then upon earth, who professed to worship that one Supreme Being, of whose nature and attributes certain individuals only amongst the Gentile nations entertained suitable conceptions.

Whilst all the known world were idolaters by establishment, the Jews alone were Unitarians upon system. Their history was most wonderful, for it undertook to give a relation of things, whereof no human records could possibly be taken, and all, who received it for truth, must receive it as the relation of God himself, for how else should men obtain a knowledge of the Creator's thoughts and operations in the first formation of all things? Accordingly we find their inspired historian, after he has brought down his narration to the journal of his own time, holding conferences with God himself, and receiving through his immediate communication certain laws and commandments, which he was to

deliver to the people, and according to which they
were to live and be governed. In this manner Moses
appears as the commissioned legislator of a Theo-
cracy, impowered to work miracles in confirmation
of his vicegerent authority, and to denounce the
most tremendous punishments upon the nation, so
highly favoured, if in any future time they should
disobey and fall off from these sacred statutes and
ordinances.

A people under such a government, set apart and
distinguished from all other nations by means so
supernatural, form a very interesting object for our
contemplation, and their history abounds in events
no less extraordinary and miraculous than the revelation itself of those laws, upon which their constitution was first established: their tedious capti-
vities, their wonderful deliverances, the administration of their priests and prophets, their triumphs and
successes, whilst adhering to God's worship, and
their deplorable condition, when they corrupted his
service with the impurities of the idolatrous nations,
whom they drove from their possessions, form a
most surprizing chain of incidents, to which the
annals of no other people upon earth can be said to
bear resemblance.

Had it suited the all-wise purposes of God, when
he revealed himself to this peculiar people, to have
made them the instruments for disseminating the
knowledge of his true religion and worship over
the Gentile world, their office and administration
had been glorious indeed; but this part was either
not allotted to them, or justly forfeited by their degenerate and abandoned conduct: disobedient and
rebellious against God's ordinances, they were so far
from propagating these imparted lights to the neighbouring nations, that they themselves sunk into their
darkness, and whilst all the land was over-run with

idols, few were the knees which bowed to the living, true and only God.

Moses, their inspired lawgiver, judge and prophet, is generally said to have delivered to them no doctrine of a future state: I am aware there is a learned author now living, one of their nation, *David Levi* by name, who controverts this assertion; it is fit therefore I should leave it in reference to his future proofs, when he shall see proper to produce them; in the mean time I may fairly state it upon this alternative, that if Moses did not impart the doctrine abovementioned, it was wholly reserved for future special revelation; if he did impart it, there must have been an obstinate want of faith in great part of the Jewish nation, who knowingly professed a contrary doctrine, or else there must have been some obscurity in Moses's account, if they innocently misunderstood it: The Sadducees were a great portion of the Jewish community, and if they were instructed by their lawgiver to believe and expect a future state, it is high matter of offence in them to have disobeyed their teacher; on the other hand, if they were not instructed to this effect by Moses, yet having been taught the knowledge of one all-righteous God, it becomes just matter of surprize, how they came to overlook a consequence so evident.

NUMBER LXIV.

From the review we have taken of the state of mankind in respect to their religious opinions at the Christian æra it appears, that the Gentile world was systematically devoted to idolatry, whilst the remnant of the Jewish tribes professed the worship of the true God; but at the same time there did not exist on earth any other temple dedicated to God's service, save that at Jerusalem. The nation so highly favoured by him, and so enlightened by his immediate revelations, was in the lowest state of political and religious declension; ten out of their twelve tribes had been carried away into captivity, from which there has to this hour been no redemption, and the remaining two were brought under the Roman yoke, and divided into sects, one of which opposed the opinion of the other, and maintained that there was to be no resurrection of the dead: the controversy was momentous, for the eternal welfare of mankind was the object of discussion, and who was to decide upon it? the worshippers of the true God had one place only upon earth, wherein to call upon his name; the groves and altars of the idols occupied all the rest: who was to restore his worship? who was to redeem mankind from almost total ignorance and corruption? Where was *the light*, that was *to lighten the Gentiles?* reason could do no more; it could only argue for the probability of a future state of rewards and punishments, but demonstration was required; an evidence, that might remove all doubts, and this was not in the power of man to furnish: some Being therefore must appear of more than human talents to instruct mankind, of more than human authority to reform them: the world was lost, unless it should please God to interpose, for the work was above human hands, and nothing but the power which created the world, could save the world.

Let any man cast his ideas back to this period, and ask his reason, if it was not natural to suppose that the Almighty Being, to whom this general ruin and disorder must be visible, would in mercy to his creatures send some help amongst them; unless it had been his purpose to abandon them to destruction, we may presume to say he surely would: is it then with man to prescribe in what particular mode and form that redemption should come? Certainly it is not with man, but with God only; he, who grants the vouchsafement, will direct the means: be these what they may, they must be preternatural and miraculous, because we have agreed that it is beyond the reach of man by any natural powers of his own to accomplish: a special inspiration then is requisite; some revelation it should seem, we know not what, we know not how, nor where, nor whence, except that it must come from God himself: what if he sends a Being upon earth to tell us his immediate will, to teach us how to please him, and to convince us of the reality of a future state? that Being then must come down from him, he must have powers miraculous, he must have qualities divine and perfect, he must return on earth from the grave, and personally shew us that he has survived it, and is corporeally living after death: will this be evidence demonstrative? who can with-

stand it? he must be of all men most obstinately
bent upon his own destruction, who should attempt to hold out against it; he must prefer darkness to light, falsehood to truth, misery to happiness, hell to heaven, who would not thankfully
embrace so great salvation.

Let us now apply what has been said to the appearance of that person, whom the Christian Church
believes to have been the true Messias of God, and
let us examine the evidences, upon which we assert
the divinity of his mission and the completion of its
purposes.

In what form and after what manner was he
sent amongst us? was it by natural or preternatural means? if his first appearance is ushered in by
a miracle, will it not be an evidence in favour of
God's special revelation? If he is presented to the
world in some mode superior to and differing from
the ordinary course of nature, such an introduction
must attract to his person and character a more
than ordinary attention: if a miraculous and mysterious Being appears upon earth, so compounded of
divine and human nature as to surpass our com-
prehension of his immediate essence, and at the same
time so levelled to our earthly ideas, as to be visibly
born of a human mother, not impregnated after the
manner of the flesh, but by the immediate Spirit of
God, in other words the son of a pure virgin, shall
we make the mysterious incarnation of such a preternatural being a reason for our disbelief in that revelation, which without a miracle we had not given
credit to? We are told that the birth of Christ was
in this wise; the fact rests upon the authority of the
evangelists who describe it: the Unitarians, who
profess Christianity with this exception, may dispute the testimony of the sacred writers in this particular, and the Jews may deny their account *in toto,*

but still if Christ himself performed miracles, which the Jews do not deny, and if he rose from the dead after his crucifixion, which the Unitarians admit, I do not see how either should be staggered by the miracle of his birth : for of the Jews I may demand, whether it were not a thing as credible for God to have wrought a miracle at the birth of Moses for instance, as that he should afterwards empower that prophet to perform, not one only, but many miracles? To the Unitarians I would candidly submit, if it be not as easy to believe the incarnation of Christ as his resurrection, the authorities for each being the same? Let the authorities therefore be the test?

I am well aware that the silence of two of the evangelists is stated by the Unitarians amongst other objections against the account, and the non-accordance of the genealogies given by Saint Matthew and Saint Luke is urged against the Christian Church by the author of *Lingua Sacra*, in a pamphlet lately published, in the following words—' The Evangelist Saint Matthew in the first chapter of his gospel gives us the genealogy of Christ, and Luke in the third chapter of his gospel does the same; but with such difference, that an unprejudiced person would hardly think they belonged to one and the same person; for the latter not only differs from the former in almost the whole genealogy from Joseph to David, but has also added a few more generations, and likewise made Jesus to descend from Nathan the son of David instead of Solomon.'—(Levi's Letter to Dr. Priestley, p. 81.)

The learned Jew is founded in his observation upon the non-accordance of these pedigrees, but not in applying that to Christ, which relates only to Joseph. Saint Matthew gives the genealogy of Joseph, whom he denominates ' the husband of

Mary, of whom was born Jesus, who is called
Christ,' chap. i. v. 16. Saint Luke with equal precision says, that 'Jesus himself began to be about
thirty years of age, being, as was supposed, the son
of Joseph.' Now when it is thus clear that both
these genealogies apply to Joseph, and both these
evangelists expressly assert that Jesus was born of
an immaculate virgin, I do not think it a fair state-
ment to call it the genealogy of Christ for the purpose of discrediting the veracity of these evangelists
in points of faith or doctrine, merely because they
differ in a family catalogue of the generations of
Joseph, one of which is carried up to Adam, and
the other brought down from Abraham. The gospel historians, as I understand them, profess seve-
rally to render a true account of Christ's mission,
comprising only a short period of his life; within
the compass of this period they are to record the
doctrines he preached, the miracles he performed,
and the circumstances of his death, passion, and
resurrection; to this undertaking they are fairly
committed; this they are to execute as faithful re-
porters, and if their reports shall be found in any
essential matter contradictory to each other or themselves, let the learned author late mentioned, or any
other opponent to Christianity, point it out, and
candour must admit the charge; but in the matter
of a pedigree, which appertains to Joseph, which
our Church universally omits in its service, which
comprises no article of doctrine, and which, being
purely matter of family record, was copied probably
from one roll by Matthew, and from another by
Luke, I cannot in truth and sincerity see how the
sacred historians are impeached by the non-agree-
ment of their accounts. We call them the *inspired*
writers, and when any such trivial contradiction as
the above can be fixed upon them by the enemies of

our faith, the word is retorted upon us with triumph; but what has inspiration to do with the genealogy of Joseph, *the supposed*, not the real, father of Jesus? And indeed what more is required for the simple narration of any facts than a faithful memory, and sincere adherence to truth?

Let this suffice for what relates to the birth of Christ, and the different ways in which men argue upon that mysterious event: if his coming was foretold, and if his person and character fully answer to those predictions, no man will deny the force of such an evidence: if we are simply told that 'a virgin did conceive and bear a son,' it is a circumstance so much out of the ordinary course of nature to happen, that it requires great faith in the veracity of the relater to believe it; but if we are possessed of an authentic record of high antecedent antiquity, wherein we find it expressly predicted, that such a circumstance shall happen, and that a 'virgin shall conceive and bear a son,' it is such a confirmation of the fact, that wonderful as it is, we can no longer doubt the truth of the historians who attest it. Now it is not one, but many prophets, who concur in foretelling the coming of the Messias; his person, his office, his humility and sufferings, his ignominious death and the glorious benefits resulting from his atonement, are not merely glanced at with enigmatic obscurity, but pointedly and precisely announced. Had such evidences met for the verification of any historical event unconnected with religion, I suppose there is no man, who could compare the one with the other, but would admit its full concordance and completion; and is it not a strange perverseness of mind, if we are obstinate in doubting it, only because we are so deeply interested to believe it?

I have said there was but one temple upon earth,

where the only true and living God was worshipped,
the temple at Jerusalem : the Jews had derived and
continued this worship from the time of Abraham,
and to him the promises were made, that ' in his
seed all the nations of the world should be blessed.'
Where then are we naturally to look for the Messias but from the stock of Abraham, from the descendants of that family, in which alone were preserved the knowledge and worship of the only true
God? If therefore the religion, which Christ founded, does in fact hold forth that blessing to all the
nations of the world, then was that promise fulfilled
in the person of Christ, ' who took upon him the
seed of Abraham.'

NUMBER LXV.

WE are next to enquire if the character and commission of the Messias were marked by such per-
formances, as might well be expected from a person,
whose introduction into the world was of so extraordinary a nature.

We are told by one of the sacred historians, that
' the Jews came round about him and said unto him,
how long dost thou make us to doubt ? If thou be
the Christ, tell us plainly : Jesus answered them, I
told you, and ye believed not ; the works that I do
in my Father's name, they bear witness of me.'

In this passage Christ himself appeals to his
works done in the name of God, to witness against
all cavils for his being the true Messias. The same
question was put to him by the disciples of the Bap-

tist, ' Art thou he that should come, or do we look
for another ?' The same appeal is made to his works
in the reply he gives to these inquirers.

It follows next in order that we should ask what
these works were, and it so happens, that the person
who performed them, has himself enumerated them
in the following words: ' The blind receive their
sight and the lame walk, the lepers are cleansed and
the deaf hear, the dead are raised up and the poor
have the gospel preached unto them.' These are
works it must be acknowledged of a most benevolent
sort; they are not indeed so splendid as the miraculous act of dividing the Red Sea for the people of
Israel to march through it, and again commanding
it to close upon their pursuers in the rear and swallow up the army of Pharaoh ; they are not of so
tremendous a character as those afflicting plagues
with which Moses punished the Egyptians ; but
would these, or such as these, have been characteristic of a mediator ? Christ came to save and not to
destroy the world, and the works above described
are no less merciful in their nature, than miraculous.

When the Jews therefore tauntingly assert the superior magnificence of the miracles wrought by
Moses, which we admit to have been in all respects
suitable to the commission which Moses was en-
charged with, they should with equal candor admit,
that the less splendid, but more salutary, miracles
of Christ, were no less suited to the merciful commission, which he came amongst us to perform.
There is indeed more horrible grandeur in the spectacle of a vast army swallowed up by the sea, mira-
culously divided into a wall on each side of those
who passed through it ; but who will say that God's
power is not as wonderfully and conspicuously displayed in restoring dead Lazarus to life, as in drowning Pharaoh and his host ? Surely it is as great a

miracle to give life to the dead, as it is to put the living to death.

The miracles of Christ were performed without ostentation and display, yet they were of such general notoriety, that the Jews themselves did not, and do not even now, deny their being wrought by him, but ascribed them to the aid and agency of the Devil: a miserable subterfuge indeed! But this is not all: a contemporary writer of that nation, David Levi, in his letter to Dr. Priestley asserts, that there was not only ' no such necessity' for the miracles of Jesus as for those of Moses, but ' that they were scarcely just or rational, and consequently cannot be offered as proofs of his divine mission in comparison with that of Moses.' p. 67. 68.

In support of this assertion the learned controversialist observes, ' that as to the miracles of Moses, there was the greatest necessity for them; for instance, the plagues he brought upon the Egyptians were necessary for the redemption of the Jewish nation; as was the dividing of the Red Sea, and the drowning the Egyptians for their further deliverance from them; the manna from heaven and the water from the rock were necessary for their subsistence in the wilderness; the same of all the rest.'

This we may admit in its full force; but as the miracles which Christ wrought were altogether as *necessary* for the proof of his divine mission, as these of Moses for the proof of his; a man must be very partial to his own nation, who will assert, that the deliverance of the Jews from their captivity in Egypt, was a more important object than the redemption of lost mankind. We will not doubt but it was *necessary* the Egyptian host should be drowned, because it seemed good to God so to punish their obduracy, and extricate the Jewish tribes; but it is no less *necessary*, that mankind should believe in Christ, if they are to be saved through his means, and for the confirmation of that *necessary* faith, these miracles were performed: the author of the objection, who himself asserts that Moses delivered the important doctrine of a future state, will not deny that the belief of a future state is a *necessary* belief; and if it be so, it must follow that Christ's resurrection and appearance upon earth after his crucifixion, (a miracle I presume as great and striking as any wrought by the hand of Moses) was as pertinent to that general end, as the wonders in the land of Egypt and at the Red Sea were to the particular purpose of rescuing the Jews out of their captivity.

If we grant that Moses, as this objector intimates, did impart the doctrine of a future state, Christ did more by exemplifying it in his own person, and against such evidence we might presume even a Sadducee would not hold out. Now as so large a portion of the Jewish nation were still in the avowed disbelief of that doctrine, which our opponent believes was taught them by their great prophet and lawgiver himself, surely he must of force allow, that the resurrection of Christ was to them at least, and to all who like them did not credit the doctrine of a life to come, a *necessary* miracle.

Where such a teacher as Moses had failed to persuade, what less than a miracle could conquer their infidelity? Unless, indeed, our author shall join issue with Abraham in his reply to Dives, as recorded in the words of Christ, and maintain with him, that as they would not believe the word of Moses, 'neither would they be persuaded, though one actually rose from the dead.'

And now I will more closely animadvert upon the bold assertion of David Levi, the Jew, (whose hostile opinions we tolerate) that the miracles of

Christ, the Savior of the world (whose religion we profess) were ' scarcely just or rational.'

Our faith is at issue ; our established church falls to the ground, our very sovereign becomes no longer the *defender of our faith*, but rather the defender of our folly, if this contemner of Christ, this alien, who assaults our religion, whilst he is living under the protection of our laws, shall, with one stroke of an audacious pen, undermine the strong foundation of our belief.

Let us hear how this modern caviller confutes those miracles, which his forefathers saw and did not dare to deny.

He takes two out of the number, and if there is any merit in the selection, he is beholden to his correspondent for it : these are, first, ' the driving the devils out of the man possessed, and sending them into the herd of swine ;' Mat. viii. 28. Secondly, ' the curse pronounced upon the barren fig-tree ;' Mark xi. 13.

Upon the first of these he has the following stricture—' This I think was not strictly just, for as according to your (Dr. Priestley's) opinion, he was but a man and a prophet, I would willingly be informed what right he had to destroy another man's property in the manner he did by sending the devils into them, and so causing them to run violently into the sea and perish ?'

This miracle is recorded also by Saint Mark, v. 1. and again by Saint Luke, viii. 26. What Saint Matthew calls the country of the Gergesenes, the other two evangelists call the country of the Gadarenes, and St. Luke adds that it is over against Galilee ; this country, as I conceive, was within the boundaries of the half tribe of Manasseh, on the other side of Jordan, and is by Strabo called Gadarida,

lib. 16. Now Moses both in Leviticus xi. and
Deuteronomy xiv. prohibits swine, as one of the
unclean beasts: ' Of their flesh shall ye not eat, and
their carcase shall ye not touch; they are unclean
to you.' Isaiah also states it as a particular sin and
abomination in the Jews, whom he calleth a ' rebellious people, a people that provoketh me to anger
continually to my face; which remain among the
graves and lodge in the monuments, which eat
swine's flesh.' lxv. 2, 3, 4. And again, ' They that
sanctify themselves and purify themselves in the
gardens, behind one tree in the midst, eating swine's
flesh, &c. shall be consumed together, saith the
Lord. lxvi. 17. Eleazar the scribe, ' when con-
strained to open his mouth and eat swine's flesh,
chose rather to die gloriously, than to live stained
with such an abomination.' 2 Macc. vi. 18. 19.
The seven brethren also, who were compelled to the
like abomination, declared, ' they were ready to die
rather than to transgress the laws of their fathers.'
This being the law of Moses with respect to this
proscribed animal, and such being the corruptions
of the people in violating that law, I am at a loss to
discover the *injustice* of the miracle; seeing what
abominations these creatures had occasioned amongst
the Jews, so as to draw down the denunciations of
the prophet Isaiah, repeatedly urged in the passages
above quoted; and it is with particular surprize I
meet the charge from one, who is himself a Jew, and
who, I must presume, would die the death of Eleazar
rather than be defiled with such abominable food.
It would be hard indeed if Christ, whom he arraigns
for abolishing the Mosaical dispensation in one part
of his argument, should in another be accused of
wrong and injury for conforming to it: but any
wretched shift shall be resorted to for matter of
railing against Christ, and rather than not feed his

spleen at all, he will feed it upon swine's flesh: let
the learned Jew first prove to me that a hog was not
an abomination to his countrymen, and it will then
be time enough to debate upon the *injustice* of destroying them; meanwhile I shall not be disposed
to allow of any damages for the swine in question at
the suit and prosecution of a Jew.

His second attack is pointed against the miracle
of the fig-tree, which was blasted at the word of
Christ.

Though Saint Matthew as well as Saint Mark,
records this miracle, yet, for reasons sufficiently obvious, he refers to the latter, who says, ' that when
Christ came to it he found nothing but leaves; for
the time of figs was not yet.'   His argument upon
this passage is as follows: ' Hence it is manifest,
that he required the tree to produce fruit out of season, and which would have been contrary to the in-
tent of its Creator; and therefore he, as a dutiful
son, curses the innocent and guiltless tree for doing
that, which his father had commanded it to do, viz.
to bear fruit in its proper season:' In this paragraph our Jew has quickened his argument with
some facetious irony, and he follows it with an air
of exultation as well as insult: ' If, after this, Christians should still persist in the miracle, according to
the letter of the story, much good may it do them;
but I am sure it will never be the means of converting
the unbelieving Jews to the Christian faith.'

I close with him in opinion that this miracle will
not be the means of converting his unbelieving brethren to Christianity; for how can I hope, that what
their fathers saw and yet believed not, should at this
distant period gain belief from their posterity? I also
join with him in saying (and I suspect I say it with
somewhat more sincerity) *much good may it do* to
all those Christians, who persist in their belief of it!

A descendant of those who murdered Christ, may act in character, when he insults his miracles and ridicules his person, but a believer in Christ will be an imitator of his patience.

It is now time to dismiss the irony and apply to the argument. This simply turns upon Saint Mark's interjectional observation, not noticed by Saint Matthew in his account, viz. ' that the time of figs was not yet :' He says, that Jesus being hungry saw a fig-tree afar off, having leaves, and came if haply he might find any thing thereon : By this it appears that the tree was in leaf, and Jesus approached it with the expectation of finding something thereon; but when he found nothing but leaves he said unto it, ' No man eat fruit of thee hereafter for ever !' And his disciples heard it : these came again the next morning, and passing by the fig-tree saw it dried up from the roots; which when Peter remarked as a completion of the miracle, Jesus said to them all, ' Have faith in God !'

In these important words we have the moral of the act. The tree, which this reviler takes upon himself to say, was *commanded* by God *to bear fruit in its proper season*, was on the contrary commanded by God to bear fruit no more, but serve a nobler purpose by witnessing to the miraculous power of Christ : and now if *an innocent and guiltless tree* was blasted out of season by the word of Christ for the purpose of inspiring the beholders with *Faith in God*, the benefit conferred upon human nature may well atone for the injury done to vegetable nature; though I am free to acknowledge to its pathetic advocate, that, as a Jew, he has undertaken a more cleanly cause, than when he before stood forth in defence of the hogs : as well may he bewail *the innocent and guiltless trees* and grain of Egypt, which were smitten by the hail, when Moses called it down upon

the land, if such be his tender feelings toward the
productions of the earth, as this single fig-tree: till
he can convince us that the deliverance of the Jews
from their Egyptian bondage was a more important
object than the redemption of the world, he will find
it hard to make a reasoning man allow, that this
single fig-tree, even though it had no right to bear
fruit, hath a stronger appeal to justice against the
miracle of Christ, *than every herb of the field that
was smitten*, every guiltless and innocent *tree of the
field that was broken* by the stretching forth of the
rod of Moses.

Thus then stands the account between Christ and
his accuser; the Jewish nation lost a tree, and mankind gained—a Saviour!

NUMBER LXVI.

IF it were necessary to enter into a more literal defence of the miracle of the blasted fig-tree, I see no
absolute reason to conclude with the caviller, that
Christ required the tree to produce fruit out of season and act against its nature; for *if the time of
figs* be the gathering or harvest of figs, it was more
reasonable to expect fruit from this tree before the
time of plucking, than after it; and as this fruit
was no small article in the produce and traffick of
Judæa, we may well conclude *the time of figs*, mentioned by Saint Mark, was like the vintage in the
wine countries; and I apprehend it would not be
an unreasonable expectation to find a cluster of
grapes on a vine, before the time of vintage was
come. This construction of the words will seem

the more reasonable, when we remark that Saint
Matthew, who records the miracle, takes no account of this circumstance, and that Saint Mark,
who states it, states also that Christ in his hunger
applied to the tree, 'if haply he might find any
thing thereon,' which implies expectation.

But our Jew hath suggested a better method of
performing the miracle, by commanding fruit from
a withered tree instead of blasting a living one;
which, says he, 'if Jesus had done, it would have
been such an instance of his power, as to have rendered the proof of the miracle indisputable.'

Here let him stand to his confession, and I take
him at his word: I agree with him in owning that
the miracle, as he states it, would have been indisputable, had Christ given life and fruit to a withered
tree; and I demand of him to agree with me, that
the miracle was indisputable, when the same Christ
gave breath and life to dead Lazarus.

But alas! I can hardly expect that the raising a
dead tree to life would have been thus successful,
though even infidelity asserts it, when the miracle
of restoring a dead man to life hath not silenced his
cavils, but left him to quibble about hogs and figs,
and even in the face of his own confession to arraign
the Saviour of the world as 'unjust and irrational'
through the channel of a Christian press: neither
am I bound to admit, that his correction of the miracle would in any respect have amended it; for, as
an instance of Christ's miraculous power, I can see
no greater energy in the act of enlivening a dead
tree, than in destroying a living one by the single
word of his command.

I must yet ask patience of the reader, whilst I
attend upon this objector to another cavil started
against this miracle of the fig-tree, in the account of

which he says there is a contradiction of dates between Saint Matthew and Saint Mark, for that in the former it appears ' Christ first cast the buyers and sellers out of the temple, and on the morrow cursed the fig-tree; whereas, according to Saint Mark, it was transacted before the driving them out of the temple, and such a manifest contradiction must greatly affect the credibility of the history.'

Whether or not a day's disagreement in the dates would so ' greatly affect the credibility of the history,' we are not called upon to argue, because it will be found that no such contradiction exists.

Saint Mark agrees with Saint Matthew in saying, that ' Jesus entered into Jerusalem, and into the temple,' and on the morrow cursed the fig-tree; he then adds that he returned to Jerusalem, and drove the buyers and sellers out of the temple: Again, the next morning, he and his disciples passed by the fig-tree, and saw it dried up from the roots: This is told in detail.

Saint Matthew agrees with Saint Mark in saying Jesus went into the temple the day before he destroyed the fig-tree, but he does not break the narrative into detail, as Saint Mark does; for as he relates the whole miracle of the fig-tree at once, comprising the events of two days in one account, so doth he give the whole of what passed in the temple at once also.

Both Evangelists agree in making Christ's entrance into the temple antecedent to his miracle; but Saint Matthew with more brevity puts the whole of each incident into one account; Saint Mark more circumstantially details every particular: And this is the mighty contradiction, which David Levi hath discovered in the sacred historians, upon which he exultingly pronounces, that ' he is confident there are a number of others as glaring as this; but which he has not, at present, either time or inclination to point out.'

These menaces I shall expect he will make good, for when his time serves to point them out, I dare believe his inclination will not stand in the way.

In the meantime, let it be remembered, that David Levi stands pledged as the author of an unsupported charge against the veracity of the Evangelists, and let every faithful Christian, to whom those holy records are dear, but most of all the proper guardians of our Church, be prepared to meet their opponent and his charge.

But our caviller hath not yet done with the Evangelists, for he asserts that ' they are not only contradictory to each other, but are inconsistent with themselves; for what can be more so than Matthew i. 18. with Matthew xiii. 55.?

Now mark the contradiction! ' The birth of Jesus was on this wise; when as his mother Mary was espoused to Joseph, before they came together, she was found with child of the Holy Ghost, chap. i. 18. The other text is found in chap. xiii. 55: ' Is not this the carpenter's son? is not his mother Mary? and his brethren James and Joses and Simon and Judas?'

Need any child be told, that in the first text Saint Matthew speaks, and in the second the cavilling Jews? who then can wonder if they disagree? As well we might expect agreement between truth and falsehood, between the Evangelist and David Levi, as between two passages of such opposite characters. Is this the man, who is to confute the holy scriptures? Weak champion of an unworthy cause!

What he means by an inconsistency between Luke i. 34, 35, and Luke xiv. 22, I cannot understand, and conclude there must be an error of the press, of which I think no author can have less reason to complain than David Levi.

These two unprosperous attacks being the whole of what he attempts upon the inconsistency of the sacred historians with themselves, I shall no longer detain my readers, than whilst I notice one more cavil, which this author points against the divine mission of Christ, as compared with that of Moses, viz. ' That God speaking with Moses face to face in the presence of six hundred thousand men, besides women and children, as mentioned in Exod. xix. 9, was such an essential proof of the divine mission of Moses, as is wanting on the part of Jesus ;' and therefore he concludes, that taking the miracles of Moses and this colloquy with the Supreme Being together, the evidences for him are much stronger than for Christ.

A man, who does not instantly discern the futility of this argument, must forget all the several incidents in the history of Christ, where the voice of God audibly testifies to his divine mission ; for instance, Matth. iii. 16, 17. ' And Jesus, when he was baptized, went up straitway out of the water, and lo ! the heavens were opened unto him, and he saw the Spirit of God descending like a dove, and lighting upon him ; and lo ! a voice from heaven, saying, This is my beloved Son, in whom I am well pleased.' The same is repeated by Mark, i. 10, 11. ; again by Luke, iii. 21, 22. ; again by John, i. 32, 33, 34.

If these supernatural signs and declarations do not evince the superiority of Christ's mission above that of Moses ; if Christ, to whom angels ministered, when the devil in despair departed from him, Christ, who was transfigured before his disciples, ' and his face did shine as the sun, and his raiment was white as the light, and behold ! there appeared

unto them Moses and Elias talking with him; *Christ,
at whose death* the vail of the temple was rent in
twain from the top to the bottom, and the earth
did quake, and the rocks rent, and the graves were
opened, and many bodies of saints, which slept,
arose, and came out of the graves after his resurrection, and went into the holy city, and appeared unto
many;' in conclusion, if Christ, whose resurrection
was declared by angels, seen and acknowledged by
many witnesses, and whose ascension into heaven
crowned and completed the irrefragable evidence of
his divine mission; if Christ, whose prophecies of
his own death and resurrection, of the destruction of
Jerusalem and the subsequent dispersion of the Jews,
have been and are now so fully verified, cannot, as
our caviller asserts, meet the comparison with Moses,
then is the Redeemer of lost mankind a less sublime
and important character than the legislator of the
Jews.

I have now attempted in the first place to discover how far the world was illuminated by right
reason before the revelation of Christ took place;
for had men's belief been such, and their practice
also such as Christianity teaches, the world had not
stood in need of a Redeemer.

The result of this enquiry was, that certain persons have expressed themselves well and justly upon
the subject of God and religion in times antecedent
to the Christian æra, and in countries where idolatry was the established worship:

That the nation of the Jews was a peculiar nation, and preserved the worship of the true and
only God, revealed in very early time to their fathers, but that this worship from various circumstances and events, in which they themselves were
highly criminal, had not been propagated beyond
the limits of a small tract, and that the temple of

Jerusalem was the only church in the world, where God was worshipped, when Christ came upon earth:

That from the almost universal diffusion of idolatry, from the unworthy ideas men had of God and religion, and the few faint notions entertained amongst them of a future state of rewards and punishments, the world was in such deplorable error, and in such universal need of an instructor and redeemer, that the coming of Christ was most seasonable and necessary to salvation:

That there were a number of concurrent prophecies of an authentic character in actual existence, which promised this salvation to the world, and depicted the person of the Messias, who was to perform this mediatorial office in so striking a manner, that it cannot be doubted but that all those characteristics meet and are fulfilled in the person of Christ:

That his birth, doctrines, miracles, prophecies, death and passion, with other evidences, are so satisfactory for the confirmation of our belief in his divine mission, that our faith as Christians is grounded upon irrefragable proofs:

Lastly, that the vague opinions of our own dissenting brethren, and the futile cavils of a recent publication by a distinguished writer of the Jewish nation, are such weak and impotent assaults upon our religion, as only serve to confirm us in it the more.

If I have effected this to the satisfaction of the serious reader, I shall be most happy; and as for those who seek nothing better than amusement in these volumes, I will apply myself without delay to the easier task of furnishing them with matter more suited to their taste.

NUMBER LXVII.

Musa dedit fidibus Divos, puerosque Deorum,
Et pugilem victorem, et equum certamine primum,
Et juvenum curas, et libera vina referre.

HORAT.

IN times of very remote antiquity, when men were not so lavish of their wit as they have since been, Poetry could not furnish employment for more than *Three Muses*; but as business grew upon their hands and departments multiplied, it became necessary to enlarge the commission, and a board was constituted consisting of *nine* in number, who had their several presidencies allotted to them, and every branch of the art poetic thenceforth had its peculiar patroness and superintendent.

As to the specific time when these three senior goddesses called in their six new assessors, it is matter of conjecture only ; but if the poet Hesiod was, as we are told, the first who had the honour of announcing their names and characters to the world, we may reasonably suppose this was done upon the immediate opening of their new commission, as they would hardly enter upon their offices without apprising all those, whom it might concern, of their accession.

Before this period, the three eldest sisters condescended to be *maids of all work* ; and if the work became more than they could turn their hands to, they have nobody but themselves and their fellow deities to complain of; for had they been content to have let the world go on in its natural course, mere mortal

poets would not probably have overburthened either
it or them; but when Apollo himself (who being
their president should have had more consideration
for their ease) begot the poet Linus in one of his
terrestrial frolics, and endowed him with hereditary
genius, he took a certain method to make work for
the muses: accordingly, we find the chaste Calliope
herself, the eldest of the sisterhood, and who should
have set a better example to the family, could not
hold out against this heavenly bastard, but in an
unguarded moment yielded her virgin honours to
Linus, and produced the poet Orpheus: such an
instance of celestial incontinence could not fail to
shake the morals of the most demure; and even the
cold goddess Luna caught the flame, and smuggled
a bantling into the world, whom, maliciously
enough, she named Musæus, with a sly design no
doubt of laying her child at the door of the Par-
nassian nunnery.

Three such high-blooded bards as Linus, Orpheus, and Musæus, so fathered and so mothered,
were enough to people all Greece with poets and
musicians; and in truth they were not idle in
their generation, but like true patriarchs spread
their families over all the shores of Ionia and
the islands of the Archipelago: it is not therefore to be wondered at, if the three sister muses,
who had enough to do to nurse their own children and descendents, were disposed to call in other
helpmates to the task, and whilst Greece was in
its glory, it may well be supposed that all the
nine sisters were fully employed in bestowing upon
every votary a portion of their attention, and answering every call made upon them for aid and inspiration: much gratitude is due to them from their
favoured poets, and much hath been paid, for even
to the present hour they are invoked and worshipped

by the sons of verse, whilst all the other deities of Olympus have either abdicated their thrones, or been dismissed from them with contempt; even Milton himself in his sacred epic invokes the *heavenly muse,* who inspired Moses *on the top of Horeb or of Sinai*; by which he ascribes great antiquity as well as dignity to the character he addresses.

The powers ascribed to Orpheus were, under the veil of fable, emblems of his influence over savage minds, and of his wisdom and eloquence in reclaiming them from that barbarous state: upon these impressions civilization and society took place: the patriarch, who founded a family or tribe, the legislator, who established a state, the priest, prophet, judge, or king, are characters, which, if traced to their first sources, will be found to branch from that of poet: the first prayers, the first laws, and the earliest prophecies were metrical; prose hath a later origin, and before the art of writing was in existence, poetry had reached a very high degree of excellence, and some of its noblest productions were no otherwise preserved than by tradition. As to the sacred quality of their first poetry the Greeks are agreed, and to give their early bards the better title to inspiration, they feign them to be descended from the Gods; Orpheus must have profited by his mother's partiality, and Linus may well be supposed to have had some interest with his father Apollo. But to dwell no longer on these fabulous legends of the Greeks, we may refer to the books of Moses for the earliest and most authentic examples of sacred poetry: every thing that was the immediate effusion of the prophetic spirit seems to have been chaunted forth in dithyrambic measure; the valedictory blessings of the Patriarchs, when dying, the songs of triumph and thanksgiving after victory are metrical, and high as the antiquity of the

sacred poem of Job undoubtedly is, such nevertheless is its character and construction, as to carry
strong internal marks of its being written in an advanced state of the art.

The poet therefore, whether Hebrew or Greek,
was in the earliest ages a sacred character, and his
talent a divine gift, a celestial inspiration : men regarded him as the ambassador of Heaven and the
interpreter of its will. It is perfectly in nature,
and no less agreeable to God's providence, to suppose that even in the darkest times some minds of
a more enlightened sort should break forth, and be
engaged in the contemplation of the universe and its
author: from meditating upon the works of the
Creator, the transition to the act of praise and adoration follows as it were of course : these are operations of the mind, which naturally inspire it with a
certain portion of rapture and enthusiasm, rushing
upon the lips in warm and glowing language, and
disdaining to be expressed in ordinary and vulgar
phrase; the thoughts become inflated, the breast
labours with a passionate desire to say something
worthy of the ear of Heaven, something in a more
elevated tone and cadence, something more harmonious and musical; this can only be effected by
measured periods, by some chaunt, that can be repeated in the strain again and again, grateful at
once to the ear and impressive on the memory ;
and what is this but poetry ? Poetry then is the
language of prayer, an address becoming of the
Deity ; it may be remembered ; it may be repeated
in the ears of the people called together for the purposes of worship ; this is a form that may be fixt
upon their minds, and in this they may be taught
to join.

The next step in the progress of poetry from the
praise of God is to the praise of men : illustrious

characters, heroic actions are singled out for celebration; the inventors of useful arts, the reformers
of savage countries, the benefactors of mankind, are
extolled in verse, they are raised to the skies; and
the poet, having praised them as the first of men
whilst on earth, deifies them after death, and, conscious that they merit immortality, boldly bestows
it, and assigns to them a rank and office in heaven
appropriate to the character they maintained in life;
hence it is that the merits of a Bacchus, a Hercules,
and numbers more are amplified by the poet, till
they become the attributes of their divinity, altars
are raised and victims immolated to their worship.
These are the fanciful effects of poetry in its second
stage: religion over-heated turns into enthusiasm;
enthusiasm forces the imagination into all the visi-
onary regions of fable, and idolatry takes possession
of the whole Gentile world. The Egyptians, a
mysterious dogmatizing race, begin the work with
symbol and hieroglyphic; the Greeks, a vain ingenious people, invent a set of tales and fables for
what they do not understand, embellish them with
all the glittering ornaments of poetry, and spread
the captivating delusion over all the world.

In the succeeding period we review the poet in
full possession of this brilliant machinery, and with
all Olympus at his command: surrounded by
Apollo and the muses, he commences every poem
with an address to them for protection: he has a
deity at his call for every operation of nature; if he
would roll the thunder, Jupiter shakes Mount Ida
to dignify his description; Neptune attends him in
his car, if he would allay the ocean; if he would
let loose the winds to raise it, Æolus unbars his
cave; the spear of Mars and the ægis of Minerva
arm him for the battle; the arrows of Apollo sca[t]
ter pestilence through the air; Mercury flies u[p]

the messages of Jupiter; Juno raves with jealousy, and Venus leads the Loves and Graces in her train. In this class, we contemplate Homer and his inferior brethren of the epic order; it is their province to form the warrior, instruct the politician, animate the patriot; they delineate the characters and manners; they charm us with their descriptions, surprize us with their incidents, interest us with their dialogue; they engage every passion in its turn, melt us to pity, rouse us to glory, strike us with terror, fire us with indignation; in a word, they prepare us for the drama, and the drama for us.

A new poet now comes upon the stage; he stands in person before us: he no longer appears as a blind and wandering bard, chaunting his rhapsodies to a throng of villagers collected in a group about him, but erects a splendid theatre, gathers together a whole city as his audience, prepares a striking spectacle, provides a chorus of actors, brings music, dance, and dress to his aid, realizes the thunder, bursts open the tombs of the dead, calls forth their apparitions, descends to the very regions of the damned, and drags the Furies from their flames to present themselves personally to the terrified spectators: such are the powers of the drama; here the poet reigns and triumphs in his highest glory.

The fifth denomination gives us the lyric poet chaunting his ode at the public games and festivals, crowned with olive and encompassed by all the wits and nobles of his age and country: here we contemplate Stesichorus, Alcæus, Pindar, Callistratus; sublime, abrupt, impetuous, they strike us with the shock of their electric genius; they dart from earth to heaven; there is no following them in their flights; we stand gazing with surprize, their boldness awes us, their brevity confounds us; their sudden transitions and ellipses escape our apprehen-

sion; we are charmed we know not why, we are
pleased with being puzzled, and applaud although
we cannot comprehend. In the lighter lyric we
meet Anacreon, Sappho, and the votaries of Bacchus and Venus; in the grave, didactic, solemn
class we have the venerable names of a Solon, a
Tyrtæus, and those, who may be styled the dema-
gogues in poetry: Is liberty to be asserted, licen-
tiousness to be repressed? Is the spirit of a nation to
be roused? It is the poet not the orator must give
the soul its energy and spring: Is Salamis to be recovered? It is the elegy of Solon must sound the
march to its attack. Are the Lacedemonians to
be awakened from their lethargy? It is Tyrtæus,
who must sing the war-song and revive their languid courage.

Poetry next appears in its pastoral character; it
affects the garb of shepherds and the language of
the rustic: it represents to our view the rural landscape and the peaceful cottage: it records the labours, the amusements, the loves of the village
nymphs and swains, and exhibits nature in its sim-
plest state: it is no longer the harp or the lyre, but
the pipe of the poet, which now invites our attention: Theocritus, leaning on his crook in his russet
mantle and *clouted brogues*, appears more perfectly
in character than the courtly Maro, who seems more
the shepherd of the theatre than of the field. I have
yet one other class in reserve for the epigrammatist,
but I will shut up my list without him, not being
willing that poetry, which commences with a
prayer, should conclude with a pun.

NUMBER LXVIII.

Taste may be considered either as sensitive or mental; and under each of these denominations is sometimes spoken of as natural, sometimes as acquired; I propose to treat of it in its intellectual construction only, and in this sense Mr. Addison defines it to be that faculty of the soul, which discerns the beauties of an author with pleasure, and the imperfections with dislike.

This definition may very properly apply to the faculty which we exercise in judging and deciding upon the works of others; but how does it apply to the faculty exercised by those who produced those works? How does it serve to develope the taste of an author, the taste of a painter or a statuary? And yet we may speak of a work of taste with the same propriety, as we do of a man of taste. It should seem therefore as if this definition went only to that denomination of taste, which we properly call an acquired taste; the productions of which generally end in imitation, whilst those of natural taste bear the stamp of originality : another characteristic of natural taste will be simplicity; for how can nature give more than she possesses, and what is nature but simplicity? Now when the mind of any man is endued with a fine natural taste, and all means of profiting by other men's ideas are out of the question, that taste will operate by disposing him to select the fairest subjects out of what he sees either for art or imagination to work upon : Still his production will be marked with simplicity; but as it is the province of taste to separate deformity or vulgarity from what is merely simple, so according to the nature of his mind who possesses it, beauty or sublimity will be the result of the operation : If his taste inclines him to what is fair and elegant in nature, he will produce beauty ; if to what is lofty, bold and tremendous, he will strike out sublimity.

Agreeably to this, we may observe in all literary and enlightened nations, their earliest authors and artists are the most simple : First, adventurers represent what they see or conceive with simplicity, because their impulse is unbiassed by emulation, having nothing in their sight either to imitate, avoid, or excel : on the other hand, their successors are sensible that one man's description of nature must be like another's, and in their zeal to keep clear of imitation, and to outstrip a predecessor, they begin to compound, refine, and even to distort. I will refer to the Venus de Medicis and the Laöcoon for an illustration of this : I do not concern myself about the dates or sculptors of these figures ; but in the former we see beautiful simplicity, the fairest form in nature, selected by a fine taste, and imitated without affectation or distortion, and as it should seem without even an effort of art : In the Laöcoon we have a complicated plot ; we unravel a maze of ingenious contrivance, where the artist has compounded and distorted nature in the ambition of surpassing her.

Virgil possessed a fine taste according to Mr. Addison's definition, which I before observed applies only to an *acquired taste* : He had the ' faculty of discerning the beauties of an author with pleasure, and the imperfections with dislike : He had also the faculty of *imitating* what he *discerned* ; so that I cannot verify what I have advanced by any stronger instance than his. I should think there

does not exist a poet, who has gone such lengths in
imitation as Virgil; for to pass over his pastoral
and bucolic poems, which are evidently drawn
from Theocritus and Hesiod, with the assistance of
Aratus in every thing that relates to the scientific
part of the signs and seasons, it is supposed that his
whole narrative of the destruction of Troy, with
the incident of the wooden horse and the episode
of Sinon, are an almost literal translation of Pisan-
der the epic poet, who in his turn perhaps might
copy his account from the Ilias Minor; (but this
last is mere suggestion). As for the Æneid, it
does little else but reverse the order of Homer's
epic, making Æneas's voyage precede his wars in
Italy, whereas the voyage of Ulysses is subsequent
to the operations of the Iliad. As Apollo is made
hostile to the Greeks, and the cause of his offence
is introduced by Homer in the opening of the
Iliad, so Juno in the Æneid stands in his place
with every circumstance of imitation. It would
be an endless task to trace the various instances
throughout the Æneid, where scarce a single incident can be found which is not copied from Homer: Neither is there greater originality in the exe-
cutive parts of the poem, than in the constructive;
with this difference only, that he has copied passages from various authors, Roman as well as
Greek, though from Homer the most. Amongst
the Greeks, the dramatic poets Æschylus, Sophocles, and principally Euripides, have had the greatest share of his attention; Aristophanes, Menander, and other comic authors, Callimachus and
some of the lyric writers, also may be traced in his
imitations. A vast collection of passages from En-
nius chiefly, from Lucretius, Furius, Lucilius, Pacuvius, Suevius, Nævius, Varius, Catullus, Accius
and others of his own nation, has been made by

Macrobius in his Saturnalia, where Virgil has done little else but put their sentiments into more elegant verse; so that in strictness of speaking we may say of the Æneid, 'that it is a miscellaneous compilation of poetical passages, composing all together an epic poem, formed upon the model of Homer's Iliad and Odyssey: abounding in beautiful versification, and justly to be admired for the fine *acquired taste* of its author, but devoid of originality either of construction or execution.' Besides its general inferiority as being a copy from Homer, it particularly falls off from its original in the conception and preservation of character: It does not reach the sublimity and majesty of its model, but it has in a great degree adopted the simplicity, and entirely avoided the rusticity of Homer.

Lucan and Claudian in later ages were perhaps as good versifiers as Virgil, but far inferior to him in that fine acquired taste, in which he excelled: They are ingenious, but not simple; and execute better than they contrive. A passage from Claudian, which I shall beg the reader's leave to compare with one from Virgil (where he personifies the evil passions and plagues of mankind, and posts them at the entrance of hell, to which Æneas is descending) will exemplify what I have said; for at the same time that it will bear a dispute, whether Claudian's description is not even superior to Virgil's in poetical merit, yet the judicious manner of introducing it in one case, and the evident want of judgment in the other, will help to shew, that the reason why we prefer Virgil to Claudian, is more on account of his superiority of taste than of talents.

Claudian's description stands in the very front of his poem on Ruffinus; Virgil's is woven into his fable, and will be found in the sixth book of his Æneid, as follows:

Vestibulum ante ipsum, primisque in faucibus Orci,
Luctus, et ultrices posuere cubilia Curæ;
Pallentesque habitant Morbi, tristisque Senectus,
Et Metus, et malesuada Fames, et turpis Egestas,
Terribiles visu formæ; Lethumque, Laborque;
Tum consanguineus Lethi Sopor, et mala mentis
Gaudia, mortiferumque adverso in limine Bellum,
Ferreique Eumenidum thalami, et Discordia demens
Vipereum crinem vittis innexa cruentis.

VIRGIL.

Just in the gates, and in the jaws of Hell,
Revengeful Cares and sullen Sorrows dwell,
And pale Diseases, and repining Age;
Want, Fear, and Famine's unresisted rage;
Here Toils, and Death, and Death's half-brother, Sleep,
Forms terrible to view, their centry keep:
With anxious Pleasures of a guilty mind,
Deep Frauds before, and open Force behind:
The Furies iron beds, and Strife that shakes
Her hissing tresses, and unfolds her snakes.

DRYDEN

Protinus infernas ad limina tetra sorores
Concilium deforme vocat; glomerantur in unum
Innumeræ pestes Erebi, quascunque sinistro
Nox genuit fœtu: Nutrix Discordia belli;
Imperiosa Fames; leto vicina Senectus;
Impatiensque sui Morbus; Livorque secundis
Anxius, est scisso Mærens velamine Luctus,
Et Timor, et cæco præceps Audacia vultu;
Et luxus populator opum; cui semper adhærens
Infelix humili gressu comitatur Egestas;
Fædaque Avaritiæ complexæ pecora matris
Insomnes longo veniunt examine Curæ.

CLAUDIAN.

The infernal council, at Alecto's call
Conven'd, assemble in the Stygian hall;
Myriads of ghastly plagues, that shun the light,
Daughters of Erebus and gloomy Night:
Strife war-compelling; Famine's wasting rage;
And Death just hovering o'er decrepid Age;
Envy, Prosperity's repining foe,
Restless Disease, and self-dishevell'd Woe,
Rashness, and Fear, and Poverty, that steals
Close as his shadow at the Spendthrift's heels;
And Cares, that clinging to the Miser's breast,
Forbid his sordid soul to taste of rest.

The productions of the human genius will borrow their complexion from the times in which they originate. Ben Jonson says, ‘ that the players often mentioned it as an honour to Shakspeare, that in his writing (whatsoever he penned) he never blotted out a line. My answer hath been (adds he) Would he had blotted out a thousand! which they thought a malevolent speech. I had not told posterity this, but for their ignorance, who chose that circumstance to commend their friend by, wherein he most faulted ; and to justify mine own candour, for I loved the man, and do honour his memory on this side idolatry as much as any : He was indeed honest, and of an open and free nature; had an excellent phantasie, brave notions and gentle expressions, wherein he flowed with that facility, that sometime it was necessary he should be stopped ; *Sufflaminandus erat*, as Augustus said of Haterius : His wit was in his own power ; would the rule of it had been so too !’

I think there can be no doubt but this kind of indignant negligence with which Shakspeare wrote, was greatly owing to the slight consideration he had for his audience. Jonson treated them with the dictatorial haughtiness of a pedant : Shakspeare with the carelessness of a gentleman who wrote at his ease, and gave them the first flowings of his fancy without any dread of their correction. These were times in which the poet indulged his genius without restraint ; he stood alone and super-eminent, and wanted no artificial scaffold to raise him above the heads of his contemporaries ; he was natural, lofty, careless, and daringly incorrect. Place the same man in other times, amongst a people polished almost into general equality, and he shall begin to hesitate and retract his sallies ; for in this respect poetical are like military excursions, and it

makes a wide difference in the movements of a skil-
ful general, whether he is to sally into a country
defended by well disciplined troops, or only by
an irregular mob of unarmed barbarians. Shakspeare might vault his Pegasus without a rein;
mountains might rise and seas roll in vain before
him; Nature herself could neither stop nor circum-
scribe his career. The modern man of verse mounts
with the precaution of a riding-master, and prances
round his little circle full-bitted and caparisoned in
all the formality of a review. Whilst he is thus
pacing and piaffering with every body's eyes upon
him, his friends are calling out every now and
then—'Seat yourself firm in the saddle! Hold
your body straight! Keep your spurs from his sides
for fear he sets a kicking! Have a care he does not
stumble: there lies a stone, here runs a ditch;
keep your whip still, and depend upon your bit, if
you have not a mind to break your neck!'—On
the other quarter his enemies are bawling out—
'How like a taylor that fellow sits on horseback!
Look at his feet, look at his arms! Set the curs
upon him; tie a cracker to his horse's tail, and
make sport for the spectator!'—All this while
perhaps the poor devil could have performed pass-
ably well, if it were not for the mobbing and hal-
looing about him: Whereas Shakspeare mounts
without fear, and starting in the jockey phrase at
score, cries out, ' Stand clear, ye sons of earth! or
by the beams of my father Apollo, I'll ride over
you, and trample you into dust!'

NUMBEB LXIX.

Nil intentatum nostri liquere poetæ :
Nec minimum meruere decus, vestigia Græca
Ausi deserere, et celebrare domestica facta.

                                                    HORAT.

THERE are two very striking characters delineated by our great dramatic poet, which I am desirous of bringing together under one review, and these are Macbeth and Richard the Third.

The parts, which these two persons sustain in their respective dramas, have a remarkable coincidence : Both are actuated by the same guilty ambition in the opening of the story : both murder their lawful sovereign in the course of it : and both are defeated and slain in battle at the conclusion of it : Yet these two characters, under circumstances so similar, are as strongly distinguished in every passage of their dramatic life by the art of the poet, as any two men ever were by the hand of nature.

Let us contemplate them in the three following periods ; viz. The premeditation of their crime ; the perpetration of it ; and the catastrophe of their death.

Duncan the reigning king of Scotland has two sons : Edward the fourth of England has also two sons ; but these kings and their respective heirs do not affect the usurpers Macbeth and Richard in the same degree, for the latter is a prince of the blood royal, brother to the king, and next in consanguinity to the throne after the death of his elder brother the Duke of Clarence : Macbeth on the contrary is not in the succession—

                    And to be king
Stands not within the prospect of belief.

His views therefore being further removed and more out of hope, a greater weight of circumstances should be thrown together to tempt and encourage him to an undertaking so much beyond *the prospect of his belief.* The art of the poet furnishes these circumstances, and the engine, which his invention employs, is of a preternatural and prodigious sort. He introduces in the very opening of his scene a troop of sybils or witches, who salute Macbeth with their divinations, and in three solemn prophetic gratulations hail him Thane of Glamis, Thane of Cawdor, and King hereafter!

> By Sinel's death I know I'm Thane of Glamis;
> But how of Cawdor?

One part of the prophecy therefore is true; the remaining promises become more deserving of belief. This is one step in the ladder of his ambition, and mark how artfully the poet has laid it in his way: No time is lost; the wonderful machinery is not suffered to stand still, for behold a verification of the second prediction, and a courtier thus addresses him from the king—

> And for an earnest of a greater honour,
> He bade me from him call thee Thane of Cawdor.

The magic now works to his heart, and he cannot wait the departure of the royal messenger before his admiration vents itself aside—

> Glamis, and Thane of Cawdor!
> The greatest is behind.

A second time he turns aside, and unable to repress the emotions, which this second confirmation of the predictions has excited, repeats the same secret observation—

> Two truths are told
> As happy prologues to the swelling act
> Of the imperial theme.

A soliloquy then ensues, in which the poet judiciously opens enough of his character to shew the spectator that these preternatural agents are not superfluously set to work upon a disposition prone to evil, but one that will have to combat many compunctious struggles before it can be brought to yield even to oracular influence. This alone would demonstrate (if we needed demonstration) that Shakspeare, without resorting to the antients had the judgment of ages as it were instinctively. From this instant we are apprised that Macbeth meditates an attack upon our pity as well as upon our horror, when he puts the following question to his conscience—

> Why do I yield to that suggestion,
> Whose horrid image doth unfix my hair,
> And make my seated heart knock at my ribs
> Against the use of nature?

Now let us turn to Richard, in whose cruel heart no such remorse finds place : he needs no tempter : There is here no *dignus vindice nodus*, nor indeed any *knot* at all, for he is already practised in murder; Ambition is his ruling passion, and a crown is in view, and he tells you at his very first entrance on the scene—

> I am determined to be a villain.

We are now presented with a character full formed and compleat for all the savage purposes of the drama ;

> *Impiger iracundus inexorabilis, acer.*

The barriers of conscience are broken down, and the soul, hardened against shame, avows its own depravity—

> Plots have I laid, inductions dangerous,
> To set my brother Clarence and the king
> In deadly hate the one against the other.

He observes no gradations in guilt, expresses no hesitation, practises no refinements, but plunges into blood with the familiarity of long custom, and gives orders to his assassins to dispatch his brother Clarence with all the unfeeling tranquillity of a Nero or Caligula. Richard, having no longer any scruples to manage with his own conscience, is exactly in the predicament, which the dramatic poet Diphilus has described with such beautiful simplicity of expression—

Ὅςις γὰρ αὐτὸς αὐτὸν ἐκ αἰσχύνεται,
Συνειδὸϑ᾽ αὐτῷ φαῦλα διαπεπραγμένῳ,
Πῶς τόν γε μηδὲν εἰδότ᾽ αἰσχυνϑήσεται.

The wretch who knows his own vile deeds, and yet fears not himself, how should he fear another, who knows them not?

It is manifest therefore that there is an essential difference in the developement of these characters, and that in favour of Macbeth: In his soul cruelty seems to dawn, it breaks out with faint glimmerings, like a winter-morning, and gathers strength by slow degrees: In Richard it flames forth at once, mounting like the sun between the tropics, and enters boldly on its career without a herald. As the character of Macbeth has a moral advantage in this distinction, so has the drama of that name a much more interesting and affecting cast: The struggles of a soul, naturally virtuous, whilst it holds the guilty impulse of ambition at bay, affords the noblest theme for the drama, and puts the creative fancy of our poet upon a resource, in which he has been rivalled only by the great father of tragedy Æschylus in the prophetic effusions of Cassandra, the incantations of the Persian Magi for raising the ghost of Darius, and the imaginary terrific forms of his furies; with all which our countryman probably had no acquaintance, or at most a very obscure one.

When I see the names of these two great luminaries of the dramatic sphere, so distant in time but so nearly allied in genius, casually brought in contact by the nature of my subject, I cannot help pausing for a while in this place to indulge so interesting a contemplation, in which I find my mind balanced between two objects, that seem to have equal claims upon me for my admiration. Æschylus is justly styled the father of tragedy, but this is not to be interpreted as if he was the inventor of it: Shakspeare with equal justice claims the same title, and his originality is qualified with the same exception: The Greek tragedy was not more rude and undigested when Æschylus brought it into shape, than the English tragedy was when Shakspeare began to write: If therefore it be granted that he had no aids from the Greek theatre (and I think this is not likely to be disputed) so far these great masters are upon equal ground. Æschylus was a warrior of high repute, of a lofty generous spirit, and deep as it should seem in the erudition of his times: In all these particulars he has great advantage over our countryman, who was humbly born, of the most menial occupation, and, as it is generally thought, unlearned. Æschylus had the whole epic of Homer in his hands, the Iliad, Odyssey, and that prolific source of dramatic fable, the Ilias Minor; he had also a great fabulous creation to resort to amongst his own divinities, characters ready defined, and an audience, whose superstition was prepared for every thing he could offer; he had therefore a firmer and broader stage, (if I may be allowed the expression) under his feet, than Shak-

speare had : His fables in general are Homeric, and
yet it does not follow that we can pronounce for
Shakspeare that he is more original in his plots, for
I understand that late researches have traced him in
all or nearly all : Both poets added so much machinery and invention of their own in the conduct
of their fables, that whatever might have been the
source, still their streams had little or no taste of the
spring they flowed from. In point of character we
have better grounds to decide, and yet it is but justice to observe, that it is not fair to bring a mangled
poet in comparison with one who is entire : In his
divine personages Æschylus has the field of heaven,
and indeed of hell also, to himself; in his heroic and
military characters he has never been excelled ; he
had too good a model within his own bosom to fail
of making those delineations natural : In his imaginary being also he will be found a respectable,
though not an equal, rival of our poet ; but in the
variety of character, in all the nicer touches of nature, in all the extravagancies of caprice and humour, from the boldest feature down to the minutest foible, Shakspeare stands alone : such persons as he delineates never came into the contemplation of Æschylus as a poet ; his tragedy has no
dealing with them ; the simplicity of the Greek
fable, and the great portion of the drama filled up
by the chorus, allow of little variety of character ;
and the most which can be said of Æschylus in
this particular is, that he never offends against nature or propriety, whether his cast is in the terrible
or pathetic, the elevated or the simple.   His versification with the intermixture of lyric composition
is more various than that of Shakspeare ; both are
lofty and sublime in the extreme, abundantly metaphorical, and sometimes extravagant :—

———*Nubes et inania captat.*

This may be said of each poet in his turn; in each the critic, if he is in search for defects, will readily enough discover—

In scenam missus magno cum pondere versus.

Both were subject to be hurried on by an uncontroulable impulse, nor could nature alone suffice for either: Æschylus had an apt creation of imaginary beings at command—

He could call spirits from the vasty deep,

and they *would come*—Shakspeare, having no such creation in resource, boldly made one of his own; if Æschylus therefore was invincible, he owed it to his armour, and that, like the armour of Æneas, was the work of the gods: but the unassisted invention of Shakspeare seized all and more than superstition supplied to Æschylus.

NUMBER LXX.

Ille profecto
Reddere personæ scit convenientia cuique.

HORAT.

We are now to attend Macbeth to the perpetration of the murder, which puts him in possession of the crown of Scotland; and this introduces a new personage on the scene, his accomplice and wife: she thus developes her own character—

Come, all you spirits,
That tend on mortal thoughts, unsex me here,
And fill me from the crown to the toe topful

Of direst cruelty; make thick my blood,
Stop up the access and passage to remorse,
That no compunctious visitings of nature
Shake my fell purpose, nor keep peace between
Th' effect and it. Come to my woman's breasts,
And take my milk for gall, you murth'ring ministers,
Wherever in your sightless substances
You wait on nature's mischief: come, thick night,
And pall thee in the dunnest smoke of hell!

Terrible invocation! Tragedy can speak no stronger language, nor could any genius less than Shakspeare's support a character of so lofty a pitch, so sublimely terrible at the very opening.

The part which Lady Macbeth fills in the drama has a relative as well as positive importance, and serves to place the repugnance of Macbeth in the strongest point of view; she is in fact the auxiliary of the witches, and the natural influence, which so high and predominant a spirit asserts over the tamer qualities of her husband, makes those witches but secondary agents for bringing about the main action of the drama. This is well worth a remark; for if they, which are only artificial and fantastic instruments, had been made the sole or even principal movers of the great incident of the murder, nature would have been excluded from her share in the drama, and Macbeth would have become the mere machine of an uncontroulable necessity, and his character, being robbed of its free agency, would have left no moral behind: I must take leave therefore to anticipate a remark, which I shall hereafter repeat, that when lady Macbeth is urging her Lord to the murder, not a word is dropt by either of the witches or their predictions. It is in these instances of his conduct that Shakspeare is so wonderful a study for the dramatic poet. But I proceed—

Lady Macbeth in her first scene, from which I have already extracted a passage, prepares for an at-

tempt upon the conscience of her husband, whose
nature she thus describes—

> Yet do I fear thy nature;
> It is too full o'th' milk of human kindness
> To catch the nearest way.

He arrives before she quits the scene, and she receives him with consummate address—

> Great Glamis! worthy Cawdor!
> Greater than both by the All-hail hereafter!

These are the very gratulations of the witches; she
welcomes him with confirmed predictions, with the
tempting salutations of ambition, not with the
softening caresses of a wife—

> *Macb.* Duncan comes here to night.
> *Lady.* And when goes hence?
> *Macb.* To-morrow, as he purposes.
> *Lady.* Oh never
> 　　　Shall sun that morrow see!

The rapidity of her passion hurries her into immediate explanation, and he, consistently with the character she had described, evades her precipitate
solicitations with a short indecisive answer—

> We will speak further——

His reflections upon this interview, and the dreadful
subject of it, are soon after given in soliloquy, in
which the poet has mixt the most touching strokes
of compunction with his meditations: he reasons
against the villainy of the act, and honour jointly
with nature assails him with an argument of double
force—

> He's here in double trust;
> First as I am his kinsman and his subject,
> Strong both against the deed; then as his host,
> Who shou'd against the murtherer shut the door,
> Not bear the knife himself.

This appeal to nature, hospitality and allegiance,
was not without its impression; he again meets his
lady, and immediately declares—

> We will proceed no further in this business.

This draws a retort upon him, in which his tergi-
versation and cowardice are satirized with so keen
an edge, and interrogatory reproaches are pressed so
fast upon him, that catching hold in his retreat of
one small but precious fragment in the wreck of innocence and honour, he demands a truce from her
attack, and with the spirit of a combatant, who has
not yet yielded up his weapons, cries out—

> Pr'ythee, peace!

The words are no expletives; they do not fill up a
sentence, but they form one: they stand in a most
important pass; they defend the breach her ambition
has made in his heart; a breach in the very citadel
of humanity; they mark the last dignified struggle
of virtue, and they have a double reflecting power,
which in the first place shews that nothing but the
voice of authority could stem the torrent of her invective, and in the next place announces that something, worthy of the solemn audience he had demanded, was on the point to follow—and worthy it
is to be a standard sentiment of moral truth expressed
with proverbial simplicity, sinking into every heart
that hears it—

> I dare do all, that may become a man,
> Who dares do more is none.

How must every feeling spectator lament that a
man should fall from virtue with such an appeal
upon his lips!

Οὐκ ἔϛιν ȣ̓δεὶς δειλός, ὁ δεδοικὼς νόμον.

PHILONIDES.

'A man is not a coward because he fears to be unjust,' is the sentiment of an old dramatic poet.

Macbeth's principle is honour; cruelty is natural to his wife; ambition is common to both; one passion favourable to her purpose has taken place in his heart; another still hangs about it, which being adverse to her plot, is first to be expelled, before she can instil her cruelty into his nature. The sentiment above quoted had been firmly delivered, and was ushered in with an apostrophe suitable to its importance; she feels its weight; she perceives it is not to be turned aside with contempt, or laughed down by ridicule, as she had already done where weaker scruples had stood in the way; but, taking sophistry in aid, by a ready turn of argument she gives him credit for his sentiment, erects a more glittering though fallacious logic upon it, and by admitting his objection cunningly confutes it—

> What beast was't then
> That made you break this enterprize to me?
> When you durst do it, then you were a man,
> And to be more than what you were, you wou'd
> Be so much more than man.

Having thus parried his objection by a sophistry calculated to blind his reason and enflame his ambition, she breaks forth into such a vaunting display of hardened intrepidity, as presents one of the most terrific pictures that was ever imagined—

> I have given suck, and know
> How tender 'tis to love the babe that milks me;
> I wou'd, whilst it was smiling in my face,
> Have pluckt my nipple from its boneless gums,
> And dasht its brains out, had I but so sworn
> As you have done to this.

This is a note of horror, screwed to a pitch that bursts the very sinews of nature; she no longer combats with human weapon, but seizing the flash of the lightning extinguishes her opponent with the stroke : here the controversy must end, for he must either adopt her spirit, or take her life : he sinks under the attack, and offering nothing in delay of execution but a feeble hesitation, founded in fear— ' If we should fail'—he concludes with an assumed ferocity, caught from her and not springing from himself—

> I am settled, and bend up
> Each corporal agent to this terrible feat.

The strong and sublime strokes of a master impressed upon this scene make it a model of dramatic composition, and I must in this place remind the reader of the observation I have before hinted at, that no reference whatever is had to the auguries of the witches : it would be injustice to suppose that this was other than a purposed omission by the poet ; a weaker genius would have resorted back to these instruments ; Shakspeare had used and laid them aside for a time ; he had a stronger engine at work, and he could proudly exclaim—

> We defy auguries !——

Nature was sufficient for that work, and to shew the mastery he had over nature, he took his human agent from the weaker sex.

This having passed in the first act, the murder is perpetrated in the succeeding one. The introductory soliloquy of Macbeth, the chimera of the dagger, and the signal on the bell, are awful preludes to the deed. In this dreadful interim Lady Macbeth, the great superintending spirit, enters to support the dreadful work. It is done ; and he returns appalled with sounds ; he surveys his bloody hands with horror ; he starts from her proposal of going back to besmear the guards of Duncan's chamber, and she

snatches the reeking daggers from his trembling
hands to finish the imperfect work—

> Infirm of purpose,
> Give me the daggers!

She returns on the scene, the deed which he revolted
from is performed, and with the same unshaken
ferocity she vauntingly displays her bloody trophies,
and exclaims—

> My hands are of your colour, but I shame
> To wear a heart so white.

Fancied noises, the throbbings of his own quail-
ing heart, had shaken the constancy of Macbeth; real
sounds, the certain signals of approaching visiters,
to whom the situation of Duncan must be revealed,
do not intimidate her; she is prepared for all trials,
and coolly tells him—

> I hear a knocking
> At the south entry: Retire we to our chamber;
> A little water clears us of this deed.
> How easy is it then !

The several incidents thrown together in this scene
of the murder of Duncan, are of so striking a sort as
to need no elucidation : they are better felt than described, and my attempts point at passages of more
obscurity, where the touches are thrown into shade,
and the art of the author lies more out of sight.

Lady Macbeth being now retired from the scene,
we may in this interval, as we did in the conclusion
of the former paper, permit the genius of Æschylus
to introduce a rival murderess on the stage.

Clytemnestra has received her husband Agamem-
non, on his return from the capture of Troy, with
studied rather than cordial congratulations. He op-
poses the pompous ceremonies she had devised for

the display of his entry, with a magnanimous contempt of such adulation—

> Sooth me not with strains
> Of adulation, as a girl; nor raise
> As to some proud barbaric king, that loves
> Loud acclamations echoed from the mouths
> Of prostrate worshippers, a clamorous welcome:
> Spread not the streets with tapestry; 'tis invidious;
> These are the honours we shou'd pay the gods;
> For mortal men to tread on ornaments
> Of rich embroidery—no; I dare not do it:
> Respect me as a man, not as a god.
>
> POTTER's ÆSCHYLUS.

These are heroic sentiments, but in conclusion the persuasions of the wife overcome the modest scruples of the hero, and he enters his palace in the pomp of triumph; when soon his dying groans are echoed from the interior scene, and the adultress comes forth besprinkled with the blood of her husband to avow the murder—

> I struck him twice, and twice
> He groan'd; then died: a third time as he lay
> I gor'd him with a wound; a grateful present
> To the stern god, that in the realms below
> Reigns o'er the dead: there let him take his seat.
> He lay; and spouting from his wounds a stream
> Of blood, bedew'd me with these crimson drops.
> I glory in them, like the genial earth,
> When the warm showers of heav'n descend, and wake
> The flowrets to unfold their vermeil leaves.
> Come then, ye reverend senators of Argos,
> Joy with me, if your hearts be turn'd to joy,
> And such I wish them.
>
> POTTER.

NUMBER LXXI.

Ille per extentum funem mihi posse videtur
Ire poeta, meum qui pectus inaniter angit,
Irritat, mulcet, falsis terroribus implet,
Ut magus ; et modo me Thebis, modo ponit Athenis.
　　　　　　　　　　　　　　　　　　HORAT.

RICHARD perpetrates several murders, but as the poet has not marked them with any distinguishing circumstances, they need not be enumerated on this occasion. Some of these he commits in his passage to power, others after he has seated himself on the throne. Ferociousness and hypocrisy are the prevailing features of his character, and as he has no one honourable or humane principle to combat, there is no opening for the poet to develope those secret workings of conscience, which he has so naturally done in the case of Macbeth.

The murder of Clarence, those of the queen's kinsmen, and of the young princes in the Tower, are all perpetrated in the same stile of hardened cruelty. He takes the ordinary method of hiring ruffians to perform his bloody commissions, and there is nothing which particularly marks the scenes, wherein he imparts his purposes and instructions to them; a very little management serves even for Tirrel, who is not a professional murderer, but is reported to be——

　　　　——a discontented gentleman,
　Whose humble means match not his haughty spirit.

With such a spirit Richard does not hold it necessary to use much circumlocution, and seems more in dread of delay than disappointment or discovery—

R. Is thy name Tirrel?
T. James Tirrel, and your most obedient subject.
R. Art thou indeed?
T. Prove me, my gracious lord.
R. Dar'st thou resolve to kill a friend of mine?
T. Please you, I had rather kill two enemies.
R. Why then thou hast it; two deep enemies,
   Foes to my rest and my sweet sleep's disturbers,
   Are they that I would have thee deal upon:
   Tirrel, I mean those bastards in the Tower.

If the reader calls to mind by what circumspect and slow degrees King John opens himself to Hubert under a similar situation with this of Richard, he will be convinced that Shakspeare considered preservation of character too important to sacrifice on any occasion to the vanity of fine writing; for the scene he has given to John, a timorous and wary prince, would ill suit the character of Richard. A close observance of nature is the first excellence of a dramatic poet, and the peculiar property of him we are reviewing.

In these two stages of our comparison, Macbeth appears with far more dramatic effect than Richard, whose first scenes present us with little else than traits of perfidiousness, one striking incident of successful hypocrisy practised on the Lady Anne, and an open unreserved display of remorseless cruelty. Impatient of any pause or interruption in his measures, a dangerous friend and a determined foe:—

Effera torquebant avidæ præcordia curæ
Effugeret ne quis gladios;
Crescebat scelerata sitis; prædæque recentis
Incæstus flagrabat amor, mullusque petendi
Cogendive pudor: crebris perjuria nectit
Blanditiis; sociat perituro fœdere dextras:
Si semel e tantis poscenti quisque negasset,
Effera prætumido quatiebat corda furore.

CLAUDIAN.

> The sole remorse his greedy heart can feel
> Is if one life escapes his murdering steel :
> That, which should quench, inflames his craving thirst,
> The second draught still deepens on the first ;
> Shameless by force or fraud to work his way,
> And no less prompt to flatter than betray :
> This hour makes friendships which he breaks the next,
> And every breach supplies a vile pretext
> Basely to cancel all concessions past,
> If in a thousand you deny the last.

Macbeth has now touched the gaol of his ambition—

> Thou hast it now ; King, Cawdor, Glamis, all
> The weyward sisters promis'd——

The auguries of the witches, to which no reference had been made in the heat of the main action, are now called to mind with many circumstances of galling aggravation, not only as to the prophecy, which gave the crown to the posterity of Banquo, but also of his own safety from the gallant and noble nature of that general—

> Our fears in Banquo
> Stick deep, and in his royalty of nature
> Reigns that, which wou'd be fear'd.

Assassins are provided to murder Banquo and his son, but this is not decided upon without much previous meditation, and he seems prompted to the act more by desperation and dread, than by any settled resolution or natural cruelty. He convenes the assassins, and in a conference of some length works round to his point, by insinuations calculated to persuade them to dispatch Banquo for injuries done to them, rather than from motives which respect himself; in which scene we discover a remarkable preservation of character in Macbeth, who by this artifice strives to blind his own conscience and throw the guilt upon theirs : in this as in the former ac-

tion there is nothing kingly in his cruelty; in one
he acted under the controuling spirit of his wife,
here he plays the sycophant with hired assassins, and
confesses himself under awe of the superior genius
of Banquo—

    ——Under him
My genius is rebuk'd, as it is said
Antony's was by Cæsar.

There is not a circumstance ever so minute in the
conduct of this character, which does not point out
to a diligent observer how closely the poet has adhered to nature in every part of his delineation: accordingly we observe a peculiarity in the language
of Macbeth, which is highly characteristic; I mean
the figurative turn of his expressions, whenever his
imagination strikes upon any gloomy subject—

    Oh! full of scorpions is my mind, dear wife!

And in this state of self-torment every object of solemnity, though ever so familiar, becomes an object
of terror; night, for instance, is not mentioned by
him without an accompaniment of every melancholy
attribute, which a frighted fancy can annex—

    Ere the bat hath flown
His cloister'd flight, ere to black Hecate's summons
The shard-born beetle with his drowsy hums
Hath rung *Night's* yawning peal, there shall be done
A deed of dreadful note.

It is the darkness of his soul that makes the night so
dreadful, the *scorpions in his mind* convoke these
images—but he has not yet done with it—

    Come, sealing *Night!*
Skarf up the tender eye of pitiful day;
And with thy bloody and invisible hand
Cancel and tear to pieces that great bond,
Which keeps me pale.   Light thickens, and the crow
Makes wing to the rooky wood.
Good things of day begin to droop and drowse,
Whilst *Night's* black agents to their prey do rouse.

The critic of language will observe that here is a re-
dundancy and crowd of metaphors, but the critic
of nature will acknowledge that it is the very truth
of character, and join me in the remark which
points it out.

In a tragedy so replete with murder, and in the
display of a character so tortured by *the scorpions of
the mind*, as this of Macbeth, it is naturally to be
expected that a genius like Shakspeare's will call in
the dead for their share in the horror of the scene.
This he has done in two several ways; first, by the
apparition of Banquo, which is invisible to all but
Macbeth; secondly, by the spells and incantations
of the witches, who raise spirits, which in certain
enigmatical predictions shadow out his fate; and
these are followed by a train of unborn revelations
drawn by the power of magic from the womb of
futurity before their time.

It appears that Lady Macbeth was not a party in
the assassination of Banquo, and the ghost, though
twice visible to the murderer, is not seen by her.
This is another incident highly worthy a particular
remark; for by keeping her free from any partici-
pation in the horror of the sight, the poet is enabled
to make a scene aside between Macbeth and her,
which contains some of the finest speakings in the
play. The ghost in Hamlet, and the ghost of Darius in Æschylus are introduced by preparation and
prelude, this of Banquo is an object of surprize as
well as terror, and there is scarce an incident to be
named of more striking and dramatic effect: it is
one amongst various proofs, that must convince
every man, who looks critically into Shakspeare,
that he was as great a master in art as in nature:
how it strikes me in this point of view, I shall take
the liberty of explaining more at length.

The murder of Duncan is the main incident of

this tragedy; that of Banquo is subordinate: Duncan's blood was not only the first so shed by Macbeth, but the dignity of the person murdered, and the aggravating circumstances attending it, constitute a crime of the very first magnitude: for these reasons it might be expected, that the spectre most likely to haunt his imagination, would be that of Duncan; and the rather because his terror and compunction were so much more strongly excited by this first murder, perpetrated with his own hands, than by the subsequent one of Banquo, palliated by evasion and committed to others. But when we recollect that Lady Macbeth was not only his accomplice, but in fact the first mover in the murder of the king, we see good reason why Duncan's ghost could not be called up, unless she, who so deeply partook of the guilt, had also shared in the horror of the appearance; and as visitations of a peculiar sort were reserved for her in a later period of the drama, it was a point of consummate art and judgment to exclude her from the affair of Banquo's murder, and make the more susceptible conscience of Macbeth figure this apparition in his mind's eye without any other witness to the vision.

I persuade myself these will appear very natural reasons, why the poet did not raise the ghost of the king in preference, though it is reasonable to think it would have been a much more noble incident in his hands, than this of Banquo. It now remains to examine whether this is more fully justified by the peculiar situation reserved for Lady Macbeth, to which I have before adverted.

The intrepidity of her character is so marked, that we may well suppose no waking terrors could shake it, and in this light it must be acknowledged a very natural expedient to make her vent the agonies of her conscience in sleep. Dreams have been a dramatic expedient ever since there has been a drama; Æschylus recites the dream of Clytemnestra immediately before her son Orestes kills her; she fancies she has given birth to a dragon—

> This new-born dragon, like an infant child,
> Laid in the cradle seem'd in want of food;
> And in her dream she held it to her breast:
> The milk he drew was mixt with clotted blood.
>
> POTTER.

This which is done by Æschylus, has been done by hundreds after him; but to introduce upon the scene the very person, walking in sleep, and giving vent to the horrid fancies, that haunt her dream, in broken speeches expressive of her guilt, uttered before witnesses, and accompanied with that natural and expressive action of washing the blood from her defiled hands, was reserved for the original and bold genius of Shakspeare only. It is an incident so full of tragic horror, so daring and at the same time so truly characteristic, that it stands out as a prominent feature in the most sublime drama in the world, and fully compensates for any sacrifices the poet might have made in the previous arrangement of his incidents.

NUMBER LXXII.

Servetur ad imum
Qualis ab incepto processerit, et sibi constet.

HORAT.

MACBETH now approaches towards his catastrophe: the heir of the crown is in arms, and he must defend valiantly what he has usurped villainously. His natural valour does not suffice for this trial; he resorts to the witches; he conjures them to give answer to what he shall ask, and he again runs into all those pleonasms of speech, which I before remarked: the predictions he extorts from the apparitions are so couched as to seem favourable to him, at the same time that they correspond with events, which afterwards prove fatal. The management of this incident has so close a resemblance to what the poet Claudian has done in the instance of Ruffinus's vision the night before his massacre, that I am tempted to insert the passage—

Ecce videt diras alludere protinus umbras,
Quas dedit ipse neci; quarum quæ clarior una
Visa loqui—Proh! surge toro; quid plurima volvis
Anxius? hæc requiem rebus, finemque labori
Allatura dies: Omni jam plebe redibis
Altior, et læti manibus portabere vulgi—
Has canit ambages. Occulto fallitur ille
Omine, nec capitis fixi præsagia sensit.

A ghastly vision in the dead of night
Of mangled, murder'd ghosts appall his sight;
When hark! a voice from forth the shadowy train
Cries out—Awake! what thoughts perplex thy brain?
Awake, arise! behold the day appears,
That ends thy labours, and dispels thy fears:
To loftier heights thy tow'ring head shall rise,
And the glad crowd shall lift thee to the skies—
Thus spake the voice: he triumphs, nor beneath
Th' ambiguous omen sees the doom of death.

Confiding in his auguries Macbeth now prepares for battle: by the first of these he is assured—

That none of woman born
Shall harm Macbeth.

By the second prediction he is told—

Macbeth shall never vanquisht be, until
Great Birnam-wood to Dunsinane's high hill
Shall come against him.

These he calls *sweet boadments !* and concludes—

> To sleep in spite of thunder.

This play is so replete with excellencies, that it would exceed all bounds, if I were to notice every one; I pass over therefore that incomparable scene between Macbeth, the Physician and Seyton, in which the agitations of his mind are so wonderfully expressed, and, without pausing for the death of Lady Macbeth, I conduct the reader to that crisis, when the messenger has announced the ominous approach of Birnam-wood—A burst of fury, an exclamation seconded by a blow is the first natural explosion of a soul so stung with *scorpions* as Macbeth's: the sudden gust is no sooner discharged, than nature speaks her own language, and the still voice of conscience, like reason in the midst of madness, murmurs forth these mournful words—

> I pall in resolution, and begin
> To doubt the equivocation of the fiend,
> That lies like truth.

With what an exquisite feeling has this darling son of nature here thrown in this touching, this pathetic sentence, amidst the very whirl and eddy of conflicting passions! Here is a study for dramatic poets; this is a string for an actor's skill to touch; this will discourse sweet music to the human heart, with which it is finely unisoned when struck with the hand of a master.

The next step brings us to the last scene of Macbeth's dramatic existence: Flushed with the blood of Siward he is encountered by Macduff, who crosses him like his evil genius—Macbeth cries out—

> Of all men else I have avoided thee.

To the last moment of character the faithful poet

supports him : he breaks off from single combat, and in the tremendous pause, so beautifully contrived to hang suspense and terror on the moral scene of his exit, the tyrant driven to bay, and panting with the heat and struggle of the fight, vauntingly exclaims—

Macb. As easy may'st thou the intrenchant air
With thy keen sword impress, as make me bleed :
Let fall thy blade on vulnerable crests,
I bear a charmed life, which must not yield
To one of woman born.
Macd.   Despair thy charm !
And let the angel, whom thou still hast serv'd,
Tell thee Macduff was from his mother's womb
Untimely ripp'd.
Macb. Accursed be that tongue that tells me so !
For it hath cow'd my better part of man.

There sinks the spirit of Macbeth—

Behold ! where stands
Th' usurper's cursed head !

How completely does this coincide with the passage already quoted !

Occulto fallitur ille
Omine, nec CAPITIS FIXI *præsagia sentit.*

Let us now approach the tent of Richard. It is matter of admiration to observe how many incidents the poet has collected in a small compass, to set the military character of his chief personage in a brilliant point of view. A succession of scouts and messengers report a variety of intelligence, all which, though generally of the most alarming nature, he meets not only with his natural gallantry, but sometimes with pleasantry, and a certain archness and repartee, which is peculiar to him throughout the drama.

It is not only a curious, but delightful task to

examine by what subtle and almost imperceptible touches Shakspeare contrives to set such marks upon his characters, as give them the most living likenesses that can be conceived. In this, above all other poets that ever existed, he is a study and a model of perfection: the great distinguishing passions every poet may describe; but Shakspeare gives you their humours, their minutest foibles, those little starts and caprices, which nothing but the most intimate familiarity brings to light: other authors write characters like historians; he like the bosom friend of the person he describes. The following extracts will furnish an example of what I have been saying.

Ratcliff informs Richard that a fleet is discovered on the western coast, supposed to be the party of Richmond—

K. Rich. Some light-foot friend post to the Duke of Norfolk;
          Ratcliff, thyself; or Catesby—Where is he?
Cates. Here, my good lord.
K. Rich. Catesby, fly to the Duke.
Cates. I will, my lord, with all convenient haste.
K. Rich. Ratcliff, come hither; post to Salisbury ;
          When thou com'st thither—*Dull, unmindful villain!*
                                        (To Catesby,)
          Why stay'st thou here, and go'st not to the Duke?
Cates. First, mighty liege, tell me your highness' pleasure,
          What from your grace I shall deliver to him.
K. Rich. Oh, true, good Catesby!

I am persuaded I need not point out to the reader's sensibility the fine turn in this expression, *Good Catesby!* How can we be surprised if such a poet makes us in love even with his villains?—Ratcliff proceeds—

Rat. What may it please you shall I do at Salisbury?
K. Rich. Why, what wou'dst thou do there before I go?
Rat. Your highness told me I shou'd post before.
K. Rich. My mind is chang'd.

These fine touches can escape no man, who has an
eye for nature.   Lord Stanley reports to Richard—

> *Stanl.* Richmond is on the seas.
> *K. Rich.* There let him sink, and be the seas on him !
>   White-liver'd runagate, what doth he there ?

This reply is pointed with irony and invective:
there are two causes in nature and character for
this; first, Richard was before informed of the
news; his passion was not taken by surprize, and
he was enough at ease to make a play upon Stanley's words—*on the seas*—and retort—*be the seas on
him !*—Secondly, Stanley was a suspected subject,
Richard was therefore interested to shew a contempt of his competitor before a man of such
doubtful allegiance.   In the spirit of this impression he urges Stanley to give an explicit answer to
the question—*What doth he there?* Stanley endeavours to evade by answering that he *knows not but by
guess :* the evasion only strengthens Richard's suspicions, and he again pushes him to disclose what
he only guesses—*Well, as you guess*—Stanley replies—

> He makes for England, here to claim the crown.
> *K. Rich.* Is the chair empty ? Is the sword unsway'd ?
>   Is the king dead? the empire unpossess'd ?
>   What heir of York is there alive but we ?
>   And who is England's king but great York's heir ?
>   Then tell me what makes he upon the sea ?

What a cluster of characteristic excellencies are
here before us? All these interrogatories are *ad ho-
minem*; they fit no man but Stanley, they can be
uttered by no man but Richard, and they can flow
from the conceptions of no poet but the poet of
nature.

Stanley's whole scene ought to be investigated,
for it is full of beauties, but I confess myself exhausted with the task, and language does not suffice

to furnish fresh terms of admiration, which a closer scrutiny would call forth.

Other messengers succeed Lord Stanley, Richard's fiery impatience does not wait the telling, but taking the outset of the account to be ominous, he strikes the courier, who proceeding with his report concludes with the good tidings of Buckingham's dispersion—Richard instantly retracts and says—

> Oh ! I cry thee mercy.
> There is my purse to cure that blow of thine.

This is another trait of the same cast with that of *Good Catesby*.

Battles are of the growth of modern tragedy; I am not learned enough in the old stage to know if Shakspeare is the inventor of this bold and bustling innovation; but I am sure he is unrivalled in his execution of it, and this of Bosworth-field is a master-piece. I shall be less particular in my present description of it, because I may probably bring it under general review with other scenes of the like sort.

It will be sufficient to observe, that in the catastrophe of Richard nothing can be more glowing than the scene, nothing more brilliant than the conduct of the chief character : he exhibits the character of a perfect general, in whom however ardent courage seems the ruling feature; he performs every part of his office with minute attention, he enquires if certain alterations are made in his armour, and even orders what particular horse he intends to charge with : he is gay with his chief officers, and even gracious to some he confides in : his gallantry is of so dazzling a quality, that we begin to feel the pride of Englishmen, and, overlooking his crimes, glory in our courageous king : Richmond is one of those civil, conscientious gentlemen, who are not very apt to captivate a spectator, and Richard, loaded as he is with enormities, rises in the comparison, and I suspect carries the good wishes of many of his audience into action, and dies with their regret.

As soon as he retires to his tent the poet begins to put in motion his great moral machinery of the ghosts. Trifles are not made for Shakspeare; difficulties, that would have plunged the spirit of any other poet, and turned his scenery into inevitable ridicule, are nothing in his way; he brings forward a long string of ghosts, and puts a speech into each of their mouths without any fear of consequences. Richard starts from his couch, and before he has shaken off the terrors of his dream, cries out—

> Give me another horse!—Bind up my wounds!—
> Have mercy, Jesu!—Soft, I did but dream—
> O coward conscience—&c.

But I may conclude my subject; every reader can go on with the soliloquy, and no words of mine can be wanted to excite their admiration.

NUMBER LXXIII.

WHEN it had entered into the mind of Shakspeare, to form an historical play upon certain events in the reign of Henry the Fourth of England, the character of the Prince of Wales recommended itself to his fancy, as likely to supply him with a fund of dramatic incidents; for what could invention have more happily suggested than this character, which history presented ready to his hands? a riotous disorderly young libertine, in whose nature lay hidden those seeds of heroism and ambition, which were to burst forth at once to the astonishment of the world, and to atchieve the conquest of France. This prince, whose character was destined to exhibit a revolution of so brilliant a sort, was not only in himself a very tempting hero for the dramatic poet, who delights in incidents of novelty and surprize, but also offered to his imagination a train of attendant characters, in the persons of his wild comrades and associates, which would be of themselves a drama. Here was a field for invention wide enough even for the genius of Shakspeare to range in. All the humours, passions, and extravagancies of human life might be brought into the composition, and when he had grouped and personified them to his taste and liking, he had a leader ready to place at the head of the train, and the truth of history to give life and interest to his drama.

With these materials ready for creation the great artist sat down to his work; the canvas was spread before him, ample and capacious as the expanse of his own fancy; nature put her pencil into his hand, and he began to sketch. His first concern was to give a chief or captain to this gang of rioters; this would naturally be the first outline he drew. To fill up the drawing of this personage he conceived a voluptuary, in whose figure and character there should be an assemblage of comic qualities: in his person he should be bloated and blown up to the size of a Silenus, lazy, luxurious, in sensuality a satyr, in intemperance a bacchalian: As he was to stand in the post of a ringleader amongst thieves and cutpurses, he made him a notorious liar, a swaggering coward, vain-glorious, arbitrary, knavish, crafty, voracious of plunder, lavish of his gains, without credit, honour or honesty, and in debt to every body about him: As he was to be the chief seducer and misleader of the heir apparent of the crown, it was incumbent on the poet to qualify him for that part in such a manner as should give probability and even a plea to the temptation; this was only to be done by the strongest touches and the highest colourings of a master; by hitting off a humour of so happy, so facetious and so alluring a cast, as should tempt even royalty to forget itself, and virtue to turn reveller in his company. His lies, his vanity and his cowardice, too gross to deceive, were to be so ingenious as to give delight; his cunning evasions, his witty resources, his mock solemnity, his vapouring self consequence, were to furnish a continual feast of laughter to his royal companion; he was not only to be witty himself, but the cause of wit in other people; a whetstone for raillery; a buffoon, whose very person was a jest: Compounded of these humours, Shakspeare produced the character of Sir John Falstaff: a character, which neither ancient nor modern comedy has ever equalled, which was so much the favourite of its author as to be introduced in three several plays, and which is likely to be the idol of the English stage, as long as it shall speak the language of Shakspeare.

This character almost singly supports the whole comic plot of the first part of Henry the fourth; the poet has indeed thrown in some auxiliary humours in the persons of Gadshill, Peto, Bardolph, and Hostess Quickly; the two first serve for little else except to fill up the action, but Bardolph as a butt to Falstaff's raillery, and the hostess in her wrangling scene with him, when his pockets had been emptied as he was asleep in the tavern, give occasion to scenes of infinite pleasantry: Poins is contrasted from the rest of the gang, and as he is made the companion of the prince, is very properly represented as a man of better qualities and morals than Falstaff's more immediate hangers on and dependants.

The humour of Falstaff opens into full display upon his very first introduction with the prince; the incident of the robbery on the highway, the scene in Eastcheap in consequence of that ridiculous encounter, and the whole of his conduct during the action with Percy, are so exquisitely pleasant, that upon the renovation of his dramatic life in the second part of Henry the Fourth, I question if the humour does not in part evaporate by continuation; at least I am persuaded that it flattens a little in the outset, and though his wit may not flow less copiously, yet it comes with more labour and is farther fetched. The poet seems to have been sensible how difficult it was to preserve the vein as rich as at first, and has therefore strengthened his comic plot in the second play with several new recruits, who may take a share with Falstaff, to whom he no longer entrusts the whole burthen of the humour. In the front of these auxiliaries stands Pistol, a character so new, whimsical and extravagant, that if it were not for a commentator now living, whose very extraordinary researches, amongst our old authors, have supplied us with passages to illuminate the strange rhapsodies which Shakspeare has put into his mouth, I should for one have thought Antient Pistol as wild and imaginary a being as Caliban; but I now perceive, by the help of these discoveries, that the character is made up in great part of absurd and fustian passages from many plays, in which Shakspeare *was versed and perhaps* had been a performer: Pistol's dialogue is a tissue of old tags of bombast, like the middle comedy of the

Greeks, which dealt in parody. I abate of my astonishment at the invention and originality of the
poet, but it does not lessen my respect for his in-
genuity. Shakspeare founded his bully in parody,
Jonson copied his from nature, and the palm seems
due to Bobadil upon a comparison with Pistol;
Congreve copied a very happy likeness from Jonson, and by the fairest and most laudable imitation
produced his Noll Bluff, one of the pleasantest hu-
mourists on the comic stage.

Shallow and Silence are two very strong auxiliaries to this second part of Falstaff's humours, and
though they do not absolutely belong to his family,
they are nevertheless near of kin, and derivatives
from his stock : Surely two pleasanter fellows never
trode the stage : they not only contrast and play
upon each other, but Silence sober and Silence
tipsy make the most comical reverse in nature ;
never was drunkenness so well introduced or so
happily employed in any drama : The dialogue
between Shallow and Falstaff, and the description
given by the latter of Shallow's youthful frolicks,
are as true nature and as true comedy as man's invention ever produced : The recruits are also in the
literal sense the recruits of the drama. These personages have the further merit of throwing Falstaff's character into a new cast, and giving it the
seasonable relief of variety.

Dame Quickly also in this second part resumes
her rôle with great comic spirit, but with some va-
riation of character, for the purpose of introducing
a new member into the troop in the person of Doll
Tearsheet, the common trull of the times. Though
this part is very strongly coloured, and though the
scene with her and Falstaff is of a loose as well as
ludicrous nature, yet if we compare Shakspeare's
conduct of this incident with that of the dramatic

writers of his time, and even since his time, we must confess he has managed it with more than common care, and exhibited his comic hero in a very ridiculous light, without any of those gross indecencies which the poets of his age indulged themselves in without restraint.

The humour of the Prince of Wales is not so free and unconstrained as in the first part ; though he still demeans himself in the course of his revels, yet it is with frequent marks of repugnance and self-consideration, as becomes the conqueror of Percy, and we see his character approaching fast towards a thorough reformation ; but though we are thus prepared for the change that is to happen, when this young hero throws off the reveller and assumes the king, yet we are not fortified against the weakness of pity, when the disappointment and banishment of Falstaff takes place, and the poet executes justice upon his inimitable delinquent, with all the rigour of an unrelenting moralist. The reader or spectator, who has accompanied Falstaff through his dramatic story, is in debt to him for so many pleasant moments, that all his failings, which should have raised contempt, have only provoked laughter, and he begins to think they are not natural to his character, but assumed for his amusement. With these impressions we see him delivered over to mortification and disgrace, and bewail his punishment with a sensibility, that is only due to the sufferings of the virtuous.

As it is impossible to ascertain the limits of Shakspeare's genius, I will not presume to say he could not have supported his humour, had he chosen to have prolonged his existence through the succeeding drama of Henry the Fifth; we may conclude, that no ready expedient presented itself to his fancy, and he was not apt to spend much pains in searching for such: He therefore put him to death, by which he fairly placed him out of the reach of his contemporaries, and got rid of the trouble and difficulty of keeping him up to his original pitch, if he had attempted to carry him through a third drama, after he had removed the Prince of Wales out of his company, and seated him on the throne. I cannot doubt but there were resources in Shakspeare's genius, and a latitude of humour in the character of Falstaff, which might have furnished scenes of admirable comedy by exhibiting him in his disgrace, and both Shallow and Silence would have been accessaries to his pleasantry: Even the field of Agincourt, and the distress of the king's army before the action, had the poet thought proper to have produced Falstaff on the scene, might have been as fruitful in comic incidents as the battle of Shrewsbury: this we can readily believe from the humours of Fluellen and Pistol, which he has woven into his drama; the former of whom is made to remind us of Falstaff, in his dialogue with Captain Gower, when he tells him that—' As Alexander is kill his friend Clytus, being in his ales and his cups, so also Harry Monmouth, being in his right wits and his goot judgements, is turn away the fat Knight with the great pelly-doublet: He was full of jests and gypes and knaveries, and mocks; I am forget his name.—Sir John Falstaff.—That is he.'—This passage has ever given me a pleasing sensation, as it marks a regret in the poet to part with a favourite character, and is a tender farewel to his memory: It is also with particular propriety that these words are put into the mouth of Fluellen, who stands here as his substitute, and whose humour, as well as that of Nym, may be said to have arisen out of the ashes of Falstaff.

NUMBER LXXIV.

I was surprised the other day to find our learned
poet Ben Jonson had been poaching in an obscure
collection of love-letters, written by the sophist
Philostratus in a very rhapsodical stile, merely for
the purpose of stringing together a parcel of unnatural far-fetched conceits, more calculated to disgust a man of Jonson's classic taste, than to put
him upon the humble task of copying them, and
then fathering the translation. The little poem he
has taken from this despicable sophist is now become a very popular song, and is the ninth in his
collection intitled The Forest.

I will take the liberty of inserting Jonson's translation, and compare it with the original, stanza by
stanza—

I.

Drink to me only with thine eyes,
  And I will pledge with mine,
Or leave a kiss but in the cup,
  And I'll not look for wine.

PHILOSTRATUS, Letter XXIV.

'Ἐμοὶ δὲ μόνοις πρόπινε τοῖς ὄμμασιν—Drink to me
with thine eyes only. 'Εἰ δὲ βέλει, τοῖς χείλεσι
προσφέρεσα, πλήρου φιλημά των τό ἔκπωμα, καὶ ὕ τως
δίδε. Or if thou wilt, putting the cup to thy lips,
fill it with kisses, and so bestow it upon me.'

II.

The thirst that from the soul doth rise,
　　Demands a drink divine,
But might I of Jove's nectar sip,
　　I wou'd not change for thine.

Phil. Letter XXV.

'Ἐγω, ἐπειδὰν ἴδω σε, διψῶ, καὶ τὸ ἔκπωμα κατέχων, καὶτὸ μὲι ἐ προσάγω τοῖς χείλεσι σε δὲ οἶδα πίνω. I, as soon as I behold thee, thirst, and taking hold of the cup, do not indeed apply that to my lips for drink, but thee.'

III.

I sent thee late a rosy wreath,
　　Not so much honouring thee,
As giving it a hope that there
　　It might not withered be.

Phil. Letter XXX.

'Πέπομφά σοι ςέφανον ῥόδων, ἐ σὲ τιμῶν (καὶ τῦτο μὲνγὰς) ἀλλ' αὐτοῖς τι χαριζόμενος τοῖς ῥόδοις, ἵνα μὴ μαρανθῆ. I send thee a rosy wreath, not so much honouring thee (though this also is in my thoughts) as bestowing favour upon the roses, that so they might not be withered.'

IV.

But thou thereon didst only breathe,
　　And sent'st it back to me,
Since when it grows and smells I swear
　　Not of itself, but thee.

Phil. Letter XXXI.

'Εἰ δὲ βούλει τί φίλω χαρίζεσθαι, τὰ λείψανα αὐτῶν ἀντίπεμψον, μηκέτι πνέοντα ῥόδον μόνον ἀλλὰ καὶ σε. If thou wouldst do a kindness to thy lover, send back the reliques of the roses [I gave thee], for they will smell no longer of themselves only, but of thee.'

When the learned poet published his love-song without any acknowledgment to Philostratus, I hope the reason of his omitting it was because he did not chuse to call the public curiosity to a perusal of such unseemly and unnatural rhapsodies, as he had condescended to copy from.

Now I am upon the subject of Ben Jonson, I shall take notice of two passages in The Induction on the Stage, prefixed to his play of Bartholomew Fair, in which he gives a sly glance at Shakspeare —' And then a substantial watch to have stolen in upon them, and taken them away with mistaking words, as the fashion is in the stage practice.' It is plain he has Dogberry and Verges in his eye, and no less so in the following, that he points his ridicule against Caliban and the romance of The Tempest—' If there be never a servant-monster in the fair who can help it, *he says*, nor a nest of anticks? He is loth to make nature afraid in his plays, like those that beget tales, Tempests, and such like drolleries, to mix his head with other mens heels.' If any of our commentators upon Shakspeare have anticipated my remark upon these instances of Jonson's propensities to carp at their favourite poet, I have overlooked the annotation, but when I find him recommending to his audience such a farrago of vulgar ribaldry as Bartholomew Fair, by pretending to exalt it above such exquisite productions as The Tempest and Much Ado about Nothing, it is an act of warrantable retaliation to expose his vanity.

It is not always however that he betakes himself to these masked attacks upon that sublime genius,

which he professed to admire almost to idolatry, it
must be owned he sometimes meets him upon
equal ground, and nobly contends with laudable
emulation for the chaplet of victory : What I now
particularly have in my eye is his Masque of the
Queens.

Many ingenious observations have been given to
the public upon Shakspeare's Imaginary Beings;
his Caliban, Ariel, and all his family of witches,
ghosts, and fairies, have been referred to as examples of his creative fancy, and with reason has his
superiority been asserted in the fabrication of these
preternatural machines ; and as to the art with
which he has woven them into the fables of his
dramas, and the incidents he has produced by their
agency, he is in these particulars still more indis-
putably unrivalled; the language he has given to
Caliban, and no less characteristically to his Ariel, is
so original, so inimitable, that it is more like magic
than invention, and his fairy poetry is as happy as
it can be : It were a jest to compare Æschylus's
ghost of Darius, or any ghost that ever walked,
with the perturbed spirit of Hamlet : Great and
merited encomiums have also been passed upon the
weird sisters in that wonderful drama, and a decided preference given them over the famous
Erichtho of Lucan : Preferable they doubtless are,
if we contemplate them in their dramatic characters, and take into our account the grand and awful commission, which they bear in that scene of
tragic terror; but of their poetical superiority, simply considered, I have some doubts ; let me add to
this, that when the learned commentator was in-
stancing Lucan's Erichtho, it is matter of some
wonder with me, how he came to overlook Jonson's
witches in the Masque of the Queens.

As he has not however prevented me of the honour of bringing these two poetic champions together into the lists, I will avail myself of the occasion, and leave it with the spectators to decide upon the contest. I will only, as their herald, give notice that the combatants are enchanters, and he that has no taste for necromancy, nor any science in the terms of the art, has no right to give his voice upon the trial of skill.

SHAKSPEARE.

1st Witch Where has thou been, sister?
2d —— Killing swine.
3d —— A sailor's wife had chesnuts in her lap,
And mouncht, and mouncht, and mouncht—Give me, quoth I !
Aroint thee, witch, the rump-fed ronyon cries.
Her husband 's to Aleppo gone, master o' th' Tyger ;
But in a sieve I'll thither sail,
And like a cat without a tail,
I'll do—I'll do—I'll do.
2d Witch. I'll give thee a wind.
3d —— Thou art kind,
1st —— And I another.
3d —— I myself have all the other,
And the very points they blow,
All the quarters that they know
I' th' shipman's card.
I will drain him dry as hay,
Sleep shall neither night nor day
Hang upon his pent-house lid ;
He shall live a man forbid ;
Weary sev'n-nights nine times nine
Shall he dwindle, peak and pine ;
Tho' his bark cannot be lost,
Yet it shall be tempest tost.
Look, what I have.
2d —— Shew me, shew me.
3d —— Here I have a pilot's thumb,
Wreckt as homeward he did come.
1st —— A drum, a drum !
Macbeth doth come.
All. The weird sisters hand in hand,

Posters of the sea and land,
Thus do go about, about,
Thrice to thine and thrice to mine,
And thrice again to make up nine.
Peace! the charm's wound up.

JONSON.

Dame. Well done, my hags!—
But first relate me what you have sought,
Where you have been and what you have brought.

1st Hag. I have been all day looking after
A raven feeding upon a quarter;
And soon as she turn'd her beak to the south,
I snatcht this morsel out of her mouth.

2d Hag. I last night lay all alone
O' th' ground to hear the mandrake grone,
And pluckt him up, though he grew full low,
And as I had done the cock did crow.

6th Hag. I had a dagger; what did I with that?
Kill'd an infant, to have his fat;
A piper it got at a church-ale,
I bade him again blow wind in it's tail.

7th Hag. A murderer yonder was hung in chains,
The sun and the wind had shrunk his veins;
I bit off a sinew, I clipt his hair,
I brought off his rags that danc'd in the air.

8th Hag. The scrich-owl's eggs and the feathers black,
The blood of the frog, and the bone in his back,
I have been getting, and made of his skin
A purset to keep Sir Cranion in.

9th Hag. And I ha' been plucking (plants among)
Hemlock, henbane, adder's tongue,
Night shade, moon-wort, libbard's-bane,
And twice by the dogs was like to be ta'en.

11th Hag. I went to the toad, breeds under the wall,
I charm'd him out, and he came at my call,
I scratcht out the eyes of the owl before,
I tore the bat's wing—What wou'd you have more?'

Dame. Yes, I have brought (to help our vows)
Horned poppy, cypress boughs,
The fig-tree wild, that grows on tombs,
And juice that from the larch-tree comes,
The basilisk's blood, and the viper's skin—
And now our orgies let's begin!

SHAKSPEARE'S CHARM.

1st Witch. Thrice the brinded cat hath mew'd.
2d —— Twice and once the hedge-pig whin'd.
3d —— Harper cries, 'tis time! tis time!'
1st —— Round about the cauldron go,
In the poison'd entrails throw.
——Toad, that under the cold stone
Days and nights has thirty-one
Swelter'd venom sleeping got,
Boil thou first i' th' charmed pot.
　All. Double, double, toil and trouble,
Fire burn and cauldron bubble!
　2d Witch. Fillet of a fenny snake
In the cauldron boil and bake;
Eye of newt and toe of frog,
Wool of bat and tongue of dog,
Adder's fork and blind-worm's sting,
Lizard's leg and owlet's wing,
For a charm of powerful trouble,
Like a hell broth, boil and bubble!
　All. Double, double, toil and trouble,
Fire burn and cauldron bubble!
　3d Witch. Scale of dragon, tooth of wolf,
Witch's mummy, maw and gulf
Of the ravening salt-sea shark,
Root of hemlock, digg'd i' th' dark;
Liver of blaspheming Jew,
Gall of goat, and slips of yew
Sliver'd in the moon's eclipse,
Nose of Turk and Tartar's lips,
Finger of birth-strangled babe,
Ditch delivered of a drab,
Make the gruel thick and slab;
Add thereto a tyger's chawdron
For th' ingredients of our cauldron.
　All. Double, double, toil and trouble,
Fire burn and cauldron bubble!
　1st Witch. Cool it with a baboon's blood——
Then the charm is firm and good.

JONSON'S CHARM.

The owl is abroad, the bat and the toad,
    And so is the cat-a-mountain,
The ant and the mole sit both in a hole,
    And frog peeps out of the fountain.
The dogs they do bay and the timbrels play,
    The spindle is now a-turning,
The moon it is red and the stars are fled,
    And all the sky is a burning.

2d Charm.

Deep, oh deep, we lay thee to sleep,
We leave thee drink by, if thou chance to be dry,
Both milk and blood, the dew and the flood.
We breathe in thy bed, at the foot and the head;
We cover thee warm, that thou take no harm,
And when thou dost wake, dame earth shall quake, &c.

3d Charm.

A cloud of pitch, a spur and a switch,
To haste him away, and a whirlwind play
Before and after, with thunder for laughter,
And storms of joy, of the roaring boy,
His head of a drake, his tail of a snake.

4th Charm.

About, about and about!
Till the mists arise and the lights fly out:
The images neither be seen nor felt,
The woollen burn and the waxen melt;
Sprinkle your liquors upon the ground,
And into the air : Around, around !
    Around, around !
    Around, around !
    Till a music sound,
    And the pace be found
    To which we may dance
    And our charms advance.

I should observe that these quotations from Jonson are selected partially and not given in continua-

tion, as they are to be found in the Masque, which is much too long to be given entire: they are accompanied with a commentary by the author, full of dæmonological learning, which was a very courtly study in the time of James the first, who was an author in that branch of superstitious pedantry.

I am aware there is little to gratify the reader's curiosity in these extracts, and still less to distract his judgment in deciding between them: they are so far curious however as they shew how strongly the characters of the poets are distinguished even in these fantastic specimens; Jonson dwells upon authorities without fancy, Shakspeare employs fancy and creates authorities.

NUMBER LXXV.

Usus vetusto genere, sed rebus novis.
PROLOG. PHÆD. FAB. LIB. V.

BEN JONSON in his prologue to the comedy of *The Fox* says that he wrote it in the short space of five weeks, his words are—

> To these there needs no lie but this his creature,
> Which was two months since no feature;
> And tho' he dares give them five lives to mend it,
> 'Tis known five weeks fully penn'd it.

This he delivers in his usual vaunting stile, spurning at the critics and detractors of his day, who thought to convict him of dulness by testifying in fact to his diligence. The magic movements of Shakspeare's muse had been so noted and applauded for their surprising rapidity, that the public had

contracted a very ridiculous respect for hasty productions in general, and thought there could be no
better test of a poet's genius, than the dispatch and
facility with which he wrote; Jonson therefore affects to mark his contempt of the public judgment
for applauding hasty writers, in the couplet preceding those above quoted—

> And when his plays come out, think they can flout 'em
> With saying, He was a year about them.

But at the same time that he shews this contempt
very justly, he certainly betrays a degree of weakness in boasting of his poetical dispatch, and seems
to forget that he had noted Shakspeare with something less than friendly censure, for the very quality
he is vaunting himself upon.

Several comic poets since his age have seemed to
pride themselves on the little time they expended on
their productions; some have had the artifice to
hook it in as an excuse for their errors, but it is no
less evident what share vanity has in all such apo-
logies: Wycherley is an instance amongst these, and
Congreve tells of his expedition in writing the *Old
Bachelor*, yet the same man afterwards, in his letter
to Mr. Dryden, pompously pronounces, that to
write one perfect comedy should be the labour of
one entire life, produced from a concentration of
talents which hardly ever met in any human person.

After all it will be confessed, that the production
of such a drama as *The Fox*, in the space of five
weeks, is a very wonderful performance; for it must
on all hands be considered as the master-piece of a
very capital artist, a work, that bears the stamp of
elaborate design, a strong and frequently a sublime
vein of poetry, much sterling wit, comic humour,
happy character, moral satire, and unrivalled erudition; a work—

Quod non imber edax, non aquilo impotens
Possit diruere, aut innumerabilis
Annorum series et fuga temporum.

In this drama the learned reader will find himself
for ever treading upon classic ground; the foot of
the poet it so fitted and familiarized to the Grecian
sock, that he wears it not with the awkwardness of
an imitator, but with all the easy confidence and
authoritative air of a privileged Athenian: exclusive
of Aristophanes, in whose volume he is perfect, it
is plain that even the gleanings and broken fragments of the Greek stage had not escaped him; in
the very first speech of Volpone's, which opens the
comedy, and in which he rapturously addresses
himself to his treasure, he is to be traced most decidedly in the fragments of Menander, Sophocles
and Euripides, in Theognis and in Hesiod, not to
mention Horace. To follow him through every
one would be tedious, and therefore I will give a
sample of one passage only; Volpone is speaking to
his gold—

> Thou being the best of things and far transcending
> All stile of joy in children, parents, friends—
> Thy looks when they to Venus did ascribe,
> They should have given her twenty thousand Cupids,
> Such are thy beauties and our loves.

Let the curious reader compare this with the following fragment of Euripides's Bellerophon, and
he will find it almost a translation.

> Ὦ χρυσὲ δεξίωμα κάλλιϛον βροτοῖς,
> Ὡς ἐδὲ μήτηρ ἡδονὰς τοίας ἔχειε,
> Οὐ παῖδες ἀνθρώποισιν, ὀυ φίλος πατὴρ.
> Εἰ δ᾽ ἡ Κύπρις τοιοῦτον ὀφθαλμοῖς ὁρᾶ,
> Οὐ θαῦμ᾽ ἔρωτας μυρίους αὐτὴν τρέφειν.

Cicero made a selection of passages from the
Greek dramatic authors, which he turned into Latin

verse for the purpose of applying them, as occasion
should offer, either in his writings or pleadings,
and our learned countryman seems on his part to
have made the whole circle of Greek and Roman
poets his own, and naturalized them to our stage.
If any learned man would employ his leisure in
following his allusions through this comedy only, I
should think it would be no unentertaining task.

The Fox is indubitably the best production of
its author, and in some points of substantial merit
yields to nothing, which the English stage can oppose to it : there is a bold and happy spirit in the
fable, it is of moral tendency, female chastity and
honour are beautifully displayed, and punishment
is inflicted on the delinquents of the drama with
strict and exemplary justice : The characters of the
Heredipetæ, depicted under the titles of birds of
prey, Voltore, Corbaccio and Corvino, are warmly
coloured, happily contrasted, and faithfully supported from the outset to the end. Volpone, who
gives his name to the piece, with a fox-like crafti-
ness deludes and gulls their hopes by the agency of
his inimitable Parasite, or (as the Greek and Roman authors expressed it) by his Fly, his Mosca ;
and in this finished portrait Jonson may throw the
gauntlet to the greatest masters of antiquity ; the
character is of classic origin ; it is found with the
contemporaries of Aristophanes, though not in any
comedy of his now existing ; the Middle Drama-
tists seem to have handled it very frequently, and
in the New Comedy it rarely failed to find a place ;
Plautus has it again and again, but the aggregate
merit of all his Parasites will not weigh in the scale
against this single Fly of our poet : The incident
of his concealing Bonario in the gallery, from
whence he breaks in upon the scene to the rescue of
Celia and the detection of Volpone, is one of the

happiest contrivances, which could possibly be devised, because, at the same time that it produces the catastrophe, it does not sacrifice Mosca's character in the manner most villains are sacrificed in comedy, by making them commit blunders, which do not correspond with the address their first representation exhibits, and which the audience has a right to expect from them throughout, of which the Double Dealer is amongst others a notable instance. But this incident of Bonario's interference does not only not impeach the adroitness of the Parasite, but it furnishes a very brilliant occasion for setting off his ready invention and presence of mind in a new and superior light, and serves to introduce the whole machinery of the trial and condemnation of the innocent persons before the court of Advocates : In this part of the fable the contrivance is inimitable, and here the poet's art is a study, which every votarist of the dramatic muses, ought to pay attention and respect to ; had the same address been exerted throughout, the construction would have been a matchless piece of art, but here we are to lament the haste of which he boasts in his prologue, and that rapidity of composition, which he appeals to as a mark of genius, is to be lamented as the probable cause of incorrectness, or at least the best and most candid plea in excuse of it : For who can deny that nature is violated by the absurdity of Volpone's unseasonable insults to the very persons, who had witnessed falsely in his defence, and even to the very Advocate, who had so successfully defended him ? Is it in character for a man of his deep cunning and long reach of thought to provoke those, on whom his all depended, to retaliate upon him, and this for the poor triumph of a silly jest ? Certainly this is a glaring defect, which every body

must lament, and which can escape nobody. The
poet himself knew the weak part of his plot, and
vainly strives to bolster it up by making Volpone
exclaim against his own folly—

> I am caught in my own noose—

And again—

> To make a snare for mine own neck, and run
> My head into it wilfully with laughter!
> When I had newly 'scap'd, was free and clear,
> Out of mere wantonness! Oh, the dull devil
> Was in this brain of mine, when I devis'd it,
> And Mosca gave it second——
> ——————These are my fine conceits!
> I must be merry, with a mischief to me!
> What a vile wretch was I, that could not bear
> My fortune soberly! I must have my crotchets,
> And my conundrums!

It is with regret I feel myself compelled to protest against so pleasant an episode, as that which
is carried on by Sir Politic Would-be and Pe-
regrine, which in fact produces a kind of double
plot and catastrophe; this is an imperfection in the
fable, which criticism cannot overlook, but Sir
Politic is altogether so delightful a fellow, that it is
impossible to give a vote for his exclusion; the
most that can be done against him, is to lament
that he has not more relation to the main business
of the fable.

The judgment pronounced upon the criminals in
the conclusion of the play is so just and solemn,
that I must think the poet has made a wanton
breach of character, and gained but a sorry jest by
the bargain, when he violates the dignity of his
court of judges by making one of them so abject in
his flattery to the Parasite upon the idea of match-
ing him with his daughter, when he hears that Volpone has made him his heir; but this is an objec-

tion, that lies within the compass of two short
lines, spoken aside from the bench, and may easily
be remedied by their omission in representation; it
is one only, and that a very slight one, amongst
those venial blemishes—

—quas incuria fudit.

It does not occur to me that any other remark is
left for me to make upon this celebrated drama,
that could convey the slightest censure; but very
many might be made in the highest strain of commendation, if there was need of any more than general testimony to such acknowledged merit.   The
Fox is a drama of so peculiar a species, that it cannot be dragged into a comparison with the production of any other modern poet whatsoever; its construction is so dissimilar from any thing of Shakspeare's writing, that it would be going greatly out
of our way, and a very gross abuse of criticism to
attempt to settle the relative degrees of merit,
where the characters of the writers are so widely
opposite : In one we may respect the profundity of
learning, in the other we must admire the sublimity of genius; to one we pay the tribute of understanding, to the other we surrender up the possession of our hearts; Shakspeare, with ten thousand spots about him, dazzles us with so bright a
lustre, that we either cannot or will not see his
faults; he gleams and flashes like a meteor, which
shoots out of our sight before the eye can measure
its proportions, or analyse its properties—but Jonson stands still to be surveyed, and presents so bold
a front, and levels it so fully to our view, as seems
to challenge the compass and the rule of the critic,
and defy him to find out an error in the scale and
composition of his structure.

Putting aside therefore any further mention of

Shakspeare, who was a poet out of all rule, and beyond all compass of criticism, one whose excellencies are above comparison, and his errors beyond number, I will venture an opinion that this drama of The Fox is, critically speaking, the nearest to perfection of any one drama, comic or tragic, which the English stage is at this day in possession of.

NUMBER LXXVI.

IN my foregoing paper, when I remarked that Jonson in his comedy of The Fox was a close copier of the antients, it occurred to me to say something upon the celebrated drama of *The Sampson Agonistes*, which, though less beholden to the Greek poets in its dialogue than the comedy above-mentioned, is in all other particulars as compleat an imitation of the antient tragedy, as the distance of times and the difference of languages will admit of.

It is professedly built according to antient rule and example, and the author, by taking Aristotle's definition of tragedy for his motto, fairly challenges the critic to examine and compare it by that test. His close adherence to the model of the Greek tragedy is in nothing more conspicuous than in the simplicity of his diction; in this particular he has curbed his fancy with so tight a hand, that, knowing as we do the fertile vein of his genius, we cannot but lament the fidelity of his imitation; for there is a harshness in the metre of his Chorus, which to a certain degree seems to border upon pedantry and affectation; he premises that the measure is indeed of all sorts, but I must take leave to observe that in some places it is no measure at all, or such at least as the ear will not patiently endure, nor which any recitation can make harmonious. By casting out of his composition the strophe and antistrophe, those stanzas which the Greeks appropriated to singing, or in one word, by making his Chorus monostrophic, he has robbed it of that lyric beauty, which he was capable of bestowing in the highest perfection; and why he should stop short in this particular, when he had otherwise gone so far in imitation, is not easy to guess; for surely it would have been quite as natural to suppose those stanzas, had he written any, might be sung, as that all the other parts, as the drama now stands with a Chorus of such irregular measure, might be recited or given in representation.

Now it is well known to every man conversant in the Greek theatre, how the Chorus, which in fact is the parent of the drama, came in process of improvement to be woven into the fable, and from being at first the whole, grew in time to be only a part: the fable being simple, and the characters few, the striking part of the spectacle rested upon the singing and dancing of the interlude, if I may so call it, and to these the people were too long accustomed and too warmly attached, to allow of any reform for their exclusion; the tragic poet therefore never got rid of his Chorus, though the writers of the Middle Comedy contrived to dismiss their's, and probably their fable being of a more lively character, their scenes were better able to stand without the support of music and spectacle, than the mournful fable and more languid recitation of the tragedians. That the tragic authors laboured against the Chorus will appear from their efforts to expel Bacchus and his Satyrs from the stage, in which they were long time opposed by the audience, and at last, by certain in-

genious expedients, which were a kind of compro-
mise with the public, effected their point: this in
part was brought about by the introduction of a
fuller scene and a more active fable, but the Chorus
with its accompaniments kept its place, and the
poet, who seldom ventured upon introducing more
than three speakers on the scene at the same time,
qualified the sterility of his business by giving to the
Chorus a share of the dialogue, who, at the same
time that they furnished the stage with numbers,
were not counted amongst the speaking characters
according to the rigour of the usage above mentioned.   A man must be an enthusiast for antiquity,
who can find charms in the dialogue part of a Greek
Chorus, and reconcile himself to their unnatural and
chilling interruptions of the action and pathos of
the scene : I am fully persuaded they came there
upon motives of expediency only, and kept their post
upon the plea of long possession, and the attractions
of spectacle and music: in short, nature was sacrificed
to the display of art, and the heart gave up its feelings that the ear and eye might be gratified.

When Milton therefore takes the Chorus into his
dialogue, excluding from his drama the lyric strophe
and antistrophe, he rejects what I conceive to be its
only recommendation, and which an elegant contemporary in his imitations of the Greek tragedy is
more properly attentive to; at the same time it cannot be denied that Milton's Chorus subscribes more
to the dialogues, and harmonizes better with the
business of the scene, than that of any Greek tragedy we can now refer to.

I would now proceed to a review of the performance itself, if it were not a discussion, which the author of The Rambler has very ably prevented me in ;
respect however to an authority so high in criticism
must not prevent me from observing, that, when he

says—' This is the tragedy, which ignorance has admired and bigotry applauded,' he makes it meritorious in any future critic to attempt at following him over the ground he has trode, for the purpose of discovering what those blemishes are, which he has found out by superior sagacity, and which others have so palpably overlooked, as to merit the disgraceful character of ignorance and bigotry.

The principal, and in effect the only, objection, which he states, is, ' that the poem *wants a middle*, since nothing passes between the first act and the last, that either hastens or delays the death of Sampson.' This demands examination: the death of Sampson I need not describe; it is a sudden, momentary event; what can hasten or delay it, but the will of the person, who by an exertion of miraculous strength was to bury himself under the ruins of a structure, in which his enemies were assembled? To determine that will depends upon the impulse of his own spirit, or it may be upon the inspiration of Heaven: if there are any incidents in the body of the drama, which lead to this determination, and indicate an impulse, either natural on preternatural, such must be called leading incidents, and those leading incidents will constitute a middle, or in more diffusive terms the middle business of the drama. Manoah in his interview with Sampson, which the author of the Rambler denominates the second act of the tragedy, tells him

> This day the Philistines a popular feast
> Here celebrate in Gaza, and proclaim
> Great pomp and sacrifice and praises loud
> To Dagon, as their God—

Here is information of a meeting of his enemies to celebrate their idolatrous triumphs; an incident of just provocation to the servant of the living God, an opportunity perhaps for vengeance, either human or divine; if it passes without notice from Sampson, it is not to be stiled an incident, if, on the contrary, he remarks upon it, it must be one—but Sampson replies

> Dagon must stoop, and shall ere long receive
> Such a discomfit, as shall quite despoil him
> Of all these boasted trophies won on me,
> And with confusion blank his worshippers.

Who will say the expectation is not here prepared for some catastrophe, we know not what, but awful it must be, for it is Sampson which denounces the downfal of the idol, it is God who inspires the denunciation; the crisis is important, for it is that which shall decide whether God or Dagon is to triumph, it is in the strongest sense of the expression —*dignus vindice nodus*—and therefore we may boldly pronounce *Deus intersit!*

That this interpretation meets the sense of the author is clear from the remark of Manoah, who is made to say that he receives these words as a prophecy. Prophetic they are, and were meant to be by the poet, who in this use of his sacred prophecy imitates the heathen oracles, on which several of their dramatic plots are constructed, as might be shewn by obvious examples. The interview with Manoah then is conducive to the catastrophe, and the drama is not in this scene devoid of incident.

Dalilah next appears, and if whatever tends to raise our interest in the leading character of the tragedy, cannot rightly be called episodical, the introduction of this person ought not to be accounted such, for who but this person is the cause and origin of all the pathos and distress of the story? The dialogue of this scene is moral, affecting and sublime; it is also strictly characteristic.

The next scene exhibits the tremendous giant Harapha, and the contrast thereby produced is amongst

the beauties of the poem, and may of itself be termed an important incident: that it leads to the catastrophe I think will not be disputed, and if it is
asked in what manner, the Chorus will supply us
with an answer—

> He will directly to the Lords I fear,
> And with malicious counsel stir them up
> Some way or other further to afflict thee.

Here is another prediction connected with the plot
and verified by its catastrophe, for Sampson is commanded to come to the festival and entertain the re-
vellers with some feats of strength: these commands
he resists, but obeys an impulse of his mind by going
afterwards, and thereby fulfils the prophetic declaration he had made to his father in the second act.
What incident can shew more management and address in the poet, than this of Sampson's refusing
the summons of the idolaters and obeying the visitation of God's spirit.

And now I may confidently appeal to the judicious reader, whether the Sampson Agonistes is so
void of incident between the opening and conclusion as fairly to be pronounced *to want a middle*.
Simple it is from first to last, simple perhaps to a
degree of coldness in some of its parts, but to say
that nothing passes between the first act and the
last, which hastens or delays the death of Sampson,
is not correct, because the very incidents are to be
found, which conduce to the catastrophe, and but
for which it could not have come to pass.

The author of the Rambler professes to examine
the Sampson Agonistes according to the rule laid
down by Aristotle for the disposition and perfection
of a tragedy, and this rule he informs us is, that it
should have *a beginning, a middle, and an end*. An
is this the mighty purpose for which the autho-

rity of Aristotle is appealed to? If it be thus the
author of the Rambler has read the Poetics, and this
be the best rule he can collect from that treatise, I
am afraid he will find it too short a measure for the
poet he is examining, or the critic he is quoting.
Aristotle had said ' that every whole hath not
amplitude enough for the construction of a tragic fable; now by a whole, (adds he in the way of
illustration) I mean that, which hath beginning,
middle, and end.' This and no more is what he
says upon beginning, middle and end; and this,
which the author of the Rambler conceives to be a
rule for tragedy, turns out to be merely an explanation of the word *whole*, which is only one term
amongst many employed by the critic in his professed and compleat definition of tragedy. I should
add, that Aristotle gives a further explanation of the
terms, beginning, middle and end, which the author
of the Rambler hath turned into English, but in so
doing he hath inexcusably turned them out of their
original sense as well as language; as any curious
critic may be convinced of, who compares them
with Aristotle's words in the eighth chapter of the
Poetics.

Of the poetic diction of the Sampson Agonistes
I have already spoken in general; to particularize
passages of striking beauty would draw me into too
great length; at the same time, not to pass over so
pleasing a part of my undertaking in absolute silence,
I will give the following reply of Sampson to the
Chorus—

> Wherever fountain or fresh current flow'd
> Against the eastern ray, trsanslucent, pure
> With touch ethereal of heaven's fiery rod,
> I drank, from the clear milky juice allaying
> Thirst, and refresh'd; nor envy'd them the grape,
> Whose heads that turbulent liquor fills with fumes.

Of the character I may say in few words, that Sampson possesses all the terrific majesty of Prometheus chained, the mysterious distress of Oedipus, and the pitiable wretchedness of Philoctetes. His properties, like those of the first, are something above human; his misfortunes, like those of the second, are derivable from the displeasure of heaven, and involved in oracles; his condition, like that of the last, is the most abject, which human nature can be reduced to from a state of dignity and splendor.

Of the catastrophe there remains only to remark, that it is of unparalleled majesty and terror.

NUMBER LXXVII.

Dr. Samuel Johnson, in his life of Rowe, pronounces of ' The Fair Penitent, that it is one of the most pleasing tragedies on the stage, where it still keeps its turns of appearing, and probably will long keep them, for that there is scarcely any work of any poet at once so interesting by the fable, and so delightful by the language. The story, he observes, is domestic, and therefore easily received by the imagination, and assimilated to common life; the diction is exquisitely harmonious, and soft or sprightly as occasion requires.' Few people, I believe, will think this character of the Fair Penitent too lavish on the score of commendation; the high degree of public favour in which this tragedy has long stood, has ever attracted the best performers in its display. As there is no drama more frequently exhibited, or more generally read, I propose to give it a fair and

impartial examination, jointly with the more unknown and less popular tragedy from which it is
derived.

The Fair Penitent is in fable and character so
closely copied from the Fatal Dowry, that it is impossible not to take that tragedy along with it; and
it is matter of some surprize to me that Rowe should
have made no acknowledgment of his imitation
either in his dedication or prologue, or any where
else that I am apprised of.

This tragedy of the Fatal Dowry was the joint
production of Massinger and Nathaniel Field; it
takes a wider compass of fable than the Fair Penitent,
by which means it presents a very affecting scene at
the opening, which discovers young Charalois attended by his friend Romont, waiting with a petition in his hand to be presented to the judges, when
they shall meet, praying the release of his dead
father's body, which had been seized by his creditors, and detained in their hands for debts he had in-
curred in the public service, as Field Marshal of the
armies of Burgundy. Massinger, to whose share
this part of the tragedy devolved, has managed this
pathetic introduction with consummate skill and
great expression of nature ; a noble youth in the last
state of worldly distress, reduced to the humiliating
yet pious office of soliciting an unfeeling and unfriendly judge to allow him to pay the solemn rites
of burial to the remains of an illustrious father, who
had fought his country's battles with glory, and had
sacrificed life and fortune in defence of an ungrateful
state, impresses the spectator's mind with pity and
respect, which are felt through every passage of the
play : one thing in particular strikes me at the opening of the scene, which is the long silence that the
poet has artfully imposed upon his principal character (Charalois) who stands in mute sorrow with

his petition in his hand, whilst his friend Romont, and his advocate Charmi, urge him to present himself to the judges, and solicit them in person: the judges now make their entrance, they stop upon the stage; they offer him the fairest opportunity for tendering his petition and soliciting his suit: Charalois remains fixed and speechless; Romont, who is all eagerness in his cause, presses him again and again—

> Now put on your spirits—
> Now, Sir, lose not this offered means: their looks,
> Fix'd on you with a pitying earnestness,
> Invites you to demand their furtherance
> To your good purpose.

The judges point him out to each other; they lament the misfortunes of his noble house; they observe,

> It is young Charalois
> Son to the Marshal, from whom he inherits
> His fame and virtues only.
> *Romont.* Hah! They name you.
> *Dulroy.* His father died in prison two days since.
> *Rochfort.* Yes, to the shame of this ungrateful state,
> That such a master in the art of war,
> So noble and so highly meriting
> From this forgetful country, should, for want
> Of means to satisfy his creditors
> The sum he took up for the general good,
> Meet with an end so infamous.
> *Romont.* Dare you ever hope for like opportunity?

It is in vain; the opportunity passes off, and Charalois opens not his mouth, nor even silently tenders his petition.

I have, upon a former occasion, both generally and particularly observed upon the effects of dramatic silence; the stage cannot afford a more beautiful and touching instance than this before us: to say it is not inferior to the silence of Hamlet upon his first appearance, would be saying too little in its favour. I have no doubt but Massinger had this

very case in his thoughts, and I honour him no less
for the imitating, than I should have done for striking out a silence so naturally and so delicately preserved. What could Charalois have uttered to give
him that interest in the hearts of his spectators,
which their own conclusions during his affecting
silence have already impressed? No sooner are the
judges gone, than the ardent Romont again breaks
forth—

> This obstinate spleen
> You think becomes your sorrow, and sorts well
> With your black suits.

This is Hamlet himself, his *inky cloak*, and *customary
suits of solemn black*. The character of Charalois is
thus fixed before he speaks; the poet's art has given
the prejudice that is to bear him in our affections
through all the succeeding events of the fable; and a
striking contrast is established between the undis-
cerning fiery zeal of Romont and Charalois' fine
sensibility and high-born dignity of soul.

A more methodical and regular dramatist would
have stopped here, satisfied that the impression already made was fully sufficient for all the purposes
of his plot; but Massinger, according to the busy
spirit of the stage for which he wrote, is not alarmed
by a throng of incidents, and proceeds to open the
court and discuss the pleadings on the stage: the
advocate Charmi in a set harangue moves the judges
for dispensing with the rigour of the law in favour
of creditors, and for rescuing the Marshal's corpse
out of their clutches; he is brow-beaten and silenced
by the presiding judge, old Novall: the plea is then
taken up by the impetuous Romont, and urged
with so much personal insolence, that he is arrested
on the spot, put in charge of the officers of the court,
and taken to prison. This is a very striking mode
of introducing the set oration of Charalois; a son

recounting the military atchievments of a newly deceased father, and imploring mercy from his creditors and the law towards his unburied remains, now claims the attention of the court, who had been hitherto unmoved by the feeble formality of a hired pleader, and the turbulent passion of an enraged soldier. Charalois' argument takes a middle course between both; the pious feelings of a son, tempered by the modest manners of a gentleman: the creditors however are implacable, the judge is hostile, and the law must take its course.

> *Creditor.*   'Tis the city's doctrine:
> We stand bound to maintain it.
>   *Charalois.* Be constant in it;
> And since you are as merciless in your natures,
> As base and mercenary in your means
> By which you get your wealth, I will not urge
> The court to take away one scruple from
> The right of their laws, or one good thought
> In you to mend your disposition with.
> I know there is no music in your ears
> So pleasing as the groans of men in prison,
> And that the tears of widows, and the cries
> Of famish'd orphans, are the feasts that take you:
> That to be in your danger with more care
> Should be avoided than infectious air,
> The loath'd embraces of diseased women,
> A flatterer's poison, or the loss of honour.
> Yet rather than my father's reverend dust
> Shall want a place in that fair monument,
> In which our noble ancestors lie entomb'd,
> Before the court I offer up myself
> A prisoner for it : load me with those irons
> That have worn out his life; in my best strength
> I'll run to the encounter of cold hunger,
> And choose my dwelling where no sun dares enter,
> So he may be releas'd.

There was yet another incident, which the poet's passion for business and spectacle induced him to avail himself of, viz. the funeral of the Marshal;

this he displays on the stage, with a train of captains
and soldiers following the body of their general:
Charalois and Romont, under custody of their jai-
lors, appear as chief mourners, and a party of creditors are concerned in the groupe.

After this solemnity is dispatched, the poet proceeds to develop the amiable generosity of old Rochfort, who, being touched with the gallant spirit of
Romont, and still more penetrated with the filial
piety of young Charalois, delivers them both from
imprisonment and distress, by discharging the debts
of the Marshal and dismissing the creditors: this
also passes before the eyes of the spectators. Before
Charalois has given full expression to his gratitude
for this extraordinary benefaction, Rochfort follows
it with a further act of bounty, which he introduces
in the stile of a request—

> Call in my daughter—Still I have a suit to you,
> Would you requite me—
> This is my only child.

Beaumelle, Rochfort's daughter, is presented to Charalois; the scene is hurried on with a precipitation
almost without example: Charalois asks the lady,

> Fair Beaumelle, can you love me?
> *Beaumelle.* Yes, my lord.
> *Charalois.* You need not question me if I can you;
> You are the fairest virgin in Dijon,
> And Rochfort is your father.

The match is agreed upon as soon as proposed, and
Rochfort hastens away to prepare the celebration.

In this cluster of incidents I must not fail to remark, that the poet introduces young Novall upon
the scene, in the very moment when the short dialogue above quoted was passing: this Novall had
before been exhibited as a suitor to Beaumelle, and
his vain frivolous character had been displayed in a

very ridiculous and contemptible light; he is now again introduced to be a witness of his own disappointment, and his only observation upon it is— *What's this change?*—Upon the exit of the father however he addresses himself to the lady, and her reply gives the alarming hint, that makes discovery of the fatal turn which the plot is now about to take; for when Novall, turning aside to Beaumelle, by one word—*Mistress!*—conveys the reproach of inconstancy, she replies,

> Oh, Servant! Virtue strengthen me!
> Thy presence blows round my affection's vane:
> You will undo me if you speak again.　　　(Exit.)

Young Novall is left on the scene with certain followers and dependents, which hang upon his fortune, one of which (Pontalier by name) a man under deep obligations to him, yet of an honest nature, advises him to an honourable renunciation of all further hopes or attempts to avail himself of the affections of Beaumelle—

> Tho' you have sav'd my life,
> Rescu'd me often from my wants, I must not
> Wink at your follies, that will ruin you.
> You know my blunt way, and my love to truth:
> Forsake the pursuit of this lady's honour,
> Now you do see her made another man's.

This honourable advice is rejected with contempt: Novall, in whose mean bosom there does not seem a trace of virtue, avows a determined perseverance; and the poet having in this hasty manner compleated these inauspicious nuptials, closes the second act of his tragedy.

NUMBER LXXVIII.

WE have now expended two entire acts of The Fatal Dowry, in advancing to that period in the fable, at which the tragedy of The Fair Penitent opens. If the author of this tragedy thought it necessary to contract Massinger's plot, and found one upon it of a more regular construction, I know not how he could do this any otherwise, than by taking up the story at the point where we have now left it, and throwing the antecedent matter into narration; and though these two prefatory acts are full of very affecting incidents, yet the pathos which properly appertains to the plot, and conduces to the catastrophe of the tragedy, does not in strictness take place before the event of the marriage. No critic will say that the pleadings before the judges, the interference of the creditors, the distresses of Charalois, or the funeral of the Marshal, are necessary parts of the drama; at the same time no reader will deny (and neither could Rowe himself overlook) the effect of these incidents: he could not fail to foresee that he was to sacrifice very much of the interest of his fable, when he was to throw that upon narration, which his original had given in spectacle; and the loss was more enhanced by falling upon the hero of the drama; for who that compares Charalois, at the end of the second act of Massinger, with Rowe's Altamont at the opening scene of The Fair Penitent, can doubt which character has most interest with the spectators? We have seen the former in all the most amiable offices which filial piety could perform; enduring insults from his inveterate oppressors, and voluntarily surrendering himself to a prison to ransom the dead body of his father from unrelenting creditors. Altamont presents himself before us in his wedding suit, in the splendour of fortune, and at the summit of happiness; he greets us with a burst of exultation—

> Let this auspicious day be ever sacred,
> No mourning, no misfortunes happen on it;
> Let it be mark'd for triumphs and rejoicings!
> Let happy lovers ever make it holy,
> Choose it to bless their hopes and crown their wishes;
> This happy day, that gives me my Calista!

The rest of the scene is employed by him and Horatio alternately in recounting the benefits conferred upon them by the generous Sciolto; and the very same incident of the seizure of his father's corpse by the creditors, and his redemption of it, is recited by Horatio—

> When his hard creditors,
> Urg'd and assisted by Lothario's father,
> (Foe to thy house and rival of their greatness)
> By sentence of the cruel law forbade
> His venerable corpse to rest in earth,
> Thou gav'st thyself a ransom for his bones;
> With piety uncommon didst give up
> Thy hopeful youth to slaves, who ne'er knew mercy.

It is not however within the reach of this, or any other description, to place Altamont in that interesting and amiable light, as circumstances have already placed Charalois; the happy and exulting bridegroom may be an object of our congratulation, but the virtuous and suffering Charalois engages our pity, love, and admiration. If Rowe would have his audience credit Altamont for that filial piety, which marks the character he copied from, it was a small oversight to put the following expression into his mouth—

Oh, great Sciolto! Oh, my more than father!

A closer attention to character would have reminded him that it was possible for Altamont to express his gratitude to Sciolto without setting him above a father, to whose memory he had paid such devotion.

From this contraction of his plot, by the defalcation of so many pathetic incidents, it became impossible for the author of the Fair Penitent to make his Altamont the hero of his tragedy, and the leading part is taken from him by Horatio, and even by Lothario, throughout the drama. There are several other reasons, which concur to sink Altamont upon the comparison with Charalois, the chief of which arises from the captivating colours in which Rowe has painted his libertine : on the contrary, Massinger gives a contemptible picture of his young Novall ; he makes him not only vicious, but ridiculous ; in foppery and impertinence he is the counterpart of Shakspeare's Osrick ; vain-glorious, purseproud, and overbearing amongst his dependents ; a spiritless poltroon in his interview with Romont. Lothario (as Johnson observes) ' with gaiety which cannot be hated, and bravery which cannot be despised, retains too much of the spectator's kindness.' His high spirit, brilliant qualities, and fine person, are so described, as to put us in danger of false impressions in his favour, and to set the passions in opposition to the moral of the piece : I suspect that the gallantry of Lothario makes more advocates for Calista than she ought to have. There is another consideration, which operates against Altamont, and it is an indelicacy in his character, which the poet should have provided against : he marries

Calista with the full persuasion of her being averse to the match; in his first meeting with Sciolto he says—

> Oh! could I hope there was one thought of Altamont,
> One kind remembrance in Calista's breast—
> ——————I found her cold
> As a dead lover's statue on his tomb;
> A rising storm of passion shook her breast,
> Her eyes a piteous shower of tears let fall,
> And then she sigh'd as if her heart were breaking.
> With all the tenderest eloquence of love
> I begg'd to be a sharer in her grief;
> But she, with looks averse and eyes that froze me,
> Sadly replied, her sorrows were her own,
> Nor in a father's power to dispose of.

I am aware that Sciolto attempts to parry these facts, by an interpretation too gross and unbecoming for a father's character, and only fit for the lips of a Lothario; but yet it is not in nature to suppose that Altamont could mistake such symptoms, and it fixes a meanness upon him, which prevails against his character throughout the play. Nothing of this sort could be discovered by Massinger's bridegroom, for the ceremony was agreed upon and performed at the very first interview of the parties; Beaumelle gave a full and unreserved assent, and though her character suffers on the score of hypocrisy on that account, yet Charalois is saved by it: less hypocrisy appears in Calista, but hers is the deeper guilt, because she was already dishonoured by Lothario, and Beaumelle's coquetry with Novall had not yet reached the length of criminality. Add to this, that Altamont appears in the contemptible light of a suitor, whom Calista had apprized of her aversion, and to whom she had done a deliberate act of dishonour, though his person and character must have been long known to her. The case is far otherwise between Charalois and Beaumelle, who

never met before, and every care is taken by the
poet to save his hero from such a deliberate injury,
as might convey contempt; with this view the
marriage is precipitated; nothing is allowed to pass,
that might open the character of Charalois to Beaumelle : she is hurried into an assignation with Novall
immediately upon her marriage; every artifice of seduction is employed by her confidante Bellaperte,
and Aymer the parasite of Novall, to make this
meeting criminal; she falls the victim of passion,
and when detection brings her to a sense of her
guilt, she makes this penitent and pathetic appeal to
Charalois—

> Oh my fate !
> That never would consent that I should see
> How worthy thou wert both of love and duty
> Before I lost you; and my misery made
> The glass, in which I now behold your virtue——
>   With justice therefore you may cut me off,
> And from your memory wash the remembrance
> That e'er I was; like to some vicious purpose,
> Which in your better judgment you repent of,
> And study to forget——
>   ——Yet you shall find,
> Tho' I was bold enough to be a strumpet,
> I dare not yet live one : let those fam'd matrons,
> That are canoniz'd worthy of our sex,
> Transcend me in their sanctity of life,
> I yet will equal them in dying nobly,
> Ambitious of no honour after life,
> But that, when I am dead, you will forgive me.

Compare this with the conduct of Calista, and then
decide which frail fair-one has the better title to the
appellation of a *Penitent*, and which drama conveys
the better moral by its catastrophe.

There is indeed a grossness in the older poet,
which his more modern imitator has refined; but he
has only sweetened the poison, not removed its venom; nay, by how much more palatable he has

made it; so much more pernicious it is become in his tempting sparkling cup, than in the coarse deterring dose of Massinger.

Rowe has no doubt greatly outstepped his original in the striking character of Lothario, who leaves Novall as far behind him as Charalois does Altamont: it is admitted then that Calista has as good a plea as any wanton could wish, to urge for her criminality with Lothario, and the poet has not spared the ear of modesty in his exaggerated description of the guilty scene; every luxurious image, that his inflamed imagination could crowd into the glowing rhapsody, is there to be found, and the whole is recited in numbers so flowing and harmonious, that they not only arrest the passions but the memory also, and perhaps have been, and still can be, as generally repeated as any passage in English poetry. Massinger with less elegance, but not with less regard to decency, suffers the guilty act to pass within the course of his drama; the greater refinement of manners in Rowe's day did not allow of this, and he anticipated the incident; but when he revived the recollection of it by such a studied defcription, he plainly shewed that it was not from moral principle that he omitted it; and if he has presented his heroine to the spectators with more immediate delicacy during the compass of the play, he has at the same time given her greater depravity of mind; her manners may be more refined, but her principle is fouler than Beaumelle's. Calista, who yielded to the gallant gay Lothario, *hot with the Tuscan grape*, might perhaps have disdained a lover who addressed her in the holiday language which Novall uses to Beaumelle—

> Best day to Nature's curiosity!
> Star of Dijon, the lustre of all France!
> Perpetual Spring dwell on thy rosy cheeks,
> Whose breath is perfume to our continent;

See, Flora trimm'd in her varieties!——
No Autumn, nor no Age ever approach
This heavenly piece, which Nature having wrought,
She lost her needle, and did then despair
Ever to work so lively and so fair.

The letter of Calista (which brings about the discovery by the poor expedient of Lothario's dropping
it and Horatio's finding it) has not even the merit of
being characteristically wicked, and is both in its
matter and mode below tragedy. It is *Lothario's
cruelty has determined her to yield a perfect obedience to
her father, and give her hand to Altamont, in spite
of her weakness for the false Lothario.*——If the lady
had given her *perfect obedience* its true denomination, she had called it a most dishonourable
compliance; and if we may take Lothario's word
(who seems full correct enough in describing facts
and particulars) she had not much cause to complain of his being false; for he tells Rossano——

I lik'd her, would have marry'd her,
But that it pleas'd her father to refuse me,
To make this honourable fool her husband.

It appears by this that Lothario had not been *false*
to her in the article of marriage, though he might
have been *cruel* to her on the score of passion, which
indeed is confest on his part with as much *cold indifference*, as the most barefaced avowal could express.——But to return to the letter : she proceeds to
tell him—' that she could almost wish she had that
heart, and that honour to bestow with it, which he
has robbed her of'—But lest this half wish should
startle him, she adds—' But oh! I fear, could I re-
trieve them, I should again be undone by the too
faithless, yet too lovely Lothario.'—This must be
owned as full a reason as she could give why she
should only *almost wish* for her lost honour, when

she would make such an use of it, if she had it again
at her disposal.　And yet the very next paragraph
throws every thing into contradiction, for she tells
him—' this is the last weakness of her pen, and to-
morrow shall be the last in which she will indulge
her eyes.'　If she could keep to that resolution, I
must think the recovery of her innocence would
have been worth a whole wish, and many a wish;
unless we are to suppose she was so devoted to
guilt, that she could take delight in reflecting upon
it: this is a state of depravity, which human nature
hardly ever attains, and seems peculiar to Calista.
She now grows very humble, and concludes in a
stile well suited to her humility—' Lucilla shall conduct you, if you are kind enough to let me see you;
it shall be the last trouble you shall meet with from
——The lost Calista.'

It was very ill done of Horatio's curiosity to read
this letter, and I must ever regret that he has so un-
handsomely exposed a lady's private correspondence
to the world.

NUMBER LXXIX.

Though the part which Horatio takes in the business of the drama, is exactly that which falls to the
share of Romont in the Fatal Dowry, yet their characters are of a very different cast; for as Rowe
had bestowed the fire and impetuosity of Romont
upon his Lothario, it was a very judicious opposition to contrast it with the cool deliberate courage
of the sententious Horatio, the friend and brother-
in-law of Altamont.

When Horatio has read Calista's letter, which
Lothario had dropped (an accident which more frequently happens to gentlemen in comedies than in
tragedies) he falls into a very long meditation, and
closes it with putting this question to himself:

> What if I give this paper to her father?
> It follows that his justice dooms her dead,
> And breaks his heart with sorrow; hard return
> For all the good his hand has heap'd on us!
> Hold, let me take a moment's thought—

At this moment he is interrupted in his reflections by
the presence of Lavinia, whose tender solicitude
fills up the remaining part of the dialogue, and concludes the act without any decisive resolution on the
part of Horatio; an incident well contrived, and introduced with much dramatic skill and effect:
though pressed by his wife to disclose the cause of
his uneasiness, he does not impart to her the fatal
discovery he has made; this also is well in character. Upon his next entrance he has withdrawn himself from the company, and being alone, resumes
his meditation—

> What, if, while all are here intent on revelling,
> I privately went forth and sought Lothario?
> This letter may be forg'd; perhaps the wantonness
> Of his vain youth to stain a lady's fame;
> Perhaps his malice to disturb my friend.
> Oh! no, my heart forebodes it must be true.
> Methought e'en now I mark'd the starts of guilt
> That shook her soul, tho' damn'd dissimulation
> Screen'd her dark thoughts, and set to public view
> A specious face of innocence and beauty.

This soliloquy is succeeded by the much-admired
and striking scene between him and Lothario; rigid
criticism might wish to abridge some of the sententious declamatory speeches of Horatio, and shorten
the dialogue to quicken the effect; but the moral

sentiment and harmonious versification are much too charming to be treated as intruders, and the author has also struck upon a natural expedient for prolonging the dialogue, without any violence to probability, by the interposition of Rossano, who acts as a mediator between the hostile parties. This interposition is further necessary to prevent a decisive rencounter, for which the fable is not ripe; neither would it be proper for Horatio to anticipate the revenge, which is reserved for Altamont: the altercation therefore closes with a challenge from Lothario—

> West of the town a mile, amongst the rocks,
> Two hours ere noon to-morrow I expect thee;
> Thy single hand to mine.

The place of meeting is not well ascertained, and the time is too long deferred for strict probability; there are however certain things in all dramas, which must not be too rigidly insisted upon, and provided no extraordinary violence is done to reason and common sense, the candid critic ought to let them pass: this I take to be a case in point; and though Horatio's cool courage and ready presence of mind, are not just the qualities to reconcile us to such an oversight, yet I see no reason to be severe upon the incident, which is followed by his immediate recollection—

> Two hours ere noon to-morrow! Hah! Ere that
> He sees Calista.—Oh! unthinking fool!
> What if I urg'd her with the crime and danger?
> If any spark from Heav'n remain unquench'd
> Within her breast, my breath perhaps may wake it.
> Could I but prosper there, I would not doubt
> My combat with that loud vain-glorious boaster.

Whether this be a measure altogether in character with a man of Horatio's good sense and discretion,

I must own is matter of doubt with me. I think
he appears fully satisfied of her actual criminality;
and in that case it would be more natural for him to
lay his measures for intercepting Lothario, and preventing the assignation, than to try his rhetoric in
the present crisis upon the agitated mind of Calista.
As it has justly occurred to him, that he has been
over-reached by Lothario in the postponement of
the duel, the measure I suggest would naturally tend
to hasten that rencounter. Now, though the business of the drama may require an explanation between Horatio and Calista, whereupon to ground an
occasion for his interesting quarrel with Altamont,
yet I do not see any necessity to make that a preme-
ditated explanation, nor to sacrifice character by a
measure that is inconsistent with the better judgment of Horatio. The poet, however, has decreed
it otherwise, and a deliberate interview with Calista
and Horatio accordingly takes place. This, although introduced with a solemn invocation on his
part, is very clumsily conducted—

> Teach me, some Power! that happy art of speech
> To dress my purpose up in gracious words,
> Such as may softly steal upon her soul,
> And never waken the tempestuous passions.

Who can expect, after this preparation, to hear
Horatio thus break his secret to Calista?

> Lothario and Calista!—Thus they join
> Two names, which Heav'n decreed should never meet.
> Hence have the talkers of this populous city
> A shameful tale to tell for public sport,
> Of an unhappy beauty, a false fair-one,
> Who plighted to a noble youth her faith,
> When she had giv'n her honour to a wretch.

This I hold to be totally out of nature; first, because
it is a palpable departure from his resolution to use

gracious words; next, because it has a certain tendency to produce rage and not repentance; and
thirdly, because it is founded in exaggeration and
falsehood; for how is he warranted to say that the
story is the public talk and sport of the city? If it
were so, what can his interference avail? why seek
this interview?

> Why come to tell her how she might be happy?
> To sooth the secret anguish of her soul?
> To comfort that fair mourner, that forlorn one,
> And teach her steps to know the paths of peace?

No judge of nature will think he takes the means to
lead her into the *paths of peace*, by hurrying her to
the very brink of desperation. I need not enlarge
upon this observation, and shall therefore only remark, that the scene breaks up, as might be expected, with the following proof of her penitence,
and his success in persuasion—

> Henceforth, thou officious fool,
> Meddle no more, nor dare, ev'n on thy life,
> To breathe an accent that may touch my virtue:
> I am myself the guardian of my honour,
> And will not bear so insolent a monitor.

Let us now enquire how Romont (the Horatio of
Massinger) conducts this incident, a character from
whom less discretion is to be expected than from his
philosophical successor. Romont himself discovers
Beaumelle and Novall engaged in the most wanton
familiarities, and, with a warmth suitable to his
zeal, breaks up the amorous conference by driving
Novall off the scene with ineffable contempt: he
then applies himself to the lady, and with a very
natural and manly spirit says,

> ———I respect you
> Not for yourself, but in remembrance of
> Who is your father, and whose wife you now are.

She replies to him with contempt and ridicule; he resumes the same characteristic strain he set out with, and proceeds—

> My intents,
> Madam, deserve not this; nor do I stay
> To be the whetstone of your wit: preserve it
> To spend on such as know how to admire
> Such colour'd stuff.   In me there is now speaks to you
> As true a friend and servant to your honour,
> And one that will with as much hazard guard it,
> As ever man did goodness.   But then, lady,
> You must endeavour, not alone to be,
> But to appear worthy such love and service.

We have just now heard Horatio reproach Calista with the reports that were circulated against her reputation; let us compare it with what Romont says upon the same subject—

> But yet be careful!
> Detraction's a bold monster, and fears not
> To wound the fame of princes, if it find
> But any blemish in their lives to work on.
> But I'll be plainer with you : had the people
> Been learnt to speak but what even now I saw,
> Their malice out of that would raise an engine
> To overthrow your honour.   In my sight,
> With yonder painted fool I frighted from you,
> You us'd familiarity beyond
> A modest entertainment : you embrac'd him
> With too much ardour for a stranger, and
> Met him with kisses neither chaste nor comely :
> But learn you to forget him, as I will
> Your bounties to him; you will find it safer
> Rather to be uncourtly than immodest.

What avails it to attempt drawing a comparison between this conduct and that of Horatio's, where no comparison is to be made? I leave it to the reader, and decline a task at once so unnecessary and ungrateful.

When Romont finds no impression is to be made

upon Beaumelle, he me[et]er, and immediately falls into the same [t]hat Horatio had struck upon—

> Her father!—Hah!
> How if I break this to[...] cannot
> Meet with an ill constr[...] wisdom,
> Made powerful by the [...] father,
> Will warrant and give [h]is counsels.
> It shall be so.

If this step needs excuse[...]r will consider that it is a step of pre[...] he experiment however fails, and he is re[...] some asperity by Rochfort; this draws[...] between him and Charalois, which, as i[...] to transcribe, so it is throughout too ex[...]tract any part from it. I can only expr[...]rize, that the author of The Fair Penite[...]s scene before him, could conduct his [...] between Altamont and Horatio upon [...]adely different, and so much inferior: I [...]se he thought it a strong incident to ma[...]t give a blow to his friend, else he mig[...] an interview carried on with infinitely [...] both of language and character, betw[...]ois and Romont, in circumstances ex[...]ar, where no such violence was commi[...]n meditated. Was it because Pierre had [...]w to Jaffier, that Altamont was to repe[...]indignity to Horatio, for a woman, o[...]sion he had proofs not to be mistaken?[...]s a character at least as high and irritabl[...]nt, and Romont is out of all compariso[...]h and plainspoken than Horatio: Cha[...]be deceived into an opinion of Beaume[...]h for him; Altamont could not deceive[...] such a notion, and the lady had testifi[...]e of him in the strongest terms, accom[...] symptoms

which he ad described as indicating some
rooted and affliction : Could any solution
be more n what Horatio gives? Novall
was a ri temptible, that Charalois could
not, with of probability, consider him as
an object usy; it would have been a de-
gradation racter, had he yielded to such a
suspicion , on the contrary, was of all
men livi st to be apprehended by a husband, le dence or vanity be ever so great.
Rowe, i pt to *surprize*, has sacrificed nature and of character for stage-effect;
Massing serving both nature and character, has l his friends through an angry
altercati initely more spirit, more pathos
and mo c effect, and yet dismissed them
with th g animated and affecting speech
from C his friend :

    my friend;
    ou'rt mad. I must not buy
    at this rate. Had I just cause,
    durst pursue such injury
    water, earth, nay, were they all
    to chaos; but there's none.
    mont, consists in camps, not courts.
    il man ! let's meet no more:
    web of friendship I untwist.
    e, walk pale, and lock my wife
    om her birth's free liberty,
    nine to me? Yes; if I do,
    cuckold then dog me with scorn :
    hman, no Italian born.   (Exit.)

It is ltamont at least was an exception
to th on *Italian* husbands. I shall pursue t on no further, nor offer any other
rema incident of the blow given by Al-
tamo with regard to Horatio's conduct
upon ; he draws his sword, and imme-

diately suspends resentment upon the following
motive:

> Yet hold! By heav'n, his father's in his face!
> Spite of my wrongs, my heart runs o'er with tenderness,
> And I could rather die myself than hurt him.

We must suppose it was the martial attitude that
Altamont had put himself into, which brought the
resemblance of his father so strongly to the observation of Horatio, otherwise it was a very unnatural
moment to recollect it in, when he had just received
the deepest insult one man can give to another: it is
however worth a remark, that this father of Altamont should act on both sides, and yet miscarry in
his mediation; for it is but a few passages before
that Altamont says to Horatio,

> Thou wert my father's friend; he lov'd thee well;
> A venerable mark of him
> Hangs round thee, and protects thee from my vengeance.
> I cannot, dare not lift my sword against thee.

What this *mark* was is left to conjecture; but it is
plain it was as seasonable for Horatio's rescue at
this moment, as it was for Altamont a few moments
after, who had certainly overlooked it when he
struck the very friend against whom he could not,
dared not *lift his sword*.

When Lavinia's entrance has parted Altamont
and Horatio, her husband complains to her of the
ingratitude with which he has been treated, and
says—

> He, who was all to me, child, brother, friend,
> With barbarous bloody malice sought my life.

These are very extraordinary terms for a man like
Horatio to use, and seem to convey a charge very
unfit for him to make, and of a very different nature
from the hasty insult he had received; in fact it ap-

pears as if the blow had totally reversed his character, for the resolution he takes in consequence of this
personal affront, is just such an one as would be
only taken by the man who dared not to resent it—

> From Genoa, from falsehood and inconstancy,
> To some more honest distant clime we'll go;
> Nor will I be beholden to my country
> For aught but thee, the partner of my flight.

That Horatio's heroism did not consist in the ready
forgiveness of injuries, is evident from the obstinate
sullenness with which he rejects the penitent apolo-
gies of Altamont in the further progress of the play ;
I am at a loss therefore to know what colour the
poet meant to give his character, by disposing him
to quit his country with this insult unatoned for,
and the additional stigma upon him of running
away from his appointment with Lothario for the
next morning *amongst the rocks.* Had he meant to
bring him off upon the repugnance he felt of resent-
ing any injury against the son of a father, whose
image was so visible *in his face*, that his ' heart ran
o'er with fondness in spite of his wrongs, and he
could rather die than hurt him ;' surely that image
would have interceded no less powerfully for him,
when, penetrated with remorse, he intercedes for
pity and forgiveness, and even faints at his feet with
agony at his unrelenting obduracy : it would be unfair to suppose he was more like his father when he
had dealt him an insulting blow, than when he was
atoning for an injury by the most ample satisfaction
and submission.

This is the light in which the conduct of Horatio
strikes me ; if I am wrong, I owe an atonement to
the manes of an elegant poet, which, upon conviction of my error, I will study to pay in the fullest
manner I am able.

It now remains only to say a few words upon the
catastrophe, in which the author varies from his original, by making Calista destroy herself with a dagger, put into her hand for that purpose by her father : if I am to moralize upon this proceeding of
Sciolto, I know full well the incident cannot bear
up against it; a Roman father would stand the discussion better than a Christian one; and I also know
that the most natural expedient is unluckily a most
undramatic one; yet the poet did not totally overlook it, for he makes Sciolto's first thought turn
upon a convent, if I rightly understand the following passage—

> Hence from my sight! thy father cannot bear thee :
> Fly with thy infamy to some dark cell,
> Where, on the confines of eternal night,
> Mourning, misfortunes, cares and anguish dwell;
> Where ugly Shame hides her opprobrious head,
> And Death and Hell detested rule maintain;
> There howl out the remainder of thy life,
> And wish thy name may be no more remember'd.

Whilst I am transcribing these lines a doubt strikes
me that I have misinterpreted them, and yet Calista's answer seems to point to the meaning I had suggested; perhaps however they are mere ravings in
fine numbers without any determinate idea : whatever they may be, it is clear they do not go to the
length of death : he tells Altamont, as soon as she is
departed—

> 　　　I wo' not kill her ;
> Yet by the ruin she has brought upon us,
> The common infamy that brands us both,
> She sha' not 'scape.

He seems in this moment to have formed the resolution, which he afterwards puts into execution; he
prompts her to self-murder, and arms her for the
act : this may save the spectators a sight too shock-

ing to behold, but does it convey less horror to the
heart, than if he had put her to death with his own
hand? A father killing his child for incontinence
with the man whom he had not permitted to marry
her, when he solicited his consent, is an act too
monstrous to reflect upon: Is that father less a
monster, who, deliberately and after full reflection,
puts a dagger into her hand and bids her commit
self-murder? I should humbly conceive the latter
act a degree in guilt beyond the former; especially
when I hear that father coolly demanding of his victim, if she has reflected upon what may happen
after death—

>   Hast thou consider'd what may happen after it?
>   How thy account may stand, and what to answer?

A parent surely would turn that question upon his
own heart, before he precipitated his unprepared
child to so awful and uncertain an account: rage
and instant revenge may find some plea; sudden
passion may transport even a father to lift his hand
against his own offspring; but this act of Sciolto
has no shelter but in heathen authority—

>   'Tis justly thought, and worthy of that spirit,
>   That dwelt in antient Latian breasts, when Rome
>   Was mistress of the world.

Did ever poetry beguile a man into such an allusion? And to what does that piece of information
tend, *that Rome was mistress of the world?* If this is
human nature, it would almost tempt one to reply
in Sciolto's own words—

>   I cou'd curse nature.

But it is no more like nature, than the following
sentiments of Calista are like the sentiments of a *Penitent*, or a Christian—

> That I must die it is my only comfort.
> Death is the privilege of human nature,
> And life without it were not worth our taking—

And again,

> Yet Heav'n, who knows our weak imperfect natures,
> How blind with passions, and how prone to evil,
> Makes not too strict inquiry for offences,
> But is aton'd by penitence and prayer.
> Cheap recompence! here 'twou'd not be receiv'd;
> Nothing but blood can make the expiation.

Such is the catastrophe of Rowe's *Fair Penitent*, such is the representation he gives us of human nature, and such the moral of his tragedy.

I shall conclude with an extract or two from the catastrophe of The Fatal Dowry; and first, for the *penitence* of Beaumelle, I shall select only the following speech, addressed to her husband:

> I dare not move you
> To hear me speak. I know my fault is far
> Beyond qualification or excuse;
> That 'tis not fit for me to hope, or you
> To think of mercy; only I presume
> To intreat you wou'd be pleas'd to look upon
> My sorrow for it, and believe these tears
> Are the true children of my grief, and not
> A woman's cunning.

I need not point out the contrast between this and the quotations from Calista. It will require a longer extract to bring the conduct of Rochfort into comparison with that of Sciolto: the reader will observe that Novall's dead body is now on the scene, Charalois, Beaumelle, and Rochfort her father, are present. The charge of adultery is urged by Charalois, and appeal is made to the justice of Rochfort in the case.

> *Rochfort.* What answer makes the prisoner?
> *Beaumelle.* I confess

The fact I'm charg'd with, and yield myself
Most miserably guilty.

   Rochfort Heaven take mercy
Upon your soul then! It must leave your body—
—Since that the politic law provides that servants,
To whose care we commit our goods, shall die
If they abuse our trust; what can you look for,
To whose charge this most hopeful Lord gave up
All he receiv'd from his brave ancestors,
All he cou'd leave to his posterity?
His honour—Wicked woman! in whose safety
All his life's joys and comforts were lock'd up,
Which thy lust, a thief, hath now stolen from him!
And therefore——

   Charalois. Stay, just Judge—May not what's lost
By her one fault (for I am charitable,
And charge her not with many) be forgotten
In her fair life hereafter?

   Rochfort. Never, Sir!
The wrong that's done to the chaste married bed,
Repentant tears can never expiate:
And be assur'd to pardon such a sin,
Is an offence as great as to commit it.

In consequence of this the husband strikes her dead
before her father's eyes: the act indeed is horrid;
even tragedy shrinks from it, and Nature with a father's voice instantly cries out—*Is she dead then?*—
and you have kill'd her?—Charalois avows it, and
pleads his sentence for the deed; the revolting, ago-
nized parent breaks forth into one of the most pathetic, natural and expressive lamentations, that the
English drama can produce—

     ——But I pronounc'd it
As a Judge only, and a friend to justice,
And, zealous in defence of your wrong'd honour,
Broke all the ties of nature, and cast off
The love and soft affection of a father:
I in your cause put on a scarlet robe
Of red dy'd cruelty; but in return
You have advanc'd for me no flag of mercy:
I look'd on you as a wrong'd husband, but
You clos'd your eyes against me as a father.

Oh, Beaumelle! Oh, my daughter!——
　Charalois. This is madness.
　Rochfort. Keep from me!—Cou'd not one good
　　　　thought rise up
To tell you that she was my age's comfort,
Begot by a weak man, and born a woman,
And cou'd not therefore but partake of frailty?
Or wherefore did not thankfulness step forth
To urge my many merits, which I may
Object to you, since you prove ungrateful?
Flinty-hearted Charalois!——
　Charalois. Nature does prevail above your virtue.

What conclusions can I draw from these comparative examples, which every reader would not anticipate? Is there a man, who has any feeling for real nature, dramatic character, moral sentiment, tragic pathos or nervous diction, who can hesitate, even for a moment, where to bestow the palm?

NUMBER LXXX.

I WAS some nights ago much entertained with an excellent representation of Mr. Congreve's comedy of The Double Dealer. When I reflected upon the youth of the author and the merit of the play, I acknowledged the truth of what the late Dr. Samuel Johnson says in his life of this poet, that ' amongst all the efforts of early genius, which literary history records, I doubt whether any one can be produced that more surpasses the common limits of nature than the plays of Congreve.'

The author of this comedy in his dedication informs us, that he ' designed the moral first, and to that moral invented the fable;' *and does not know*

' that he has borrowed one hint of it any where.'—
' I made the plot,' says he, ' as strong as I could;
because it was single; and I made it single because
I would avoid confusion, and was resolved to preserve the three unities of the drama.' As it is impossible not to give full credit to this assertion, I
must consider the resemblance which many circumstances in The Double Dealer bear to those in a comedy of Beaumont and Fletcher, intitled Cupid's
Revenge, as a casual coincidence; and I think the
learned biographer above quoted has good reason to
pronounce of Congreve, ' that he is an original writer, who borrowed neither the models of his plot,
nor the manner of his dialogue.'

Mellafont, the nephew and heir of Lord Touchwood, being engaged to Cynthia, daughter of Sir
Paul Pliant, the traversing this match forms the object of the plot, on which this comedy of The
Double Dealer is constructed; the intrigue consists
in the various artifices employed by Lady Touchwood and her agents for that purpose.

That the object is (as the author himself states it
to be) *singly* this, will appear upon considering, that
although the ruin of Mellafont's fortune is for a
time effected by these contrivances, that are employed for traversing his marriage, yet it is rather
a measure of necessity and self-defence in Lady
Touchwood, than of original design; it springs
from the artifice of incident, and belongs more properly to the intrigue, than to the object of the plot.

The making or obstructing marriages is the common hinge on which most comic fables are contrived to turn, but in this match of Mellafont's,
which the author has taken for the ground-work of
his plot, I must observe that it would have been
better to have given more interest to an event, which
he has made the main object of the play : he has

taken little pains to recommend the parties to his spectators, or to paint their mutual attachment with any warmth of colouring. Who will feel any concern whether Mellafont marries Cynthia or not, if they themselves appear indifferent on the occasion, and upon the eve of their nuptials converse in the following strain?

Mel. You seem thoughtful Cynthia.

Cyn. I am thinking, tho' marriage makes man and wife one flesh, it leaves them still two fools, and they become more conspicuous by setting off one another.

Mel. That's only when two fools meet, and their follies are opposed.

Cyn. Nay I have known two wits meet, and by the opposition of their wit, render themselves as ridiculous as fools. 'Tis an old game we are going to play at; what think you of drawing stakes, and giving over in time?

Mel. No, hang it, that's not endeavouring to win, because it is possible we may lose—&c. &c.

This scene, which proceeds throughout in the same strain, seems to confirm Dr. Johnson's remark, that ' Congreve formed a peculiar idea of comic excellence, which he supposed to consist in gay remarks and unexpected answers—*that* his scenes exhibit not much of humour, imagery or passion; his personages are a kind of intellectual gladiators; every sentence is to ward or strike; the contest of smartness is never intermitted; and his wit is a meteor playing to and fro with alternate coruscations.'

There is but one more interview between Cynthia and Mellafont, which is the opening of the fourth act, and this is of so flat and insipid a sort, as to be with reason omitted in representation: I think therefore it may be justly observed, that this match, for the prevention of which artifices of so virulent and diabolical a nature are practised by Lady Touchwood and The Double Dealer, is not pressed upon the feelings of the spectators in so interesting a manner, as it should and might have been.

Having remarked upon the object of the plot, I shall next consider the intrigue; and for this purpose we must methodically trace the conduct of Lady Touchwood, who is the poet's chief engine, and that of her under-agent Maskwell.

The scene lies in Lord Touchwood's house, but whether in town or country does not appear. Sir Paul Pliant, his lady and daughter, are naturally brought thither, upon the day preceding Cynthia's marriage, to adjust the settlement: Lord and Lady Froth, Careless and Brisk, are visitors on the occasion; Mellafont and Maskwell are inmates: this disposition is as happy as can be devised. The incident related by Mellafont to Careless, of the attempt upon him made by Lady Touchwood, artfully prepares us to expect every thing that revenge and passion can suggest for frustrating his happiness; and it is judicious to represent Mellafont incredulous as to the criminality of Maskwell's intercourse with Lady Touchwood; for if he had believed it upon Careless's suggestion, it would have made his blindness to the character of Maskwell not only weak, (which in fact it is) but unnatural and even guilty.

Maskwell in the first act makes general promises to Lady Touchwood that he will defeat Mellafont's match—' You shall possess and ruin him too.'—The lady presses him to explain particulars; he opens no other resource but that of possessing Lady Pliant with an idea that Mellafont is fond of her—' She must be thoroughly persuaded that Mellafont loves her.'—So shallow a contrivance as this cannot escape the lady's penetration, and she naturally answers—' I don't see what you can propose from so trifling a design; for her first conversing with Mellafont will convince her of the contrary.' In fact, the author's good sense was well aware how weak this expedient is, and it seems applied to no other purpose than as an incident to help on the underplot, by bringing forward the comic effect of Lady Pliant's character, and that of Sir Paul: Maskwell himself is so fairly gravelled by the observation, that he confesses he 'does not depend upon it;' but he observes that 'it will prepare something else, and gain him leisure to lay a stronger plot; if I gain a little time, says he, I shall not want contrivance.'

In the second act this design upon Lady Pliant is played off, and Maskwell in an interview with Mellafont avows the plot, and says—' to tell you the truth, I encouraged it for your diversion.' He proceeds to say, that in order to gain the confidence of Lady Touchwood, ' he had pretended to have been long secretly in love with Cynthia;' that thereby he had drawn forth ' the secrets of her heart,' and that ' if he accomplish'd her designs, she had engaged to put Cynthia with all her fortune into his power:' he then discloses by soliloquy that his motive for *double dealing* was founded in his passion for Cynthia, and observes that ' the name of rival cuts all ties asunder and is a general acquittance.' This proceeding is in nature and is good comedy.

The third act opens with a scene between Lord and Lady Touchwood, which is admirably conceived and executed with great spirit; I question if there is any thing of the author superior to this dialogue. The design of alarming the jealousy and resentment of Lord Touchwood now appears to have originated with the lady, although Maskwell was privy to it, and ' ready for a cue to come in and confirm all, had there been occasion;' he proposes to her to say that he was ' privy to Mellafont's design, but that he used his utmost endeavours to dissuade him from it;' and on the credit he thinks to establish by this proof of his honour and honesty, he grounds another plot, which he keeps as his ultimate and most secret resource, that ' of cheating her [Lady Touchwood] *as* well as the rest.' He now reveals to Mellafont a criminal assignation with Lady Touchwood in her chamber at eight, and proposes to him to come and surprize them together, ' and then,' says he, ' it will be hard if you cannot bring her to any conditions.'

This appears to me to be a very dangerous experiment, and scarce within the bounds of nature and probability. If Maskwell, under cover of the proposal, had in view nothing more than the introduction of Mellafont into Lady Touchwood's bedchamber, there to put them together, and then to bring Lord Touchwood secretly upon them in the moment of their interview, his contrivance could not have been better laid for the purpose of confirming the impression, which that lord had received against his nephew; in which Maskwell had nothing more to do than to apprise the lady of his design, and she of course could have managed the interview to the purposes of the plot, and effectually have compleated the ruin of Mellafont: this, it should seem, would have answered his object compleatly, for he would have risen upon the ruin of Mellafont, possessed himself of Lord Touchwood's favour, bound Lady Touchwood to concealment of his villainy, and been as able to lay his train for the possession of Cynthia, as by any other mode he could chuse for obtaining her; but if he put it to the issue of a surprize upon Lady Touchwood, when she was not prepared for the management of that surprize, what was he to expect from the introduction of Lord Touchwood, but discovery and defeat? Was it not natural to suppose Mellafont would seize the opportunity of reproaching her with her criminality with Maskwell? It was for that very purpose he brings him thither; he tells him 'it will be hard if he cannot then bring her to any conditions;'—and if this was to pass under the terror of his reproaches, how could Maskwell set Lord Touchwood upon listening to their conversation, and not apprehend for a consequence apparently so unavoidable? He puts every thing to risque by proposing to Mellafont to conceal himself in Lady Touchwood's bed-chamber, whilst she is in the closet; he then meets Lord Touchwood, appoints him to come to the lobby by the bed-chamber in a quarter of an hour's time; he keeps his assignation with the lady, Mellafont starts from his hiding-place, and Maskwell escapes, but soon returns, secretly introducing Lord Touchwood to listen to the dialogue between his lady and nephew: she accidentally discovers him without his being seen by Mellafont, and turns that accidental discovery against Mellafont. What a combination of improbabilities is here fortuitously thrown together to produce this lucky incident! Could Maskwell reasonably presume upon a chance so beyond expectation? Every thing is made to turn upon the precarious point of a minute: if Lord Touchwood, who was appointed for a quarter of an hour, had anticipated that appointment, if Lady Touchwood had been less punctual to her assignation, if Mellafont had happened to have dropt one word in his uncle's hearing, charging her with his discovery, as had been agreed, or if either she had happened not to have seen Lord Touchwood, or Mellafont had seen him; in short, if any one thing had turned up, which ought to have come to pass, or otherwise than it was made to come to pass by the greatest violence to probability, Maskwell was inevitably undone: it must be owned he laid a train for his own desruction, but stage incident rescued him; and this, with the lady's adroitness, effaces the improbability, when it passes in representation, and keeps nature out of sight. Had Mellafont told the plain story to his uncle, after Lady Touchwood had so unexpectedly turned it against him, it would at least have put the plot to risque, and of this the author seems so conscious, that he does not suffer him to attempt a single word in his defence; to save his villain, he is compelled to sacrifice his hero.

It is not sufficient to say that a poet has his characters in his power, and can fashion incidents according to his own discretion; he must do no violence to nature and probability for the purposes of his plot.

Maskwell having in this manner escaped with success, begins next to put in execution his plot for obtaining Cynthia, and this constitutes the intrigue and catastrophe of the fifth act: his plan is as follows—Having imparted to Lord Touchwood his love for Cynthia by the vehicle of a soliloquy, which is to be overheard by his lordship, he proposes to himself to carry off Cynthia to St. Alban's with the chaplain in the coach, there to be married; this she is to be trepanned into by persuading her that the chaplain is Mellafont, and Mellafont is brought to co-operate, by a promise that he shall elope with Cynthia under that disguise, and that the chaplain shall be made to follow on the day after and then marry him to Cynthia; with this view Mellafont is appointed to meet Maskwell in one chamber, and Cynthia in another; the real chaplain is to be passed upon the lady for Mellafont, and Mellafont is to be left in the lurch; this plot upon Cynthia, Maskwell confides to Lord Touchwood, telling him there is no other way to possess himself of her but by surprize.

Though the author undoubtedly meant his villain should in the end outwit himself, yet he did not mean him to attempt impossibilities, and the absurdities of this contrivance are so many, that I know not which to mention first. How was Maskwell to possess himself of Cynthia by this scheme? By what force or fraud is he to accomplish the object of marrying her? We must conclude he was not quite so desperate as to sacrifice all his hopes from Lord Touchwood by any violence upon her person; there is nothing in his character to warrant the conjecture. It is no less unaccountable how Mellafont could be caught by this project, and induced to equip himself in the chaplain's gown to run off with a lady, who had pledged herself to him never to marry any other man: there was no want of consent on her part; a reconciliation with Lord Touchwood was the only object he had to look to, and how was that to be effected by this elopement with Cynthia?

The jealousy of Lady Touchwood was another rock on which Maskwell was sure to split: it would have been natural for him to have provided against this danger by binding my lord to secrecy, and the lady's pride of family was a ready plea for that purpose; when he was talking to himself for the purpose of being overheard by Lord Touchwood, he had nothing to do but to throw in this observation amongst the rest to bar that point against discovery.

The reader will not suppose I would suggest a plan of operation for *The Double Dealer* to secure him against discovery; I am only for adding probability and common precaution to his projects: I allow that it is in character for him to grow wanton with success; there is a moral in a villain outwitting himself; but the catastrophe would in my opinion have been far more brilliant, if his schemes had broke up with more force of contrivance; laid as they are, they melt away and dissolve by their own weakness and inconsistency; Lord and Lady Touchwood, Careless and Cynthia, all join in the discovery;

every one but Mellafont sees through the plot, and he is blindness itself.

Mr. Congreve, in his dedication above mentioned, defends himself against the objection to soliloquies; but I conceive he is more open to criticism for the frequent use he makes of listening; Lord Touchwood three times has recourse to this expedient.

Of the characters in this comedy Lady Touchwood, though of an unfavourable cast, seems to have been the chief care of the poet, and is well preserved throughout; her elevation of tone, nearly approaching to the tragic, affords a strong relief to the lighter sketches of the episodical persons, Sir Paul and Lady Pliant, Lord and Lady Froth, who are highly entertaining, but much more loose than the stage in its present state of reformation would endure: nothing more can be said of Careless and Brisk, than that they are the young men of the theatre, at the time when they were in representation. Of Maskwell enough has been said in these remarks, nor need any thing be added to what has been already observed upon Mellafont and Cynthia. As for the moral of the play, which the author says he designed in the first place, and then applied the fable to it, it should seem to have been his principal object in the formation of the comedy, and yet it is not made to reach several characters of very libertine principles, who are left to reform themselves at leisure; and the plot, though subordinate to the moral, seems to have drawn him off from executing his good intentions so compleatly, as those professions may be understood to engage for.

NUMBER LXXXI.

Citò scribendo non fit ut bene scribatur; bene scribendo fit ut citò.

QUINTIL. Lib. x.

THE celebrated author of the Rambler in his concluding paper says, 'I have laboured to refine our language to grammatical purity, and to clear it from colloquial barbarisms, licentious idioms and irregular combinations: something perhaps I have added to the elegance of its construction, and something to the harmony of its cadence.' I hope our language hath gained all the profit, which the labours of this meritorious writer were exerted to produce: in style of a certain description he undoubtedly excels; but though I think there is much in his essays for a reader to admire, I should not recommend them as a model for a disciple to copy.

Simplicity, ease and perspicuity should be the first objects of a young writer: Addison and other authors of his class will furnish him with examples, and assist him in the attainment of these excellencies; but after all, the style, in which a man shall write, will not be formed by imitation only; it will be the style of his mind; it will assimilate itself to his mode of thinking, and take its colour from the complexion of his ordinary discourse, and the company he consorts with. As for that distinguishing characteristic, which the ingenious essayist terms very properly *the harmony of its cadence*, that I take to be incommunicable, and immediately dependent upon the ear of him who models it. This *harmony of cadence* is so strong a mark of discrimination between authors of note in the world of letters, that we can depose to a style, whose modulation we are familiar with, almost as confidently as to the hand-writing of a correspondent. But though I think there will be found in the periods of every established writer a certain peculiar tune, (whether harmonious or otherwise) which will depend rather upon the natural ear than upon the imitative powers, yet I would not be understood to say that the study of good models can fail to be of use in the first formation of it. When a subject presents itself to the mind, and thoughts arise, which are to be committed to writing, it is then for a man to chuse whether he will express himself in simple or in elaborate diction, whether he will compress his matter or dilate it, ornament it with epithets and robe it in metaphor, or whether he will deliver it plainly and naturally in such language as a well-bred person and scholar would use, who affects no parade of speech, nor aims at any flights of fancy. Let him decide as he will, in all these cases he hath models in plenty to chuse from, which may be said to court his imitation.

For instance; if his ambition is to glitter and surprize with the figurative and metaphorical brilliancy of his period, let him tune his ear to some such passages as the following, where doctor Johnson in the character of critic and biographer is pronouncing upon the poet Congreve. ' His scenes exhibit not much of humour, imagery or passion: his personages are a kind of intellectual gladiators; every sentence is to ward or strike; the contest of smartness is never intermitted; his wit is a meteor playing to and fro with alternate coruscations.' If he can learn to embroider with as much splendor, taste and address as this and many other samples from the same master exhibit, he cannot study in a better school.

On the contrary, if simplicity be his object, and

a certain serenity of style, which seems in unison with the soul, he may open the Spectator, and take from the first paper of Mr. Addison the first paragraph that meets his eye—the following for instance —' There is nothing that makes its way more directly to the soul than *beauty*, which immediately diffuses a secret satisfaction and complacency through the imagination, and gives a finishing to any thing that is great or uncommon : the very first discovery of it strikes the mind with an inward joy, and spreads a chearfulness and delight through all its faculties.' Or again in the same essay. ' We no where meet with a more glorious or pleasing show in nature, than what appears in the heavens at the rising and setting of the sun, which is wholly made up of those different stains of light, that show themselves in clouds of a different situation.' A florid writer would hardly have resisted the opportunities, which here court the imagination to indulge its flights, whereas few writers of any sort would have been tempted on a topic merely critical, to have employed such figurative and splendid diction, as that of Doctor Johnson ; these little samples therefore, though selected with little or no care, but taken as they came to hand, may serve to exemplify my meaning, and in some degree characterize the different styles of the respective writers.

Now as every student, who is capable of copying either of these styles, or even of comparing them, must discern on which side the greater danger of miscarrying lies, as well as the greater disgrace in case of such miscarriage, prudence will direct him in his outset not to hazard the attempt at a florid diction. If his ear hath not been vitiated by vulgar habitudes, he will only have to guard against mean expressions, while he is studying to be simple and perspicuous ; he will put his thoughts into language naturally as they present themselves, giving them for the present little more than mere grammatical correction; afterwards, upon a closer review, he will polish those parts that seem rude, harmonize them where they are unequal, compress what is too diffusive, raise what is low, and attune the whole to that general cadence, which seems most grateful to his ear.

But if our student hath been smitten with the turbulent oratory of the senate, the acrimonious declamation of the bar, or the pompous eloquence of the pulpit, and shall take the lofty speakers in these several orders for his models, rather than such as address the ear in humbler tones, his passions will in that case hurry him into the florid and figurative style, to a sublime and swelling period; and if in this he excels, it must be owned he accomplishes a great and arduous task, and he will gain a liberal share of applause from the world, which in general is apt to be captivated with those high and towering images, that strike and surprize the senses. In this stile the Hebrew prophets write, ' whose discourse' (to use the words of the learned Doctor Bentley) ' after the genius of the Eastern nations, is thick set with metaphor and allegory; the same bold comparisons and dithyrambic liberty of style every where occurring—For when ' *the Spirit of God came upon them*,' and breathed a new warmth and vigour through all the powers of the body and soul: when by the influx of divine light the whole scene of Christ's heavenly kingdom was represented to their view, so that their hearts were ravished with joy, and their imaginations turgid and pregnant with the glorious ideas; then surely, if ever, their style would be strong and lofty, full of allusions to all that is great and magnificent in the kingdoms of this world.'   *(Commencement Sermon)*

—And these flights of imagination, these effusions of rapture and sublimity, will occasionally be found in the pulpit eloquence of some of our most correct and temperate writers; witness that brilliant apostrophe at the conclusion of the ninth discourse of Bishop Sherlock, than whom few or none have written with more didactic brevity and simplicity— 'Go,' (says he to the Deists) ' go to your natural religion: lay before her Mahomet and his disciples arrayed in armour and in blood, riding in triumph over the spoils of thousands, and tens of thousands, who fell by his victorious sword: shew her the cities which he set in flames, the countries which he ravaged and destroyed, and the miserable distress of all the inhabitants of the earth. When she has viewed him in this scene, carry her into his retirements; shew her the prophet's chamber, his concubines and wives; let her see his adultery, and hear him alledge revelation and his divine commission to justify his lust and oppression. When she is tired with this prospect, then shew her the blessed Jesus, humble and meek, doing good to all the sons of men, patiently instructing both the ignorant and perverse; let her see him in his most retired privacies; let her follow him to the mount, and hear his devotions and supplications to God; carry her to his table to view his poor fare, and hear his heavenly discourse: let her see him injured but not provoked; let her attend him to the tribunal, and consider the patience with which he endured the scoffs and reproaches of his enemies: lead her to his cross, and let her view him in the agony of death, and hear his last prayer for his persecutors—' *Father, forgive them, for they know not what they do.*'

This is a lofty passage in the high imperative tone of declamation; it is richly coloured, boldly contrasted and replete with imagery, and is amongst the strongest of those instances, where the orator addresses himself to the senses and passions of his hearers : but let the disciple tread this path with caution ; let him wait the call, and be sure he has an occasion worthy of his efforts before he makes them.

Allegory, personification and metaphor will press upon him his imagination at certain times, but let him soberly consult his judgment in those moments, and weigh their fitness before he admits them into his style.   As for allegory, it is at best but a kind of fairy form ; it is hard to naturalize it, and it will rarely fill a graceful part in any manly composition. With respect to personification, as I am speaking of prose only, it is but an exotic ornament, and may be considered rather as the loan of the muses than as the property of prose; let our student therefore beware how he borrows the feathers of the jay, lest his unnatural finery should only serve to make him pointed at and despised.   Metaphor, on the other hand, is common property, and he may take his share of it, provided he has discretion not to abuse his privilege, and neither surfeits the appetite with repletion, nor confounds the palate with too much variety : let his metaphor be apposite, single and unconfused, and it will serve him as a kind of rhetorical lever to lift and elevate his style above the pitch of ordinary discourse ; let him also so apply this machine, as to make it touch in as many points as possible ; otherwise it can never so poise the weight above it, as to keep it firm and steady on its proper center.

To give an example of the right use and application of this figure, I again apply to a learned author already quoted—' Our first parents having fallen from their native state of innocence, the tincture of evil, like an hereditary disease, infected all their

posterity; and the leaven of sin having once corrupted the whole mass of mankind, all the species
ever after would be soured and tainted with it; the
vicious ferment perpetually diffusing and propagating itself through all generations.'—(*Bentley,
Comm. Sermon.*)

There will be found also in certain writers a pro-
fusion of words, ramifying indeed from the same
root, yet rising into climax by their power and importance, which seems to burst forth from the over-
flow and impetuosity of the imagination: resemble-
ing at first sight what Quintilian characterises as
the '*Abundantia Juvenilis*,' but which, when tempered by the hand of a master, will upon closer
examination be found to bear the stamp of judgment under the appearance of precipitancy. I
need only turn to the famous '*Commencement Sermon*' before quoted, and my meaning will be fully
illustrated—'Let them tell us then what is the
chain, the cement, the magnetism, what they
will call it, the invisible tie of that union, whereby
matter and an incorporeal mind, things that have
no similitude or alliance to each other, can so sympathize by a mutual league of motion and sensation.
No; they will not pretend to that, for they can
frame no conceptions of it: they are sure there is
such an union from the operations and effects, but
the cause and the manner of it are too subtle and
secret to be discovered by the eye of reason: 'tis
mystery, 'tis divine magic, 'tis natural miracle,'

NUMBER LXXXII.

Defunctus jam sum, nihil, est qued dicat mihi.

TERENT.

In all ages of the world men have been in habits of praising the time past at the expence of the time present.   This was done even in the Augustan æra, and in that witty and celebrated period the *laudator temporis acti* must have been either a very splenetic, or a very silly character.

Our present grumblers may perhaps be better warranted ; but, though there may not be the same injustice in their cavilling complaints, there is more than equal impolicy in them ; for if by discouraging their contemporaries they mean to mend them, they take a very certain method of counteracting their own designs ; and if they have any other meaning, it must be something worse thsn impolitic, and they have more to answer for than a mere mistake.

Who but the meanest of mankind would wish to damp the spirit and degrade the genius of the country he belongs to ? Is any man lowered by the dignity of his own nation, by the talents of his contemporaries? Who would not prefer to live in an enlightened and a rising age, rather than in a dark and declining one ? It is natural to take a pride in the excellence of our free constitution, in the virtues of our Sovereign ; is it not as natural to sympathize in the prosperity of our arts and sciences, in the reputation of our countrymen ? But these splenetic *dampers* are for ever sighing over the decline of wit, the decline of genius, the decline of literature, when if there is any one thing that has declined rather than another, it is the wretched state of criticism, so far as they have to do with it.

As I was passing from the city the other day, I turned into a coffee-house, and took my seat at a table, next to which some gentlemen had assembled, and were conversing over their coffee. A dispute was carried on between a little prattling volatile fellow and an old gentleman of a sullen, morose aspect, who in a dictatorial tone of voice was declaiming against the times, and treating them and their puisny advocate with more contempt than either one or the other seemed to deserve: still the little fellow, who had abundance of zeal and no want of words, kept battling with might and main for the world as it goes against the world as it had gone by, and I could perceive he had an interest with the junior part of his hearers, whilst the sullen orator was no less popular amongst the elders of the party: the little fellow, who seemed to think it no good reason why any work should be decried only because the author of it was living, had been descanting upon the merit of a recent publication, and had now shifted his ground from the sciences to the fine arts, where he seemed to have taken a strong post and stood resolutely to it; his opponent, who was not a man to be tickled out of his spleen by a few fine dashes of arts merely elegant, did not relish this kind of skirmishing argument, and tauntingly cried out—' What tell you me of a parcel of gew-gaw artists, fit only to pick the pockets of a dissipated trifling age? You talk of your painters and portrait-mongers, what use are they of? Where are the philosophers and the poets, whose countenances might interest posterity to sit to them? Will they paint me a Bacon, a Newton, or a Locke? I defy

them : there are not three heads upon living shoulders in the kingdom, worth the oil that would be
wasted upon them. Will they or you find me a
Shakspeare, a Milton, a Dryden, a Pope, an Addison? You cannot find a limb, a feature, or even
the shadow of the least of them : these were men
worthy to be recorded; poets, who reached the very
topmost summits of Parnassus; our moderns are
but pismires crawling at its lowest root.'—This
lofty defiance brought our little advocate to a non-
plus; the moment was embarrassing; the champion of time past was echoed by his party with a
cry of—' No, no! there are no such men as these
now living.'—' I believe not,' he replied, ' I believe not: I could give you a score of names more,
but these are enough : honest Tom Durfey would
be more than a match for any poetaster now breath-
ing.'

In this style he went on crowing and clapping
his wings over a beaten cock, for our poor little
champion seemed dead upon the pit : he muttered
something between his teeth, as if struggling to
pronounce some name that stuck in his throat; but
either there was in fact no contemporary, whom he
thought it safe to oppose to these Goliahs in the lists,
or none were present to his mind at this moment.

Alas! thought I, your cause, my beloved contemporaries, is desperate : *Væ Victis!* You are but
dust in the scale, while this *Brennus* directs the
beam. All that I have admired and applauded in
my zeal for those with whom I have lived and still
live; all that has hitherto made my heart expand
with pride and reverence for the age and nation I
belong to, will be immolated to the manes of these
departed worthies, whom though I revere, I cannot
love and cherish with that sympathy of soul, which
I feel towards you, my dear but degenerate contemporaries!

There was a young man, sitting at the elbow of the little crest-fallen fellow, with a round clerical curl, which tokened him to be a son of the church. Having silently awaited the full time for a rally, if any spirit of resurrection had been left in the fallen hero, and none such appearing, he addressed himself to the challenger with an air so modest, but withal so impressive, that it was impossible not to be prejudiced in his favour, before he opened his cause.

' I cannot wonder,' said he, ' if the gentleman who has challenged us to produce a parallel to any one of the great names he has enumerated, finds us unprepared with any living rival to those illustrious characters: their fame, though the age in which they lived did not always appreciate it as it ought, hath yet been rising day by day in the esteem of posterity, till time hath stampt a kind of sacredness upon it, which it would now be a literary impiety to blaspheme.　There are some amongst those, whom their advocate hath named, I cannot speak or think of but with a reverence only short of idolatry.　Not this nation only but all Europe hath been enlightened by their labours: the great principle of nature, the very law upon which the whole system of the universe moves and gravitates, hath been developed and demonstrated by the penetrating, I had almost said the preternatural, powers of our immortal Newton.　The present race of philosophers can only be considered as his disciples; but they are disciples who do honour to their master: If the principle of gravitation be the grand *desideratum* of philosophy, the discovery is with him, the application, inferences and advantages of that discovery are with those who succeed him; and can we accuse the present age of being idle or unable to avail themselves of the ground he gave them? Let me remind you that our present solar system is furnished with more pla-

nets than Newton knew; that our late observations
upon the transit of the planet Venus were decisive
for the proof and confirmation of his system: that
we have circumnavigated the globe again and again;
that we can boast the researches and discoveries of a
Captain Cook, who, though he did not invent the
compass, employed it as no man ever did, and left a
map behind him, compared to which Sir Isaac Newton's was a sheet of nakedness and error: it is with
gravitation therefore as with the loadstone; their
powers have been discovered by our predecessors,
but we have put them to their noblest uses.

 ‘ The venerable names of Bacon and Locke were,
if I mistake not, mentioned in the same class with
Newton, and though the learned gentleman could
no doubt have made his selection more numerous, I
doubt if he could have made it stronger, or more to
the purpose of his own assertions.

 ‘ I have always regarded Bacon as the father of
philosophy in this country, yet it is no breach of
candour to observe, that the darkness of the age
which he enlightened, affords a favourable contrast
to set off the splendor of his talents: but do we,
who applaud him, read him? Yet if such is our veneration for times long since gone by, why do we
not? The fact is, intermediate writers have disse-
minated his original matter through more pleasing
vehicles, and we concur, whether commendably or
not, to put his volumes upon the superannuated list,
allowing him however an unalienable compensation
upon our praise, and reserving to ourselves a right
of taking him from the shelf, whenever we are disposed to sink the merit of a more recent author by
a comparison with him. I will not therefore disturb his venerable dust, but turn without further
delay to the author of the Essay upon the Human
Understanding.

'This essay, which professes to define every
thing, as it arises or passes in the mind, must ultimately be compiled from observations of its author
upon himself and within himself: before I compare the merit of this work therefore with the merit
of any other man's work of our own immediate
times, I must compare what it advances as general
to mankind, with what I perceive within my particular self; and upon this reference, speaking only
for an humble individual, I must own to my shame,
that my understanding and the author's do by no
means coincide either in definitions or ideas. I may
have reason to lament the inaccuracy or the slug-
gishness of my own senses and perceptions, but I
cannot submit to any man's doctrine against their
conviction: I will only say that Mr. Locke's metaphysics are not my metaphysics, and, as it would
be an ill compliment to any one of our contemporaries to compare him with a writer, who to me is un-
intelligible, so will I hope it can never be considered
as a reflection upon so great a name as Mr. Locke's,
not to be understood by so insignificant a man as
myself.'

'Well, sir,' cried the sullen gentleman with a
sneer, 'I think you have contrived to dispatch our
philosophers; you have now only a few obscure
poets to dismiss in like manner, and you will have
a clear field for yourself and your friends.'

NUMBER LXXXIII.

Ingeniis non ille favet, plauditque sepultis,
Nostra sed impugnat, nos nostraque lividus odit.

HORAT.

THE sarcastic speech of the old snarler, with which
we concluded the last paper, being undeserved on
the part of the person to whom it was applied, was
very properly disregarded; and the clergyman proceeded as follows:

' The poets you have named will never be mentioned by me but with a degree of enthusiasm,
which I should rather expect to be accused of carrying to excess, than of erring in the opposite extreme, had you not put me on my guard against
partiality, by charging me with it beforehand. I
shall therefore without further apology or preface
begin with Shakspeare, first named by you, and first
in fame as well as time: It would be madness in
me to think of bringing any poet now living into
competition with Shakspeare; but I hope it will
not be thought madness, or any thing resembling to
it, to observe to you, that it is not in the nature of
things possible for any poet to appear in an age so
polished as this of ours, who can be brought into
any critical comparison with that extraordinary and
eccentric genius.

' For let us consider the two great striking features of his drama, sublimity and character. Now
sublimity involves sentiment and expression; the
first of these is in the soul of the poet; it is that

portion of inspiration, which we personify when
we call it The Muse; so far I am free to acknowledge there is no immediate reason to be given,
why her visits should be confined to any age, nation or person; she may fire the heart of the poet
on the shores of Ionia three thousand years ago, or
on the banks of the Cam or Isis at the present moment; but so far as language is concerned, I may
venture to say that modern diction will never
strike modern ears with that awful kind of magic,
which antiquity gives to words and phrases no
longer in familiar use: In this respect our great
dramatic poet hath an advantage over his distant
descendants, which he owes to time, and which of
course is one more than he is indebted for to his
own pre-eminent genius. As for character, which
I suggested as one of the two most striking features
of Shakspeare's drama, (or in other words the true
and perfect delineation of nature) in this our poet
is indeed a master unrivalled; yet who will not
allow the happy coincidence of time for this perfection in a writer of the drama? The different orders of men, which Shakspeare saw and copied, are
in many instances extinct, and such must have the
charms of novelty at least in our eyes: And has
the modern dramatist the same rich and various
field of character? The level manners of a polished
age furnish little choice to an author, who now
enters on the task, in which such numbers have
gone before him, and so exhausted the materials,
that it is justly to be wondered at, when any thing
like variety can be struck out. Dramatic characters are portraits drawn from nature, and if all the
sitters have a family likeness, the artist must either
depart from the truth, or preserve the resemblance;
in like manner the poet must either invent characters,
of which there is no counterpart in existence, or

expose himself to the danger of an insipid and tiresome repetition : To add to his difficulties it so happens, that the present age, whilst it furnishes less variety to his choice, requires more than ever for its own amusement; the dignity of the stage must of course be prostituted to the unnatural resources of a wild imagination, and its propriety disturbed ; music will supply those resources for a time, and accordingly we find the French and English theatres in the dearth of character feeding upon the airy diet of sound ; but this, with all the support that spectacle can give, is but a flimsy substitute, whilst the public whose taste in the mean time becomes vitiated—

> ———media inter carmina poscunt
> Aut Ursum aut Pugiles———

the latter of which monstrous prostitutions we have lately seen our national stage most shamefully exposed to.

'By comparing the different ages of poetry in our own country with those of Greece, we shall find the effects agree in each ; for as the refinement of manners took place, the language of poetry became also more refined, and with greater correctness had less energy and force; the style of the poet, like the characters of the people, takes a brighter polish, which, whilst it smooths away its former asperities and protuberances, weakens the staple of its fabric, and what it gives to the elegance and delicacy of its complexion, takes away from the strength and sturdiness of its constitution. Whoever will compare Æschylus with Euripides, and Aristophanes with Menander, will need no other illustration of this remark.

Consider only the inequalities of Shakspeare's dramas : examine not only one with another, but compare even scene with scene in the same play. Did ever the imagination of man run riot into such wild and opposite extremes? Could this be done, or, being done, would it be suffered in the present age? How many of these plays, if acted as they were originally written, would now be permitted to pass? Can we have a stronger proof of the barbarous taste of those times, in which Titus Andronicus first appeared, than the favour which that horrid spectacle was received with? Yet of this we are assured by Ben Jonson. If this play was Shakspeare's, it was his first production, and some of his best commentators are of opinion it was actually written by him whilst he resided at Stratford upon Avon. Had this production been followed by the three parts of Henry the Sixth, by Love's Labour Lost, the two Gentlemen of Verona, the Comedy of Errors, or some few others, which our stage does not attempt to reform, that critic must have had a very singular degree of intuition, who had discovered in those dramas a genius capable of producing the Macbeth. How would a young author be received in the present time, who was to make his first essay before the public with such a piece as Titus Andronicus? Now if we are warranted in saying there are several of Shakspeare's dramas, which could not live upon our present stage at any rate, and few, if any, that would pass without just censure in many parts, were they represented in their original state, we must acknowledge it is with reason that our living authors, standing in awe of their audiences, dare not aim at those bold and irregular flights of imagination, which carried our bard to such a height of fame; and therefore it was that I ventured awhile ago to say, there can be no poet in a polished and critical age like this, who can be brought into any fair comparison with so bold and

eccentric a genius as Shakspeare, of whom we may
say with Horace—

> *Tentavit quoque rem, si digne vertere posset,*
> *Et placuit sibi, natura sublimis et acer:*
> *Nam spirat tragicum satis, et feliciter audet:*
> *Sed turpem putat in scriptis metuitque lituram.*

When I bring to my recollection the several periods of our English drama since the age of Shakspeare, I could name many dates, when it has been
in hands far inferior to the present, and were it my
purpose to enter into particulars, I should not scruple to appeal to several dramatic productions within
the compass of our own times, but as the task of
separating and selecting one from another amongst
our own contemporaries can never be a pleasant
task, nor one I would willingly engage in, I will
content myself with referring to our stock of modern acting plays; many of which having passed
the ordeal of critics, (who speak the same language
with what I have just now heard, and are continually crying down those they live with) may perhaps
take their turn with posterity, and be hereafter as
partially over-rated upon a comparison with the
productions of the age to come, as they are now
undervalued when compared with those of the ages
past.

' With regard to Milton, if we could not name
any one epic poet of our nation since his time, it
would be saying no more of us than may be said of
the world in general, from the æra of Homer to
that of Virgil. Greece had one standard epic poet;
Rome had no more; England has her Milton. If
Dryden pronounced that ' the force of nature could
no further go,' he was at once a good authority and
a strong example of the truth of the assertion : If
his genius shrunk from the undertaking, can we

wonder that so few have taken it up? Yet we will not forget Leonidas; nor speak slightly of its merit; and as death has removed the worthy author where he cannot hear our praises, the world may now, as in the case of Milton heretofore, be so much the more forward to bestow them. If the Sampson Agonistes is nearer to the simplicity of its Grecian original than either our own Elfrida or Caractacus, those dramas have a tender interest, a pathetic delicacy, which in that are wanting; and though Comus has every charm of language, it has a vein of allegory that impoverishes the mine

'The variety of Dryden's genius was such as to preclude comparison; were I disposed to attempt it. Of his dramatic productions he himself declares, 'that he never wrote any thing in that way to please himself but his All for Love.' For ever under arms, he lived in a continual state of poetic warfare with his contemporaries, galling and galled by turns; he subsisted also by expedients, and necessity, which forced his genius into quicker growth than was natural to it, made a rich harvest but slovenly husbandry; it drove him also into a duplicity of character that is painful to reflect upon; it put him ill at ease within himself, and verified the fable of the nightingale, singing with a thorn at its breast.

'Pope's versification gave the last and finishing polish to our English poetry: His lyre more sweet than Dryden's was less sonorous; his touch more correct, but not so bold; his strain more musical in its tones, but not so striking in its effect: Review him as a critic, and review him throughout, you will pronounce him the most perfect poet in our language; read him as an enthusiast and examine him in detail, you cannot refuse him your approbation, but your rapture you will reserve for Dryden.

' But you will tell me this does not apply to the question in dispute, and that instead of settling precedency between your poets, it is time for me to produce my own: For this I shall beg your excuse; my zeal for my contemporaries shall not hurry them into comparisons, which their own modesty would revolt from; it hath prompted me to intrude upon your patience, whilst I submitted a few mitigating considerations in their behalf; not as an answer to your challenge, but as an effort to soften your contempt. I confess to you I have sometimes flattered myself I have found the strength of Dryden in our late Churchill, and the sweetness of Pope in our lamented Goldsmith: Enraptured as I am with the lyre of Timotheus in the Feast of Alexander, I contemplate with awful delight Gray's enthusiastic bard—

> On a rock, whose haughty brow
> Frowns o'er old Conway's foaming flood,
> Rob'd in the sable garb of woe,
> With haggard eyes the poet stood;
> (Loose his beard and hoary hair
> Stream'd like a meteor to the troubled air)
> And with a master's hand and prophet's fire
> Struck the deep sorrows of his lyre.

Let the living muses speak for themselves; I have all the warmth of a friend, but not the presumption of a champion: the poets you now so loudly praise when dead, found the world as loud in defamation when living; you are now paying the debts of your predecessors, and atoning for their injustice; posterity will in like manner atone for your's.

' You mentioned the name of Addison in your list, not altogether as a poet I presume, but rather as the man of morals, the reformer of manners, and the friend of religion; with affection I sub-scribe my tribute to his literary fame, to his ami-able character: In sweetness and simplicity of style, in purity and perspicuity of sentiment, he is a model to all essayists. At the same time I feel the honest pride of a contemporary in recalling to your me-mory the name of Samuel Johnson, who as a moral and religious essayist, as an acute and penetrating critic, as a nervous and elaborate poet, an excellent grammarian, and a general scholar, ranks with the first names in literature.

‘ Not having named an historian in your list of illustrious men, you have precluded me from ad-verting to the histories of Hume, Robertson, Lyt-telton, Henry, Gibbon, and others, who are a host of writers, which all antiquity cannot equal.’

Here the clergyman concluded: the conversation now grew desultory and uninteresting, and I re-turned home.

END OF THE FORTY-SECOND VOLUME.

T. Gillet, Printer, Salisbury-square.

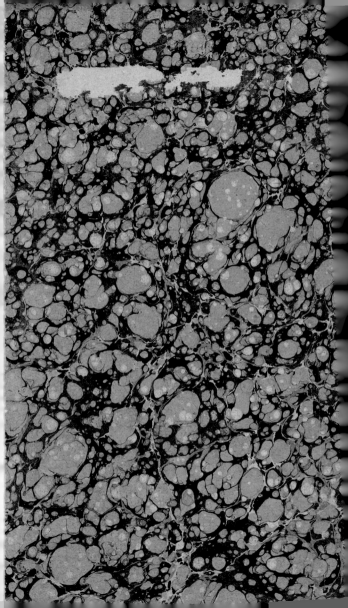